The Islamic Council of Norway and the Challenge of Representing
Islam in Europe

Muslim Minorities

Editorial Board

Jørgen S. Nielsen (*University of Copenhagen*)
Aminah McCloud (*DePaul University, Chicago*)
Jörn Thielmann (*EZIRE, Erlangen University*)

VOLUME 46

The titles published in this series are listed at *brill.com/mumi*

The Islamic Council of Norway and the Challenge of Representing Islam in Europe

Muslims under Pressure

By

Olav Elgvin

BRILL

LEIDEN | BOSTON

This is an open access title distributed under the terms of the CC BY-NC-ND 4.0 license, which permits any non-commercial use, distribution, and reproduction in any medium, provided no alterations are made and the original author(s) and source are credited. Further information and the complete license text can be found at https://creativecommons.org/licenses/by-nc-nd/4.0/

The terms of the CC license apply only to the original material. The use of material from other sources (indicated by a reference) such as diagrams, illustrations, photos and text samples may require further permission from the respective copyright holder.

This volume was supported by: The Research Council of Norway.

Cover illustration: The prime minister of Norway, Jonas Gahr Støre, visits the Islamic Cultural Center in 2023. Photo credit: Prime minister's office, Norway.

The Library of Congress Cataloging-in-Publication Data is available online at https://catalog.loc.gov
LC record available at https://lccn.loc.gov/2025014892

Typeface for the Latin, Greek, and Cyrillic scripts: "Brill". See and download: brill.com/brill-typeface.

ISSN 1570-7571
ISBN 978-90-04-70113-7 (hardback)
ISBN 978-90-04-70114-4 (e-book)
DOI 10.1163/9789004701144

Copyright 2025 by Olav Elgvin. Published by Koninklijke Brill BV, Plantijnstraat 2, 2321 JC Leiden, The Netherlands.
Koninklijke Brill BV incorporates the imprints Brill, Brill Nijhoff, Brill Schöningh, Brill Fink, Brill mentis, Brill Wageningen Academic, Vandenhoeck & Ruprecht, Böhlau and V&R unipress.
Koninklijke Brill BV reserves the right to protect this publication against unauthorized use.
For more information: info@brill.com.

This book is printed on acid-free paper and produced in a sustainable manner.

Contents

Acknowledgements IX
List of Figures XI

1 **Introduction** 1
  1.1 Internal Conflicts and Representing Islam 3
  1.2 Learning from the Norwegian Story 4
  1.3 Placing This Book in the Literature 5
  1.4 Data, Analysis and Ethics 8
  1.5 Overview of the Book: Multipolarity, Cross-Pressures and
    Unstable Institutionalisation 12

2 **Overcoming the Challenge of Multipolarity: the Road to the Islamic
  Council of Norway (1989–1993)** 16
  2.1 Foundational Research on Muslim Councils and
    Umbrella Organisations 16
  2.2 Why So Many Conflicts? 20
  2.3 Diversity vs. Multipolarity on the Muslim Field 22
  2.4 Multipolarity and Diversity among Muslims in Norway 24
  2.5 Coming Together for the First Time: the Rushdie Affair 28
  2.6 The External Impetus: the Initiative from the Church 33
  2.7 The Internal Response: the Wish to Represent Islam 38
  2.8 Overcoming Multipolarity: Idealistic Entrepreneurs
    and Post-Islamists 43

3 **Dealing with Cross-Pressures: a New Organisation Finds Its Place
  (1993–2006)** 51
  3.1 A Muslim Umbrella Organisation under Pressure 51
  3.2 The Rushdie Case Once Again: Early External Pressure 56
  3.3 Choosing Moderation and Dialogue: from Early Discourse
    to Educational Policies 58
  3.4 New Allies and a New Direction: the Battle for the Public School 64
  3.5 Internal Agreements on Contested Issues 73
  3.6 Limits to Compromise: Decoupling and Withdrawal 77
  3.7 Redefining the Muslim Interest: towards a
    Norwegian-Muslim Identity 87

VI CONTENTS

4 Unstable Institutionalisation: New Responsibilities and New Divisions (2006–2012) 91

4.1 On the Importance of Institutionalisation and the External Environment 91
4.2 Becoming a Trusted Partner: the Cartoon Affair 93
4.3 Funding with Strings Attached 97
4.4 New Responsibilities and External Expectations 101
4.5 Internal Tensions 106
4.6 Diverging Approaches: the Dialogue Path vs the Community Path 112
4.7 Unstable Institutionalisation and a Shift in Personnel 116
4.8 Internal and External Tensions 120
4.9 Emergence of the Community Path: Halal Food and Muslim Solidarity 124
4.10 Halal Certification and Financial Independence 128
4.11 Seeking Community or Seeking Allies 132

5 Towards the Split (2013–2018) 136

5.1 Deepening Conflicts 136
5.2 The Dynamic of Conflict and the Role of Individuals 139
5.3 Turning Up the Heat: the Debate over Fundamentalism and Radicalization 141
5.4 The Challenge of Multipolarity Once Again 144
5.5 Unstable Internal Institutionalisation and the Failed Intervention 147
5.6 Unstable External Institutionalisation and the New Organisation 155

6 Breaking Up and Starting Over (2018–2024) 160

6.1 Clarifying the Profile 160
6.2 Competition and Cooperation between Two Umbrella Organisations 163

7 Lessons Learned? Islamic Representation in Norway and Beyond 166

7.1 The Consequences of Islamic Representation 166
7.2 Causes for the Split 170
 7.2.1 *Multipolarity* 170
 7.2.2 *Different Ways of Responding to Cross-Pressures* 171
 7.2.3 *Unstable Institutionalisation* 172
 7.2.4 *Contingency* 172

CONTENTS VII

7.3 Comparative Outlook: Muslim Councils in Other Countries and the Case of Norway 173

    7.3.1 *France* 173

    7.3.2 *Austria* 175

    7.3.3 *Germany* 178

    7.3.4 *The UK* 181

7.4 Concluding Remarks: Better Models for Representing Islam and Muslims? 183

Appendix 1: Interview Guide 187

Appendix 2: Persons Interviewed in Depth for This Project 188

Appendix 3: Key Written Sources 189

Bibliography 222

Index 242

Acknowledgements

This book could not have been written without the generous help and support of a good number of people and institutions, to whom I am deeply thankful. It began its life as a PhD thesis, written with the support of a university grant at the Department of Comparative Politics at the University of Bergen. I owe a large debt of gratitude to my two PhD supervisors, Elisabeth Ivarsflaten and Lars Svåsand. They both combine great intelligence with intellectual openness, friendliness, and humility. Without their help and support, I doubt I would have been able to finish the thesis. Others at Sampol – too many to mention here – also provided invaluable input and critique that helped me sharpen and improve my arguments.

My second academic home – before, during, and after my PhD – has been the research institute Fafo in Oslo. During my PhD, my part-time position at Fafo was funded through a research project on Islam in Europe (*Muslim Politics and Governance of Islam*) within the SAMKUL program of the Research Council of Norway (RCN). Fafo's leadership consistently showed their support and gave me the flexibility I needed to complete the thesis. I owe particular thanks to Jon Rogstad, Hanne Kavli, and Beret Bråten. I'm grateful to be part of a collegial and supportive research group at Fafo, which makes my work as a researcher much more enjoyable.

After finishing my PhD, one option would have been to publish the thesis more or less as it was. However, following feedback from various scholars and practitioners, I decided to revise the manuscript substantially before publishing it as a book. I soon became a post-doctoral researcher on the *Cancode* project at the University of Bergen, financed by the Trond Mohn Research Foundation (grant TMS2020STG01). The project leader, Eirik Hovden, gave me a remarkable amount of freedom and flexibility during my post-doctoral years, for which I am very grateful. This made it possible for me to focus on revising the thesis – which has now become this book.

At Brill, I owe thanks to editor Nienke Brienen-Molenaar and the editors of the *Muslim Minorities* series, for believing in the project and for their patience when it took more time than planned to complete the revisions.

•••

I am also deeply grateful to my family and friends. Without the love and support my parents have provided throughout my life, I would not be where I am today. My in-laws in Algeria have also cheered me on, even from far away. My son Elias is a daily reminder that there are things in life that matter more than minor imperfections in an academic manuscript.

Finally, I am indebted to all the people I interviewed for this project, or who shared personal documents with me and thereby agreed to become subjects of research. To permit someone to study you is not – and should not be – an easy decision. I'm thankful for their trust, and I hope I've done justice to what they shared with me.

My deepest thanks, as always, go to my wife, Sara, for too many things to mention.

Oslo, April 2025

Figures

1   Mentions of 'Islam' in Norwegian print media   34

2   Mentions of "Muslims", "Pakistanis" and "Immigrants" in Norwegian print media, 1970–1994   35

3   Organisational strategies when facing conflicting demands   56

CHAPTER 1

Introduction

> We need the Muslims to be organised. That is the only way we can hold them responsible for what happens in their communities.

A Norwegian government official told me this several years ago (interview with the author, 05.01.2015). I had talked to him about Norwegian faith communities and asked about Norwegian government policies towards these communities. This official found it especially important that Muslims should become more organised. He perceived several challenges facing Muslims in Norway: discrimination and Islamophobia, radicalization, social pressure to conform to conservative norms. The answer to all this, he thought, was stronger institutionalisation and representation of Muslims in Norwegian society. They needed better representative institutions. With such institutions in place, the Norwegian authorities could hold Muslim groups accountable, with representative institutions functioning as interlocutors between the government and ordinary Muslims on the ground.

Whether he knew it or not, this official expressed a way of thinking that has become common in European policy circles during the past 20 years. As has been documented in several studies, European governments have sought to institutionalise and regulate the Islamic or Muslim presence in their countries through the empowerment of representative Islamic or Muslim councils (Bayrakli, Hafez, and Faytre 2018; Braginskaia 2015; Bruce 2018; Ciciora 2018; Godard 2015; Haddad and Golson 2007; Laurence 2009, 2012; Mattes and Rosenberger 2015; Rosenow-Williams 2012; Silvestri 2010).

These councils or organisations purport to represent Muslims, mosques or other Muslim organisations vis-à-vis the state and other actors in society. They are expected to voice the concerns of their members to the authorities or to society at large and thereby ensure that the interests of their members are considered when policy is formulated. But they are also expected to voice the concerns of the authorities and society at large to their members and constituencies and ensure that central issues for the authorities – such as violent radicalization – are addressed. In many ways, it is an *exchange relationship*: You give some, you get some.

The creation and institutionalisation of these representative councils has been well covered in the literature. None of these studies, however, have explored explicitly and in depth what has arguably been one of the most salient

© OLAV ELGVIN, 2025 | DOI:10.1163/9789004701144_002

This is an open access chapter distributed under the terms of the CC BY-NC-ND 4.0 license.

features of many of these organisations: that they have often been marked by instability, defections, conflicts or splits. The experience in many European countries is simply that it is difficult to be a Muslim Council, as I will call these organisations in this book. The conflicts have been mentioned in some of the studies, and in media reports, but they have not been looked at systematically by researchers. Some of these organisations have been split, and others have been paralyzed by internal conflicts. Some organisations have seen one of the sides prevail in the conflict, while others were able work out their internal differences. In the Islamic field, such conflicts and splits are not unique to such representative councils. Divisive conflicts have also been described in other Islamic organisations and mosques (Pfaff and Gill 2006; Shavit 2016; Warner and Wenner 2006). But Muslim Councils may seem to particularly prone to conflicts.

How can such a conflict look like? We may take the situation in France as an example. The situation of Muslims in France and Islam in France has been treated in numerous studies, partly due to the sheer size of the Muslim population in France, and partly due to the analytical interest in the French model of secularism. In France, the nationally designated Muslim council was for many years the Conseil Français du Culte Musulman (CFCM), created in 2003. It has been the subject of several studies (Bayrakli, Hafez, and Faytre 2018; Bruce 2018; Ciciora 2018; Godard 2015; Laurence 2005, 2012; Laurence and Vaisse 2007). The story of the CFCM, however, has been conflict-ridden from the very beginning. CFCM was created as a kind of federation between the various factions in French Islam – Algerian, Moroccan, Turkish, and post-Islamist. Only five years after the creation of the organisation, the Algerian faction in the CFCM decided to boycott the elections for the board of the CFCM in 2008. Three years later, in 2011, they re-joined the elections. In 2013 it was the UOIF – the largest Islamic federation in France – that decided to boycott the elections, before re-joining. In the following years, even more conflicts followed (for more on the French story, see the last chapter).

This is a fascinating and remarkable story, which has yet to be analysed in depth by researchers. But the French experience is far from unique. Similar conflicts have been documented in Muslim Councils in Germany (Bruce 2018, 135–42; Rosenow-Williams 2012, chapter 6), in the UK (Shah 2016, 12–19), in Austria (Kurier 2018), in Russia (Braginskaia 2015, 15–16), in the Netherlands (Atkinson 2016; Houten 2019), in Sweden (Sorgenfrei 2018, 105–31), in Spain (Laurence 2012, 196), and in Belgium (Dupont 2024; Loobuyck, Debeer, and Meier 2013, 69–70). But why have such conflicts occurred in these organisations? With a few exceptions, this question has not received much attention

INTRODUCTION   3

from scholars of Islam in Europe. The aim of this book is to propose some analytical answers to this question, by using the history of The Islamic Council of
Norway as a case study.

1.1   Internal Conflicts and Representing Islam

Why is it important to understand such conflicts? The reason is simple:
A Muslim Council which is paralyzed by conflicts will not be able to do its
job. If one asks what "the job" of a Muslim Council actually is, different actors
will probably provide different answers. If you ask policymakers, the response
may be that such councils have value insofar as they help achieve certain
policy goals – for example that Muslims should accept regulations on halal
food or headscarves. From the perspective of the leaders of Muslim NGOs or
mosques, the point of such councils may be to advance the collective interests
of Muslims vis-à-vis the authorities, or to fight Islamophobia. From the point of
view of actors with an interest in intercultural dialogue, the main purpose
of such councils may be to promote understanding which helps people live
side by side in diverse societies. But for all these different goals, a fundamental requirement will be that the organisation has a certain degree of stability
and institutionalisation. An organisation in which the leadership is constantly
shifting or in conflict with each other, will not be able to advance any goals. In
order to reach a goal – be it fighting against Islamophobia or helping the state
to implement certain policies – it is usually a requirement that the organisation has a minimal level of organisational and institutional stability.

Understanding conflicts and splits in Muslim councils may also be of
analytical value for understanding the Islamic landscape in Europe more generally. Muslim councils are unique kinds of organisations. They are among the
very few attempts to join together the various factions and organisations on
the Islamic field. Understanding why such attempts have proved difficult may
therefore aid us in understanding the Islamic field or landscape more generally. Conflicts in Muslim Councils may indicate what kind of cleavages and
conflicts are present and salient on the Islamic field.

Understanding why such conflicts have occurred, may also make it easier to
identify how Muslim Councils can work better. Recent history has shown that
representing Islam in Europe – as Muslim Councils have attempted to do – is
not easy. Both actors in the Muslim fields and various authorities may have an
interest in understanding how Muslim Councils and their interlocutors can
make this task easier.

1.2 Learning from the Norwegian Story

The story I will tell in this book is the trajectory of the umbrella organisation *The Islamic Council of Norway* (IRN). It was established in 1992/1993, as one of the first councils of its kind in Western Europe. Despite some rough tumbles, IRN seemed to grow stronger during its first 15–20 years. Starting out as an organisation run on a voluntary basis, it began to receive funding from the Norwegian state in 2007. It also became an increasingly important interlocutor for the authorities. Seen from the outside, IRN appeared to be a stable and secure organisation. Nevertheless, an internal conflict emerged in the 2010s. This conflict ended with a split and a public fall from grace in 2017. The government took away their funding, and an important faction within IRN broke out and started a new organisation of their own. IRN had also built up a large and successful franchise for the certification of halal food, which broke down.

Why study the history of this relatively small organisation, in a small country with a small Muslim population on the outskirts of Europe? In my training as a political scientist I have been socialized into talking about *case selection*: One should choose to study cases which can cast light on a broader family of cases, in one way or the other (Flyvbjerg 2006; Gerring 2007; Seawright and Gerring 2008). I have, however, become increasingly wary of employing such language when doing qualitative research. Most historical events have unique and contingent features which can make it difficult to generalize too strongly to other cases. It may not always be the case that an historical episode is a "case" of something else at all. Furthermore, some events or social realities are interesting and important in themselves, and we can choose to study them without justifying it with the goal of building large-scale theory. Rather than talk about case selection, I now prefer to talk about *case contribution*: the degree to which the cases or historical instances we study may contribute to our understanding of other historical events or patterns, even though we may not have chosen to study these cases based on a perfect comparativist logic.

Sometimes the answer is that a case does not provide much overall contribution to our understanding of larger phenomena. But sometimes the analysis of a certain event or social phenomenon may also help us to make sense of occurrences and events in different social contexts as well, when we carefully weigh similarities and differences across contexts. I hope that can be the case with the story I am telling in this book. In the last chapter, I therefore include a comparative outlook, where I take a short look at other *shadow cases* (Soifer 2018). In this outlook I look briefly at Muslim councils and Muslim representation in other European countries, and I discuss how insights from the Norwegian story can help us understand patterns beyond Norway.

The main message in the book is that there were three conditions which probably led to the conflicts and splits in the Islamic Council of Norway:

INTRODUCTION 5

Multipolarity on the Muslim field, *cross-pressures*, and *unstable institutionalisation* both internally and externally. Some of these conditions have been alluded to in previous research on Islam in Europe but have – with a few exceptions – not been explored in detail with regards to how they have affected conflict and cooperation in Islamic or Muslim organisations more broadly. My claim is not that other factors did not matter in the story of the IRN, or that these factors are equally important in all other cases. I do think, however, that these three factors go a long way in explaining why events unfolded as they did in the IRN, and that these three factors have played a role for instability and conflict in Muslim councils in other countries as well.

1.3 Placing This Book in the Literature

This book project started its life as a PhD thesis in political science, which I defended on December 18th 2020 (O. Elgvin 2020). For this book version, the thesis has been substantially revised in many ways. Whereas the thesis only covered developments until 2019, this book tells the story up until 2024. The book is nevertheless much shorter than the thesis, and was shortened from 400 to slightly above 200 pages. It has also been updated and analytically revised in several ways, following feedback at my PhD defence and from various people who read the thesis afterwards.

The thesis was written according to a method known among political scientists as *process tracing*: Doing history with the explicit aim of uncovering causal mechanisms which can be generalized across contexts (Beach and Pedersen 2013). When I reworked the material for this book, I realized that I had not fully succeeded in my process tracing endeavour. I was not able to pinpoint the exact mechanisms or causal chains that had occurred, despite working closely with a large amount of data over the course of several years. There were simply too many unknowns – parts of the causal chains I did not have access to – and too many contingencies that could just as well have unfolded in different ways. The more I delved into the data, the messier and more arbitrary the actual historical developments appeared. I related more and more to what the historian Bret Devereaux had written about doing history in a blog exchange with the economist Noah Smith: "efforts at strict predictability will always be overwhelmed by contingency, context and unexpected variables" (Devereaux 2022).

When revising the thesis for this book, my first instinct was to sharpen the historical angle of the work and describe the events and developments I had studied in even more empirical and historical detail. This would have necessitated accounting for all the contingencies and particular contexts, the personal quirks of the main actors involved, etc. This, however, would probably not have been that interesting to scholars outside the Norwegian context. I also realized that by temperament and training I am much more of a social and political scientist than a historian. What I have attempted to do instead is to draw out some larger analytical implications of the events I studied. I have attempted to put these analytical categories center stage, and structure the historical story I tell according to some overarching concepts and ideas. This has also involved to simplify the story I am telling: To focus on the larger aspects which may be of enduring analytical importance, and to remove events that are more peripheral. For readers who are interested in a more complete history of The Islamic Council of Norway and their relations with society at large, I refer to my PhD thesis, as well as some spin-off articles in both Norwegian and English (O. Elgvin 2022, 2023b, 2023a).

This has resulted in a book that remains anchored in political science, but also moves into the realms of Islamic and religious studies, and political sociology. The aim is not to describe exact or complete causal mechanisms, as qualitative political scientists often strive for when doing process tracing. What I aim for in is rather to engage in *analytical description*. Description is not easy or "mere", as the political scientist John Gerring put it (Gerring 2012). Good description is about identifying the most relevant or important features of a certain situation or event. Is it important for the understanding of IRN that most of the key actors have been men, for example? Probably, even though I regrettably do not devote much space to the gender dimension in this book. But was it an important feature of the early history of IRN what shoe size the founders wore? No, that was a peripheral feature that did not matter a lot. These kinds of considerations are about description – choosing what to highlight, and what to leave out, and deciding which concepts help us to make sense of the social world. Such concepts can be thought of as *social conditions* – features of the social environment on the meso- or macro-level that have an impact on how events unfold. Such social conditions are of course connected to causality. What makes something count as a *condition* is precisely that it has an impact on this event or the other. The difference is about emphasis: Trying to pinpoint exact mechanisms, as proponents of process tracing often strive for, or rather identifying larger macro conditions which have an impact via various kinds of mechanisms.

My general approach to doing social science falls within what one may label a *soft positivist* or *critical realist* tradition (Danermark, Ekstrom, and Jakobsen 2005; Fox 2008). I do think that the search for inter-subjective truth is an important goal, and this is the ambition that underlies this book. At the same time, my goals of generalization are somewhat modest, and I fully acknowledge that my own positionality and bias as a researcher matters. In analysing

INTRODUCTION

the material, I have been inspired by recent methodological writings on *analytic eclecticism* in political science and *abduction* in sociology, two approaches that share important similarities (Sil and Katzenstein 2010b, 2010a; Tavory and Timmermans 2014; Timmermans and Tavory 2012). The theoretical and methodological ideal of *abduction* – etymologically "leading away", in Latin – calls for the researcher to explicitly start with a theoretical point of departure, or knowledge of the relevant theories pertaining to the case at hand. But the ideal is to arrive at a "situational fit between observed facts and rules" (Timmermans and Tavory 2012, 171). This may call for adjusting or updating the theoretical starting point. This is the approach that has been guiding my work in both the PhD thesis and this book: Starting out with some theoretical and analytical ideas about what to look for in the data, and then to continually readjust these ideas as the research process unfolds.

In terms of academic literatures and debates, the book situates itself between several bodies of work. The literature I build on most directly is the very small literature that has covered Muslim Councils and Islamic umbrella or interest organisations more generally, in political science and sociology (Bayrakli, Hafez, and Faytre 2018; Braginskaia 2015; Bruce 2018; Ciciora 2018; Dazey 2021a; Godard 2015; Laurence 2012; Rosenow-Williams 2012). In order to understand the field and landscape that the IRN represents, I have also immersed myself in the large literature on Muslim movements and currents in Norway and Europe, and contemporary Islamic theology more broadly (Ahmed 2015; Jacobsen 2010; Jouanneau 2013; Larsen 2018; Maréchal 2008; Østberg 2003; Peter and Ortega 2014; Schiffauer 2000, 2010; Vogt 2008; Vogt, Larsen, and Moe 2011). The analytical concepts in the book, however, are mostly drawn from the field of organisational theory in sociology and political science (Ahrne and Brunsson 2008; Kraatz and Block 2008; Oliver 1991; Rosenow-Williams 2012; Scott 2013). Throughout the book, I will often talk about what the IRN or other organisations *do*, what the organisations *wants*, or what their interests *are*. This is line with a long-standing practice in the study of organisations, where organisations are often assumed to have some kind of collective agency or group agency (Gehring and Marx 2023).

I believe that this book gives a contribution to several bodies of work. Most immediately, it is a contribution to the literature on the political representation of Muslims in Europe. It engages in the discussion on Muslim councils and umbrella organisations, following important earlier contributions from Jonathan Laurence, Benjamin Bruce, Alice Ciciora, Kerstin Rosenow-Williams, Margot Dazey and Ekaterina Braginskaia (Braginskaia 2015; Bruce 2018; Ciciora 2018; Dazey 2021a; Laurence 2012; Rosenow-Williams 2012). More broadly, however, this is one of the first scholarly works to deal explicitly analytically with conflict in Muslims organisations and in the Muslim field in Europe, following earlier work by Bernard Godard, Uriya Shavit and Werner Schiffauer (Godard 2015; Schiffauer 2000; Shavit 2016). The analytical categories I place centre stage – cross-pressures, unstable institutionalisation and multipolarity – may be of value for understanding conflict among Muslims in Europe more broadly, beyond Muslim councils or umbrella organisations.

Within a broader political science debate, this book is a contribution to the literature on the political integration of Muslims in Europe. This literature has focused on issues like legal integration (Joppke 2013), value orientation and ideology among political and religious Muslim elites (Klausen 2005; March 2011), values and opinions among Muslim populations in Europe (Laurence and Vaisse 2007), willingness to include or exclude Muslims in the majority population (Ivarsflaten and Sniderman 2022), and collective organisation among Muslims (Pfaff and Gill 2006; Warner and Wenner 2006). The story I tell in this book follows Jonathan Laurence and Kerstin Rosenow-Williams (Laurence 2012; Rosenow-Williams 2012) in emphasising that the organisational meso-level matters: That representative Muslim organisations play an important role in the integration of Muslims and Islam in Europe.

1.4 Data, Analysis and Ethics

The data in this book come from several kinds of sources, and was collected over the course of several years. These sources are of varied types – archival written sources, media items, oral interviews, and field work observations. The written sources I consulted include thousands of contemporaneous newspaper records from the central Norwegian media archive *Atekst/retriever*, sources in private archives, posts on websites and social media, and scholarly literature on Islam in Norway.

The relevant scholarly literature on The Islamic Council of Norway, the Norwegian mosque landscape, and similar organisations in other European countries was an important starting point. I then continued by searching through the Norwegian media archive for all mentions of The Islamic Council of Norway, and related terms. I also read through all posts that the organisation made on their website and on social media, and I also accessed deleted posts through the Internet Archive.

Two private archives proved central. An important source of data for the first couple of decades of IRN can be found in the personal archive of Professor Oddbjørn Leirvik. Leirvik was instrumental in establishing the IRN, and was engaged in the formal dialogue between the Church of Norway and the IRN

INTRODUCTION 9

from the start. He maintained a personal archive from the very beginning, where he recorded all the letters that were sent to and from the Church of Norway concerning the IRN, minutes from meetings, as well as personal handwritten notes and scribblings from different occasions. He generously allowed me to consult those records. Another written archive I was able to consult from the 1990s was the personal archive of Bente Sandvig from the Norwegian Humanist Organisation (HEF). In the 90s there was much cooperation between the IRN and HEF. Sandvig's archive contained newspaper clippings, minutes from meetings and seminars, letters, and personal notes. She also generously allowed me to consult her archives.

I contacted the Islamic Council of Norway and asked for access to any archives they might have had. I was told by several actors that the historical archives of the IRN apparently vanished in 2010, because of the burglary of the laptop of the secretary general at the time. For the developments in recent years, when conflict was rife, I was not granted access to the internal archives of IRN. Some actors in IRN – both past and present – agreed to share some of their written records with me, such as emails, personal notes, minutes from meetings, and some key documents from the organisation that they still had in their possession. This was often done on the condition of anonymity. I approach these written sources with some caution, as some of them have been shared with me to "set the record straight" from the perspective of the actors, and may therefore omit information which does not fit the narrative they wanted to share with me. Nevertheless, many of these documents did contain information that proved vital for piecing the picture together.

I was also granted access to some official documents about the contact between IRN and Norwegian authorities, as Norwegian law mandates that communication with the authorities should generally be made available to the public upon request. I also accessed the administrative documents about IRN in the administrative Brønnøysund registries of Norway, to which organisations such as IRN are required to send reports about statutes, board members, etc.

Due to the sheer amount of written documents I surveyed, I did not do a complete coding or classification of all this written material. I used the material to build a historical timeline of the trajectory of IRN, as such an historical timeline did not yet exist. This involved reading and re-reading the material, fill in any gaps, and assess the evidence. A basic methodological principle was the use of triangulation: to use several sources of data to increase the chance of arriving at the most reasonable interpretation.

I complemented these written sources with 29 qualitative interviews with key actors, in both the IRN and external interlocutors. A full list of the interviewees is provided in appendix 1, except for two bureaucrats who asked that their names should not be published. The function of these interviews was partly to fill in gaps in the historical timeline. But I also relied on the interviews to understand more about why the events transpired as they did.

When conducting these interviews, I promised all the interviewees that it was done on the condition of anonymity; but that I could ask them to grant permission to be quoted by name on specific issues if they consented. Roughly half of these interviews were recorded, when the interviewees consented to that, and partly or fully transcribed later. I took extensive notes during the interviews which were not recorded and filled in these notes immediately after the interview. Some of the recorded interviews did not contain much important information. These interviews were partly transcribed by me, where I transcribed the most important parts and summarized what was more peripheral. The interviews which I deemed to contain essential information were fully transcribed by research assistant Malena Kyvik Martens.

To ensure anonymity when required, I will refer to the interviews in two ways. When I refer to interviewees by name, I also provide the date of the interview. When I refer to the interviewees anonymously, I assign each a letter – such as "B", or "Z". I do not provide the precise date or year for the interview for these anonymized referrals, as that could make it possible to identify some of them in conjunction with the interview list in appendix 2. The date for the interview is then provided as "2017–2019". The actors I interviewed belong roughly to three groups: current and previous key actors in IRN; current and previous key actors in organisations or institutions the IRN had much contact with, either public officials or persons in civil society; expert interviews, with external actors who had followed closely the development in the IRN, but who were not involved with IRN in a personal or professional manner.

The book also draws on some interviews I did earlier, for other research projects, and is also informed by fieldwork and over the course of many years. This fieldwork started in 2008, when I began doing work on what would become my master's thesis (Elgvin 2011). After working with that master's thesis, I made a habit of visiting mosques, Islamic organisations and organised Islamic events at regular intervals. I also kept in touch with many of the persons with whom I became acquainted at that time, both meeting them face to face and interacting with them on social media. In 2017 and 2018, I also participated as an observer in a joint programme between the municipality of Bergen and the mosques in Bergen, which was attended by imams, mosque activists, and employees in the municipality and Norwegian public services.

Even though I have tried to assess the data as objectively as possible, there is no getting around the fact that my biases and judgments as a researcher will inform this book. This is a qualitative work, where my own analysis of the

INTRODUCTION 11

events that transpired is central. In 2011 I was for example appointed to the contact/dialogue group between the Church of Norway and the Jewish community in Norway, as a lay representative from the Church (I was appointed due to the fact that I spent several years of my childhood in Jerusalem, and speak Hebrew fluently). Due to stays abroad I was not able to attend many of the meetings, and when I began working on this thesis the contact group had in any case become dormant. There is nevertheless a danger that this affiliation could predispose me to have a too positive outlook on the kind of dialogue that took place between IRN and MKR. Throughout working with the material in the book I have attempted to be mindful of such possible biases, and to think through whether the conclusions I draw are supported by the data or not.

The central question for readers of this work remains whether what I write can be trusted. The best way to achieve the trust of the reader is to ensure a sufficient level of transparency – to make "the essential components [of the] work visible to fellow scholars" (Moravcsik 2014, 48). In this thesis, this is only possible to a certain degree. As the oral interviews were done on the condition of anonymity, they cannot be made publicly available in complete form. Most of the interviews contain material that would make it easy to identify the speakers to people with some knowledge of the Islamic scene in Norway. But given that I list the people I spoke to in Appendix 2, they can in principle be contacted and asked whether what I wrote in this thesis rings true to them. I concluded that it was ethically acceptable to list the interviewees in the appendix, as long as I took care that individual citations could not be identified.

Most of the written sources, on the other hand, can in principle be made publicly available. The totality of the written sources I consulted – the Norwegian media sources, secondary literature, Leirvik's and Sandvig's personal archives, the postings on IRN's website – amounts to several thousand pages. All of these sources cannot be made easily available. What I do instead is to reproduce in an online appendix what can be regarded as key documents from the IRN. Some of these documents have been publicly available previously as well, but most have not. When providing these documents, it becomes possible for the reader to assess whether my analysis of these documents is reasonable.

In addition to the issue of transparency, it was important to think through ethical issues throughout the work with the thesis and this book. As Islam is a heavily politicized field in Norway, conducting this study required an emphasis on informed consent, privacy and confidentiality. Norwegian guidelines on research ethics state that research subjects are entitled to confidential treatment of all information about personal circumstances, and that research data should usually be anonymized (Norwegian National Research Ethics Committee 2016, 13–15). I ensured consent by telling the informants about my research project before each interview and made it clear that participation was voluntary.

An additional ethical requirement when doing qualitative research is the ideal of not causing harm to those one does research on. In this study, there is a non-negligible risk that my research may cause serious pain or stress to people who have been involved in the IRN. As will be seen in some of the next chapters, there are several actors in the IRN who experienced a heavy personal toll as a result of their involvement in the IRN, in particular relating to how they felt they were treated by the media. Some actors in the IRN have even gone through bouts of personal depression and burnout. Given that my PhD thesis and this book is the first scholarly study of the IRN, any negative depictions of particular persons may add to this stress. At the same time, it would be impossible to describe the IRN's history without talking about some of the actual persons involved. Some of them have moved on from the IRN and would maybe prefer not being associated publicly with the IRN anymore. But it would not be possible to anonymise the names of the two secretary generals of the IRN, for example, who played important roles in the organisation. How should this be balanced against the larger benefit of the study?

This is a dilemma without any definite answers. I have attempted to solve this dilemma through a delicate balancing act. Details which may put particular persons in a negative light and which I do not deem essential for understanding the trajectory of the IRN have been left out. In the cases where it was not possible to understand the trajectory of the IRN without describing particular actions by particular persons, I have included the most essential details. I have nevertheless tried to present the persons and their actions in a nuanced way, and to use wording they will hopefully be comfortable with. It is my hope that I have found a balance in the writing of the book which provides a good account of why events unfolded as they did, while at the same time respecting the persons involved and not causing them any unreasonable harm through the act of writing.

1.5 Overview of the Book: Multipolarity, Cross-Pressures and Unstable Institutionalisation

Throughout the book I elaborate on three analytical concepts, or social conditions, which led to the conflicts and splits in the Islamic Council of Norway: Multipolarity, cross-pressures and unstable institutionalisation. The book is structured in a chronological way, where each chapter deals with one important period in the history of the organisation. At the same time, the various chapters also delve into different analytical concepts.

INTRODUCTION

Chapter 2 chapter asks how and why IRN was created and deals with the late 1980s and the early 1990s. I show that IRN was created as a result from demands from both above and below – what I call a double search for representation. There were external actors who wanted to have an accountable organisation to relate to, but there were also Muslim actors who sought a representative organisation which could advance their interests. This double search for representation sowed the seeds for what would later emerge as a key challenge for the organisation; that it simultaneously faced pressure from many directions at once. In this chapter I also introduce how the concept of *multipolarity* can be used for understanding the Islamic field. The central challenge for the initiators who set up IRN was not diversity per se, i.e. that Muslims were different from each other. The challenge was rather multipolarity – the existence of several centres of power which competed with each other. It proved possible to overcome this challenge, however. The solution was to create an umbrella organisation that would not meddle too much in the internal affairs of its members.

Chapter 3 looks at how IRN developed in the consolidation phase, which lasted from roughly 1993 to 2006. This chapter surveys how the organisation attempted to balance the different demands it was facing during the first years, and the challenges it faced when doing so. Whereas the earliest discourse of IRN had an exclusionary bent to it, the organisation soon adapted to a discourse which was softer and more inclusive and aligned its goals to the political reality it faced. The organisation chose not to isolate itself but attempted to reach its goals in close cooperation with other organisations – notably the Jewish Community of Oslo, and the Norwegian Humanist Association, in addition to the Church of Norway. Analytically, the chapter introduces the concept of cross-pressures. The various members of the organisation had different goals, as had the authorities and its external dialogue partners. This led the organisation to engage in delicate balancing acts. It adjusted to demands from society at large, but nevertheless tried to find solutions that could be acceptable to most of their members.

Chapter 4 looks at the period between 2006 and 2012, in which the organisation attempted to grow and become more institutionalised. During the Cartoon Crisis in 2006 and 2007 the organisation played a role as a bridge-builder which Norwegian policy makers appreciated. As a result, the organisation received public funding for the first time and increased in visibility and standing. The main approach thus became to continue to engage in the art of balancing, along with changes in its internal discourse.

A conflict in the organisation emerged in the early 2010s, however, when new persons joined the leadership of the IRN. They had new ideas about how the organisation should be run. Under their leadership, the organisation increasingly sought a more independent profile. They sought independence from state funding by relying on income from halal certification and began to voice more criticism towards external actors. This created opposition on the part of the old leadership in IRN. Analytically, I claim that this development can be understood through the concept of *unstable institutionalisation*. Even though the organisation became institutionalised following the cartoon crisis in 2006, this institutionalisation was inherently unstable, both internally and externally. The internal structure of the organisation was not equipped to deal with the kind of conflicts and pressures that its new responsibilities could entail. The external environment, moreover, was unstable and unpredictable: actors in the organisation did not know how much they could rely on external support from the authorities. These conditions made it more likely that disagreements could become full-blown conflicts.

Chapter 5 covers how conflict and disagreements in the organisation deepened and ultimately led to a split between 2012 and 2018. In 2018, a faction decided to break out of the organisation to create the competing umbrella organisation *Muslim Dialogue Network* (MDN). The disagreements that led to the split were partly about personal conflicts. But there were also ideological disagreements over what kind of approach the organisation should pursue – an approach dedicated to soft outreach and external dialogue, or an approach dedicated to internal community building. I label these approaches *the dialogue path* and *the community path*.

Chapter 6 is short and deals with the aftermath of the split. After the split, the two competing umbrella organisations slowly moved closer to each other. After an initial fall from grace, the IRN was let back into the fold as a partner for Norwegian authorities, not least during the covid pandemic.

Chapter 7 summarises the book and discusses whether we can learn any lessons from the story of IRN regarding Muslim representation in Europe. This chapter brings together the various analytical building blocks from the book and proposes an answer to why the IRN ultimately split up. The cross-pressures the organisation was under became more intense in the 2010s and led to competing approaches of focusing on either dialogue or community building. This also made the condition of multipolarity even more challenging. The disagreement over different approaches towards society at large overlapped partly with other cleavages in the organisation, related to theology and ethnic background. This made it more difficult to arrive at compromises in the organisation that were acceptable to all. The result was a split, and one umbrella organisation became two.

The chapter includes a brief comparison with *shadow cases* from other countries – the UK, Germany, Austria and France (Soifer 2018). These shadow cases do suggest that the factors I identified in the Norwegian case have been at play in other Muslim councils as well.

The larger lesson from the story I tell in this book, I argue, is that successful representation of Muslim communities though representative councils may necessitate better institutionalisation of such organisations, and less pressure from the government and society at large. Muslim councils seem to be stable and perform well when they face predictable conditions – be it in form of guaranteed support from the state, or independence at a distance from the state. The Norwegian story also indicates that the IRN adapted to norms in mainstream society even in the 1990s, when there was less pressure from society at large and the organisation became engaged in dialogue and friendly alliances with other organisations. In the 2010s, however, when external pressure became stronger than it had ever been, the organisation went in a more inward-looking direction and ultimately split up. Getting Muslim representation to work well, for both Muslim communities and society at large, may require that authorities and society at large strikes a balance between demands and leniency towards representative Muslim organisations.

CHAPTER 2

Overcoming the Challenge of Multipolarity: the Road to the Islamic Council of Norway (1989–1993)

Why has it often proved difficult to be a Muslim council or umbrella organisation, in Norway and elsewhere? To the degree that there is an answer to be found in the existing literature, it is about diversity or pluralism among Muslims. Muslims are so different from each other and disagree on so many things, the argument goes, that cooperation becomes difficult. I begin the book by showing that this argument is too simple.

The chapter surveys how the Islamic Council of Norway came into being. What were the challenges, and how did the actors who were involved overcome these challenges? The main challenge the early actors in the IRN were facing was not about diversity per se. It was rather about multipolarity: That the Muslim field had several centres of power, who all vied for influence. But as the developments in these years show, it was not impossible to overcome this challenge. The creation of the IRN also hints about another challenge that the organisation would have to face in the years to come. It was created due to pressure from both inside and outside the Muslim field, what I call a double search for representation. Actors from the society at large asked Muslims to organise, to have someone to speak to. But Muslims also sought such organisation themselves, to defend what they saw as their interests. From the very beginning, the IRN thus faced pressure from many directions at once.

2.1 Foundational Research on Muslim Councils and Umbrella Organisations

To the degree that the research on representative Muslim councils can be said to be a defined field of research, it is largely owed to an influential series of publications by the American political scientist Jonathan Laurence (Laurence 2005, 2006, 2009, 2012, 2015; Laurence and Vaisse 2007). There were other researchers who also published valuable early studies on the emergence of such councils (Haddad and Golson 2007; Silvestri 2007), partly in dialogue with Laurence's early work, but these did not attain the same influence as Laurence's studies.

© OLAV ELGVIN, 2025 | DOI:10.1163/9789004701144_003

This is an open access chapter distributed under the terms of the CC BY-NC-ND 4.0 license.

OVERCOMING THE CHALLENGE OF MULTIPOLARITY 17

Laurence's focus from early on was on representative councils that were created from above, i.e. by the authorities and state actors. The backdrop for the interest in such councils from state authorities was what the political scientist Jytte Klausen has aptly named *the Islamic challenge*: the perception that the integration of Muslims and Islam in European societies posed some particular challenges (Klausen 2005). In Laurence's telling, policymakers thought for a long time that Muslim migrant workers would at some point return home. From the 1980s there was an increasing recognition that this was not going to happen. European governments realized that the temporary workers were not temporary, and wanted to deal with problems such as unemployment, social unrest and the nascent wave of religiously framed political violence. They therefore began to seek interlocutors who were locally grounded. At the same time, religion became a more important identity marker in Muslim populations. In his book *The Emancipation of Europe's Muslims. The State's Role in Minority Integration* (2012), Laurence describes this policy shift in the following way (italics in original): "Religion had previously been but one characteristic of this population of immigrant origin. Religion became *the* relevant characteristic for policymakers, and as such, the door through which social integration of this minority population would come to pass" (Laurence 2012, 148).

The expectation of Laurence – and many of the European government officials he interviewed – was that this would lead to moderation and adaptation in Muslim organisations and communities. Laurence saw this attempt to incorporate Muslims and Muslim organisations closer into the societal apparatus as being similar to previous attempts at corporatist incorporation of groups which had been more or less marginal in European countries: The Jewish communities in the 19th century, and labour/worker movements in the 20th century. The title of the book – the Emancipation of Europe's Muslims – is a deliberate allusion to what has been called the *Jewish emancipation* in the 19th century, when Jewish communities received rights as citizens in several European countries (Brenner et al. 2003). Laurence takes particular note of the Jewish emancipation in France under Napoleon, and the emancipation in Germany/Prussia and under Kaiser Wilhelm II. In both of these cases, Jewish emancipation consisted of a double process. Jewish communities and individuals were granted more rights as citizens. In return, the Jewish communities had to acknowledge the authority of the state and foreswear some theological ideas, such as the ban on intermarriage between Jews and non-Jews.

When Laurence began working on this topic in the early 2000s, the topic was novel and relatively unexplored. But soon other researchers also began working on the topic. Some of them emphasized that Muslim councils could also emerge from below, not only from above. Muslim actors also thought that they had interests to pursue, and that organising collectively could be a way of advancing these interests. The first articulation of this view came in 2010, before Laurence had published his major book. Emily Cochran Bech, then a PhD student in political science at Columbia University, wrote a conference paper in 2010 on Muslim councils in Europe (Bech 2010). It was a comparative case study on the emergence of Muslim councils in France, the United Kingdom, Denmark and Sweden. Bech's question was how Muslim councils emerged. This paper was never published in a journal, and the empirical analysis remained rudimentary. But some of the topics Bech focused on in her analysis would later resurface in other studies. Bech challenged what she saw as an overly state-centric tendency in the work of Laurence, in which the heavy hand of the state was seen as essential for the emergence of Muslim Councils. Based on the examples of the UK and Sweden, she claimed that such councils could also evolve from the ground up. Even though the initial impetus for the *Muslim Council of Britain* (MCB) had been gentle prodding from the Conservative Home secretary Michael Howard in 1995, it was nevertheless the Muslim organisations themselves that took charge of the process of creating the organisation (Bech 2010, 16–17). The same applied to Sweden, according to Bech. A Muslim council emerged in Sweden in 1990, which continued to function well until 2000s and 2010s – the *Swedish Muslim Council* (SMR). Even though it was not formally acknowledged as an official partner for the government, it did function as "the government's main consultative partner" [on Muslim matters], and it "represents a majority of Sweden's Muslims through its constituent organisations" (Bech 2010, 10–11). And crucially for Bech's argument, the SMR emerged largely bottom-up, it was not created top-down by the state.

A similar picture emerged in the PhD thesis of Ekaterina Braginskaia (Braginskaia 2015). Braginskaia compared Muslim councils in two very different contexts, Russia and the UK. In the UK she looked at the *Muslim Council of Britain* (MCB), and in Russia she looked at the *Russia Council of Muftis* (SMR). These councils have very different histories and make-ups, and the environments they operate within are also very different. The MCB in the UK primarily sought support horizontally and from below, and was created bottom-up. The SMR in Russia, meanwhile, primarily sought support from above, from the state and the authorities. This had to do with the opportunity structures the organisations faced. The SMR could rely on the state, but not so much on civil society and other organisations. The MCB could not rely on the state, which did not want to cooperate intimately with the organisation, and therefore turned to other organisations for support.

Political scientist Alice Ciciora (Ciciora 2018) later expanded upon these claims. She created a useful overview of all the Muslim councils in Europe defined as organisations or groups that "the state has in some manner designated to be the organisation with which it will consult" (Ciciora 2018, 336). She claimed that far from all Muslim councils were created by the state. Ciciora's claim was that the Muslim councils in Europe varied in two crucial dimensions. The first is whether the councils are generated top-down (state-created), or evolved; bottom-up. The second dimension is whether the organisation is *exclusionary* or *umbrella* – i.e. whether it includes all Muslim sects and denominations, or only some of these. According to her, Muslim councils of all types could be found across Europe.

Some studies have approached Muslim councils or representative umbrella organisations with different research questions. Political scientist Benjamin Bruce wrote a detailed historical monography on how Turkey and Morocco attempted to govern their diasporas in Europe (Bruce 2018). While it was not the primary focus of his work, he nevertheless touched upon Muslim councils in France and Germany. According to Bruce, the councils in France and Germany could only be deemed to be partially successful. They faced several internal and external obstacles that made their work difficult (Bruce 2018, 127–41).

The German Kerstin Rosenow-Williams also published a thorough book in Muslim umbrella organisations in Germany, based on her PhD thesis (Rosenow-Williams 2012, 2014). She distinguished between *umbrella organisations* and *peak organisations* (Rosenow-Williams 2012, 88). Umbrella organisations are federations of mosques and smaller Islamic associations, which is a common way to organise Islamic organisations in countries such as Germany, France and Sweden. Peak organisations, on the other hand, are essentially umbrellas of umbrellas, consolidating bodies that bring together different umbrella organisations – and come closer to what I refer to as Muslim Councils in this book. What distinguishes her study from the other studies on Muslim umbrella organisations, is that she studied their strategies and choices in depth. Drawing on insights from organisational theory in sociology, she claimed that an important factor influencing how Islamic organisations behave is the *expectation structures* they operate within (Rosenow-Williams 2012, 89). These organisations are often met with different expectations from different stakeholders. The members these organisations are supposed to represent, member mosques and individual Muslims, may wish for these organisations to take clear stances and voice their grievances. But the cooperating partners – the state, the municipalities, or other life stance communities – may expect these organisations to show themselves as responsible and cooperative players who refrain from making too many claims and demands. Rosenow-Williams' neo-institutional approach to organisations and institutions is an inspiration for this book, and I will return to her work in **chapter 3.**

2.2 Why So Many Conflicts?

None of these studies, however, have attempted to understand why there have been so many internal conflicts in Muslim councils or umbrella organisations. As was mentioned in the introduction, the existence of such conflicts has been mentioned in many publications, in countries as different as Germany (Bruce 2018, 135–42; Rosenow-Williams 2012, chapter 6), the UK (Shah 2016, 12–19), Austria (Kurier 2018), Russia (Braginskaia 2015, 15–16), the Netherlands (Atkinson 2016; Houten 2019), Sweden (Sorgenfrei 2018, 105–31), Spain (Laurence 2012, 196), and Belgium (Loobuyck, Debeer, and Meier 2013, 69–70). But there have not been systematic attempts in the research to understand why these conflicts occurred.

The only exception is what could be called a *semi-scholarly* book on Islam in France, by the French public servant Bernard Godard. He is a former official at the French Ministry of the Interior who was instrumental in setting up the Conseil Français du Culte Musulman (CFCM), who drew on his extensive experience with Muslim communities to write two books on Islam in France (Godard 2015; Godard and Taussig 2007). In the latter book, he devoted a whole chapter to developments in the CFCM and the conflicts that occurred. His perspective was that the conflicts were about *internal* reasons: Muslim organisations were simply too different from each other, in theological and political and ethnic orientation, and this made cooperation difficult. Godard did not explore whether there could be other reasons for the conflicts.

A similar argument can be found, however, in a few other works which also deal with conflicts and collective action among Muslims in Europe. In an influential article from 2006, the sociologists Steven Pfaff and Anthony J. Gill, explored the seeming lack of collective action among Muslims in Germany and Europe (Pfaff and Gill 2006). Their theoretical assumption was that Muslims «should» be likely to organise collectively, given that they have obvious collective interests in doing so. Nevertheless, this seldom happened, they claimed. They used Germany and the relations between mosques and authorities in Berlin as an example and showed that Muslims articulated their demands through narrow and small groups, and not through broad organisations or coalitions. Pfaff and Gill provided several possible explanations. Their most important explanation highlighted what they called the «decentralized character of Islam». According to them, this aspect makes it difficult for any actor to speak in the name of Islam and therefore makes it more difficult to organise Muslims across their differences.

Another influential article from the same year was written by the political scientists Carolyn Warner and Manfred Wenner. They made essentially the same claim. They too explored the political organisation of Muslims in Europe and noted a striking lack of organised collective action. Their explanation for this also had to do with the nature of Sunni Islam as a "decentralized" religion: "Islam is not conducive to large-scale, sustained collective action in the European context. Islam is a decentralized, non-hierarchical religion with multiple and often competing schools of law and social requirements" (Warner and Wenner 2006, 461). They did note that Shi'a Islam was centralized and hierarchical but claimed that this was not the case for Sunni Islam. Hence, this decentralized diversity of Sunni Islam made it difficult to come together to achieve common goals. Although Pfaff and Gill and Warner and Wenner's theory had to do with coming together, it may be extended to account for the stability/instability and functioning of Muslim councils.

An explanation along the same lines can be found in an article by the Islamologue Uriya Shavit, who explored the issue of fasting during Ramadan and how the two mosques in Iceland relate to each other (Shavit 2016). This article is particularly interesting given how small the Muslim community in Iceland is. Still, the one existing mosque split into two mosques in 2006. According to the interviews Shavit did, this split was not about doctrinal issues, but rather about personal conflicts. But after the split, doctrinal disagreement seemed to have reinforced the conflict. The split concerned a dilemma that Muslims who live in the north of Europe face during Ramadan: Should they follow the traditional ruling on fasting as it applies to Muslim lands? This rule states that one must refrain from food and water from dusk till dawn. But what happens if the sun never sets, as is the case in the Arctic during early summer? Or what happens if this leads to a fast of 18, 20 or 22 hours, like in recent years in Iceland?

This has led to two different interpretations. One interpretation is that fasting should then be done in accordance with the times of Mecca when the day surpasses 18 hours. The stricter interpretation is that as long as there is a difference between night and day – and two hours is sufficient for that, according to the adherents of this view – one should strive for fasting according to local times, as long as it does not endanger one's health. In Iceland, Shavit shows that this issue deepened the split in the small Muslim community. For some reason, the two mosques decided to opt for different approaches to fasting. This was a choice they had to make on their own, since there was no absolute authority in place to tell them what to do. One mosque follows the local hours, while the other follows Mecca. Because of this, the iftar – the breaking of the fast – occurs at different times in the two mosques in Reykjavik. The doctrinal and institutional diversity of current Western Islam, where the believers have a certain freedom in deciding which opinion to follow, seems to have played a

22 CHAPTER 2

role here – even though the split between the two mosques did not start out as a theological dispute.

2.3 Diversity vs. Multipolarity on the Muslim Field

But is diversity the best concept to use for describing the Muslim social field in European countries? The concept of diversity has often been used by scholars for describing the Muslim landscape in Western Europe is (Triandafyllidou 2010). Other scholars have used the related notion of *pluralism* (Maréchal et al. 2003, 36). Yet others have used concepts such as decentralized or non-hierarchical (Peña-Ramos and Medina 2011; Pfaff and Gill 2006; Warner and Wenner 2006). My suggestion in this book, however, is that the best way of conceptualizing the challenge of organising and collective action among Muslims in Europe is through the concept of multipolarity.

Even though the claim that Islam is a non-hierarchical religion is frequently made, it is not entirely correct. In Muslim majority societies, there have always been hierarchies and a state-governed way of organising religion, both historically and today. This is seen most clearly in the case of Shi'a Islam, which comprises approximately 10 to 13 percent of the global Muslim population. Shia Islam has a clear hierarchical and clergical structure, which goes back at least to the 18th century (Babayan 1996). It is often said that Sunni Islam does not have a church, with less formal hierarchies than the Catholics or the Shia Muslims have. But this is also a simplification. The Ottoman empire, which alongside the Mughal empire was the largest Muslim empire before the advent of modernity and European colonialism, had Islamic «curricula» beginning in the 16th century and onwards, which made clear what was and what was not deemed Islamic, and the institutions for higher religious education were controlled by the authorities (Ahmed and Filipovic 2004). In contemporary Turkey, this legacy continues with the state "church" Diyanet.

With the advent of European colonialism, new centralized ways of governing Islam were instituted (Gottschalk 2017). Decolonization and the rise of the nation state then once again led to a re-organisation of authority in Muslim-majority societies. In many countries, there were elaborate state-led attempts at organising and shaping how Islam should be interpreted and practiced. At the same time, networks and organisations emerged and organised expressions of Islam at a distance from – or in opposition to – the new Muslim states. Sufi brotherhoods had always been a fundamental feature of the organisation of Islam. In some states, such as Senegal, the Sufi brotherhoods became co-opted by the state and took part in governing (Diouf 2013). In other places they operated at a distance from the state. In addition to the Sufis, Islamist networks dominated by lay Muslims also emerged, frequently challenging the authority of the state. Claims about the "decentralized" or "non-hierarchical" nature of Sunni Islam are therefore exaggerated at best, and mistaken at worst. During the past centuries, Islam has been organised in a centralized manner in most Muslim states, both before and after colonization, and continuing after the rise of the nation state.

Still, the oft repeated claim about the decentralization of (Sunni) Islam does capture *something*, which is of relevance for understanding the Islamic field in both Europe and Norway. Sunni Islam does not have one big church. Regulation of religious affairs in Malaysia has not been managed by a "pope" in Mecca, but rather by local authorities. This is quite similar to Protestant Europe after the Reformation, where national kings wrested control of the Church from the hands of the Vatican. Because Muslims in the West come from all over the world, lines of authority may appear mixed and confusing. The institutional structure that provided clear lines of authority in their country of origin may no longer function in the same way in the new country. Transnational non-state networks may also be important. The religious backdrop against which we may understand Muslims and Islamic organisations in Western Europe is not non-hierarchical or decentralized. We might instead think of it as multipolar – an environment with several structures and organisations interacting with each other and with the society of which they are part, and where several actors wield nearly equal amounts of influence.

Conceiving of the Islamic landscape through the concept of multipolarity rather than the concept of diversity or non-hierarchy provides us with several insights. What is the difference? The concept of diversity invokes difference as the primary challenge to overcome. Muslims may simply be so different, the argument from diversity goes, that collective action becomes difficult. They come from different language groups, have different theologies, and occupy different classes and social positions. This is similar to the challenge that may arise if 10–20 people with very different culinary tastes have to agree between themselves about what to have for dinner. The argument from multipolarity, on the other hand, assumes that the challenge rather is that there are several power centers among Muslims in Europe, which compete over influence. This is similar to the challenge that may arise if three top chefs are tasked with making a dinner for a special guest, and they all want to use this opportunity to shine.

My analytical proposition is that when understanding collective action in the Muslim field in Europe, the situation with three chefs who all want to prepare a dinner is a more apt analogy than the situation with 10–20 people who have different culinary tastes. Yes, Muslims in Europe are obviously diverse and very different from each other. But if we talk of devout and practicing Muslims, at least, they also have some interests in common: Access to halal meat, Muslim holidays, Muslim burial sites, the right to bear the hijab, the right to construct mosques, etc. To the degree that they have difficulty cooperating to reach these common goals, it may not be because they are too diverse, but because there are competing centers of power who all want to have a say.

2.4 Multipolarity and Diversity among Muslims in Norway

The Islamic landscape in Norway exhibits both diversity and multipolarity. Muslims have varying types of religiosities and religious practice, and they have different national, ethnic and linguistic backgrounds. Some have migrated from Somalia; some have migrated from European countries like Bosnia or Albania. Some are first generation immigrants; some are the children of immigrants; and some are the grandchildren of immigrants. Some are native converts, and some are converts from an immigrant background. But there is also multipolarity at play. Various organisations have sought to organise and represent in the name of Muslims and Islam. At times, the relationship between these organisations have been competitive.

These tendencies could be seen from the very beginning, when Islam was established on Norwegian soil in the 1970s. The main scholarly work on organised Norwegian Islam in this period is a book on the Norwegian mosques and Muslim organisations by the historian of religion Kari Vogt originally published in 2000 (Vogt 2008), alongside some other early works on the sociological reality of Islam and Muslims in Norway (Ahlberg 1992; Jacobsen 2002; Østberg 1998). Vogt describes the organised Islam of the 80s and 90s as primarily divided along the lines of ethnicity and sectarian orientation. These divisions came to the fore gradually. In the beginning, there were so few mosques and so few Muslims that people congregated together across ethnic and theological divisions. As the number of Muslims grew in the 1970s and 1980s – and as the ethnic and linguistic diversity among the Muslims grew as well – a number of new mosques were established.

The most salient division on the Norwegian scene in the 1980s and 1990s was between what we may label as *South Asian competitors* – between *Deobandis* and *Barelwis*, and internally among Barelwis. As mentioned previously, Pakistani Muslims constituted the single largest group in Norway until well into the 2000s. The first mosque created was the Islamic Cultural Centre (ICC), which was founded by Pakistani labour migrants in 1974 (Vogt 2008, 38).

From the very beginning, the founders had sympathies with Jama'at e-Islami, an Islamist movement and party in Pakistan that also had a strong presence in the Pakistani diaspora in the UK. But according to the informants in Vogt's book, only a few people were actually members of the party (Vogt 2008, 39). The congregation was instead united by an ideological affinity and an interest in following the teachings of Abul A'la Mawdudi, the towering Islamist intellectual of Pakistan who had founded the Jama'at e-Islami. In the Norwegian context, though, ICC soon moved in a more liberal post-Islamist direction. More broadly, the ICC and the Jama'at e-Islami grew out of the *Deoband* movement in South Asia, which was founded in the late 19th century in India (Metcalf 2002). Deoband is a reformist, puritan movement, which has been critical of some traditional Sufi practices like commemorating Muslim saints.

But on the Islamic scene in South Asia, Deobandis have seen sharp competition from the Barelwi movement, which was also founded in the late 19th century (Jackson 2013; Tareen 2020). The Barelwi movement has maintained more of the traditional Sufi practices in South Asia, like singing songs together in the mosque, commemorating Muslim saints in the shrines and following spiritual leaders – the *pirs*. The Barelwis of Pakistan also created political parties, just as their Deobandi competitors did. The distinction between Deobandis and Barelwis is highlighted in Vogt's book (Vogt 2008). But Western scholarship on Islam has probably underestimated the depth of this conflict, as is documented in an excellent historical PhD thesis on this conflict by historian William Kessler Jackson (Jackson 2013). He documents several instances when central representatives from either the Deobandi or Barelwi school accused their opponents of not being Muslims (Jackson 2013). This is a very strong accusation, as apostasy from Islam is punishable in several Muslim countries.

So in 1976, only two years after the founding of the ICC, Pakistani migrants who sympathized with the Barelwi movement decided that they needed their own mosque. They founded what was soon to become the numerically largest mosque in Norway, the Central Jama'at-e-Ahl-e-Sunnat, often abbreviated as CJAS. Central Jama'at-e-Ahl-e-Sunnat congregated in several different locations for the next years, before subsequently moving to a location in Urtegata in downtown Oslo. CJAS soon became a large and influential mosque, as the clear majority of the Pakistani labour migrants were Barelwis and not Deobandis. The Barelwi congregation soon proved to be internally divided as well. In 1984 a split occurred, and some of the people in the mosque created another Barelwi mosque – the *World Islamic Mission*. This new mosque also experienced splits in the late 80s. The final major actor on the South Asian Islamic scene was the Tablighi Jamaat, often referred to as *Tabligh*. The Tabligh was founded in colonial India in the 1920s, as a puritan movement which aimed at reforming the mores and religious habits of Muslims. It is generally regarded as having grown out of the Deoband movement and is closer to the Deobandis than to Barelwis.

In addition to the Pakistani mosques, a number of Turkish mosques were founded in the 1980s. At the start of the decade, there was a single Turkish mosque, but this mosque experienced conflicts during the 1980s and split into three communities (Vogt 2008, 60). The largest community was connected to Diyanet, the official «state church» in Turkey. But the Islamist/post-Islamist Milli Görus also had a significant following, as well as the Sufi-oriented Süleymanci movement (J. Elgvin 2007). Other currents also set their mark on the Norwegian Islamic landscape during the 1980s and early 1990s, although the Pakistanis and the Turks were the largest groups numerically. In 1987, a mosque was founded by young Arabs which would later become a power centre in the Norwegian Islamic landscape, known colloquially as the Rabita-mosque (*al-Rabita al-Islamiyaa fi Norvij*) (Vogt 2008, 70). This mosque was founded by young activists who were loosely associated with the Muslim Brotherhood. Still, Rabita would soon move beyond traditional Islamism. It advocated for dialogue and reaching compromise with society at large, and attempted to avoid conflict and controversy. Throughout this book, I will therefore efer to their theological and ideological orientation as *post-Islamist*, not as *Islamist*. When using the term post-Islamism, like Werner Schiffauer did on his study on the Milli Görus (Schiffauer 2010), I want to make clear that these actors within the European context do not have any intentions of Islamising society as a whole. They come from an Islamist heritage, but their actual politics on European soil are usually very different from the politics that their Islamist brethren espouse in Muslim countries. Even though the Rabita mosque never had as many members as the largest Pakistani mosques, the level of activity was very high, and it set an outsized mark on the larger Islamic field in Norway.

There were also other kinds of mosques and Islamic associations in Norway which were established in the 1980s. Several smaller mosques catered to specific ethnic or national groups, such as the Gambian community or Turkish Kurds. Mosques from the Balkans or central Europe – from Bosnia, Kosovo or Albania – began to set their mark on the Islamic scene later on, but were not a significant presence in the 80s or the early 90s. There were some currents in Norwegian Islam, however, which were influential and had a substantial number of adherents but nevertheless stayed on the margins of the Islamic landscape more broadly. Most importantly there are the Shia: The 80s saw the foundation of a large Shia mosque, the *Anjuman e-Hussaini*. In the beginning, this mosque was dominated by Pakistani Shias. But with an influx of refugees from Iraq, Iran and Lebanon, Arab and Iranian Shias gradually became more influential. Still, the main Shia imam throughout the 80s was a Pakistani. As will be seen later in the chapter, the Shia cooperated with Sunni mosques in the fight against Rushdie's novel *Satanic verses*, but after that, they largely stayed out of the IRN, and did not cooperate much with other Sunni mosques – before rejoining in the 2010s (Elgvin 2023b).

Whereas Sunnis generally accepted the Shia as belonging to the Muslim fold, that was not the case with the quintessential outsider on the Islamic field in Norway: Ahmadiyya. Ahmadiyya is a religious community originating in Pakistan. It was founded by Ahmadi Kadiyani, a preacher who lived in present-day Lahore in the late 19th century. They define themselves as Muslims but are presently not recognized as Muslims by virtually any Muslim states or Islamic organisations. The reason is that they claim that their founder, Kadiyani, was a prophet. This is a stance which is in conflict with the traditional Islamic doctrine that Muhammad was the *seal of the prophets*, the last prophet to emerge. The first Ahmadiyya missionaries came to Norway already in the 1950s, and established a mosque in Oslo in 1980 (Vogt and Chaudry 2022).

The Islamic field thus demonstrated both diversity in terms of sectarian and theological orientation, and multipolarity in terms of competing power centres. In this regard, the Islamic field in Norway is similar to the Islamic fields in many other European countries. The organised Islamic field in Norway nevertheless has some unique features. In several European countries – such as France, Germany, and Sweden – mosques or Islamic associations are often organised through larger federations or umbrella organisations, and seldom receive funding from the state. In Norway, by contrast, the main organisational unit is the individual mosque. Mosques in Norway also receive funding from the state conditional on their formal membership size. This funding arrangement is required by law and has to do with Norway's history of having independent churches alongside the Church of Norway, which was the state church until 2012 (KUF 1995; Schmidt 2015). The independent churches and faith communities receive funding from the state based on their membership size, calculated from the sum that the Church of Norway receives. When adherents of other religions started setting up congregations in Norway in the post-war period, they were included in the same system. This means that mosques in Norway have a strong incentive to enrol people as members, and sometimes enter into a competitive relationship with each other.

The story in the rest of the chapter indicates that this multipolarity indeed can be a difficult challenge to overcome for Muslims who want seek collective representation. But the Norwegian story also shows that it is far from impossible. In this process, both internal and external factors played a role. The process

28   CHAPTER 2

that ended with the creation of the IRN did not happen solely due to an internal wish for representation, nor solely due to initiatives from external actors. It rather resulted from a *double search for representation*, from both within and without the Muslim communities themselves. This double pressure from both above and below, though, would later lead to difficulties in keeping the organisation together.

2.5   Coming Together for the First Time: the Rushdie Affair

In Norwegian public debate, it has sometimes been claimed that the IRN actually originated with the mobilization during the Rushdie affair in 1988 and 1989 (Akerhaug 2016). As this sub-chapter will show, there is a kernel of truth in this proposition. At the same time, the organisation that arose during the Rushdie affair was very different from the IRN organisation that was founded some years later.

The main facts of the affair are well known by now. The Indian-British novelist Salman Rushdie had published the novel Satanic Verses in late 1988, detailing the life of two Indian Muslims living in England, and grappling with questions of multiculturalism and belonging. Even before the publication of the novel in India, it created controversy. The title in the novel refers to a controversial episode in Islamic theological history, in which the prophet Muhammad allegedly received some verses which he thought were from God, but which actually came from heathen goddesses (Ahmed 2017). The threatening implication for orthodox Muslims was that if these verses were false, who is to know if other verses in the Quran may be false as well? As Shahab Ahmed shows, this led to the creation of an orthodoxy in which the existence of these verses was denied. By invoking these verses in the title, Rushdie was making a statement about doubt, insecurity, and ambiguity. But even though he likely did not know it, Rushdie also reproduced tropes from anti-Islamic discourses by using this title. The phrase "Satanic verses" itself was coined by a Christian Western orientalist in the 19th century who thought that the revelations Muhammad received had in fact come from Satan, not from God (Anthony 2019, 219). Muslim scholars, on the other hand, had throughout history referred to the verses as "the story of the maidens" (Anthony 2019, 216). By referring to these verses as *Satanic*, Rushdie was lending credence to tropes from orientalist anti-Islamic discourses. The novel, in many ways explorative and fantastic, also includes passages which are quite explicitly blasphemous. In one passage the narrator describes a brothel in Mecca, where the prostitutes carry the names of the wives of the prophet Muhammad. It is no wonder that Muslims perceived this as insulting.

It is nevertheless likely that very few of those who reacted against the novel had actually read it. It still created an immediate stir in India and Pakistan. Because of the tense communal relations between Muslims and Hindus on the Indian subcontinent, India and Pakistan have had strict laws on blasphemy since colonial times, which were meant to serve communal relations. In Pakistan, these laws became harsher in the 1980s during the reign of Zia-ul-Haq (Bangstad 2009, 139–85). Accusations about blasphemy regularly incited strong feelings among both Hindus and Muslims, and there have been several well-publicized cases in both countries where blasphemy accusations were brought before the law. The fact that Rushdie was Indian and Muslim in origin probably contributed to the fuss, and also the fact that Rushdie had achieved global acclaim as an author with his masterful first novel, *Midnight's Children*, which depicted the story of India from the beginning till the late 1980s. It was therefore one of «their own» who ruffled feathers.

Soon, the case went global. Ayatollah Khomeini, the spiritual and political Shia Muslim leader of Iran, published a fatwa in which he said that it was the duty of every Muslim worldwide to kill Rushdie, as well as anybody who aided in the publication of the book. A fatwa is an edict from a Muslim theologian which explains what is permitted and not permitted for a Muslim to do. When publishing a fatwa on Rushdie, Khomeini was in fact laying claim to be a normative source for every Muslim in the whole world. This quickly led to reactions in other parts of the world.

Norway was one of the Western countries with the strongest mobilization efforts against Rushdie's book (Engelstad 2013, 55). Soon after Khomeini's fatwa, an ad-hoc organisation called the Islamic Defence Council was formed. This cooperation council involved most of the mosques in Norway. For nearly one and a half year, they contested the publication of the Norwegian translation of the book. They arranged a major demonstration in Oslo on the 25.02.1989, in which nearly 3,000 people took part. This is a large number, given that there were only about 40,000 people from Muslim countries in Norway at the time, 19,000 of whom were members of the mosques (Daugstad and Østby 2009, 15). This implies that opposition against Rushdie's book must have been quite common in the various Muslim communities. The adopted slogans were «Stop Satan Rushdie» and «Respect for religion». Following that demonstration, the Defence Council decided to take the publishing house Aschehoug to court on charges of blasphemy, without much success.

The Islamic Defence Council was controversial from the very beginning. It always maintained an ambiguous view on Khomeini's fatwa and on its legality. On the one hand, they said that every Muslim in Norway had to follow Norwegian law, and that it was illegal for any Muslim to act against Rushdie or his associates. Their approach was to use legal means, and they sued Aschehoug for publishing the book. On the other hand, they refused to outright condemn the fatwa against Rushdie. The organisation was therefore met with much scepticism from other actors in Norwegian society.

For the purpose of this book, the unique feature of the Defence Council was that it was able to unite probably all of the mosques in Norway – and therefore functioned as an important precursor to the IRN. Given the multipolarity, conflicting identities and diverging interests among mosques and Muslims in Norway, how were they able to organise collectively in such a successful manner? Today, there are few publicly available written sources about the Defence Council. In her book from 2000, Vogt only mentions the Rushdie affair in passing. The journalist Ann-Magrit Austenå discusses the council in her book on the Rushdie affair from 2011, which included interviews with some of the actors (Austena 2011). Marianne Engelstad's master thesis is probably the most thorough treatment of the organisation so far, largely based on the aforementioned sources as well as newspaper articles from the period (Engelstad 2013). However, none of these authors specifically discussed the problem of collective action with regards to the Defence Council. For this thesis, I was able to access one additional source: An interview with Trond Ali Linstad, who functioned as the secretary of the council.

In my interview with Linstad, he stated that the Defence Council indeed functioned as a bridge between three of the main currents in Norwegian Islam in the 1980s: Barelwis, Deobandis and Shia. It was formed on the initiative of imam Mushtaq Ahmed Chishti in the Ahl-e-Sunnat mosque, the largest mosque in Norway. The imam, Chishti, seemingly enjoyed much authority. Linstad recounted it as follows:

> It was alama Chishti who stepped forward, and said that now we must unite, we must create a council, and we must stand against this attack on the prophet and on Islam.
>
> Interview with TROND ALI LINSTAD, 10.05.2018

Chishti was employed by the Barelwi mosque Ahl-e-Sunnat as imam in 1981. He passed away in 2002, and I never got the chance to meet him personally. But Vogt's book – and some of the interviewees I spoke to in 2017 and 2018 – depict him as an energetic, towering but also controversial figure. Later on, he become involved in long-standing conflicts. But in the 1980s, it does appear as if Chishti was the single most influential and predominant figure on the Islamic scene in Norway, and Ahl-e-Sunnat was the dominant mosque. When he called for unity and action, it appears that other actors and factions followed suit. Chishti convened a meeting, according to Linstad, and at this meeting, the agenda called for a discussion about how to proceed. At this meeting it was decided to form the Defence Council, and that imam Chishti would lead it.

The Defence Council also instituted a leadership board. It was composed of imam Chishti, and two other important figures with other sectarian orientations. The Deobandi Islamic Cultural Centre (ICC) – which was the first mosque in Norway – also joined. It was represented by imam Mehboob ur-Rehman. Rehman had been hired as imam in the ICC in 1985, and he would continue to serve as the main imam in the mosque until he retired in 2016 (Islamic Culture Centre Norway 2016). In the meantime, he would become one of the most influential Islamic figures in Norway. Lastly, the Shia also participated in the leadership board of the Defence Council. The third important religious figure was Mawlana Rizvi, who was the imam in the Anjuman e-Hussaini mosque, the largest Shia mosque in Norway. Like the other two imams, Mawlana Rizvi was also from South Asia. When these three men convened, they united the three main factions of Norwegian Islam at the time: Pakistani Barelwi Islam, Pakistani Deobandi Islam (and Islamism/post-Islamism), and Shia Islam.

Even though the Defence Council did not achieve their goal of stopping the publication of Rushdie's novel in Norway, they did achieve something else: they brought together the multipolar world of Norwegian Islam. Was this a difficult feat to bring about? According to Linstad, it was not too difficult. According to him, theological lines of demarcation was not a big deal in the Norwegian Muslim milieus of the 80s:

> I don't think it was such a demarcating line back then. I ran a Muslim community centre. On our board we had both prominent Shia Muslims and prominent Sunni Muslims, and it was never a problem.
>
> Interview with TROND ALI LINSTAD, 10.05.2018

Linstad's assessment may have been influenced by the fact that he himself never emphasized the intra-theological differences in Islam. When he converted to Islam and became a Shia in the 1980s, it was mainly because of the Iranian revolution. Shia Islam seemed ascendant, and most promising from a political standpoint. "It just felt natural, with the revolution in Iran. Also, I have never been very obsessed with literalism and all the small details in Islam. I am concerned with the big questions, with politics and society", he said in our interview. It is thus possible that Linstad downplays the sectarian fissures during the late 80s, because he never perceived them as important.

The tight cooperation in the Defence Council does nevertheless lend some credence to Linstad's assessment. But as will be shown later in the chapter, this was not to last. Only a few years later, Shias silently disappeared from the

IRN project, and there was opposition among some of the Sunnis to including them in the organisation. As I have argued in an article in The Journal of Muslims in Europe, the strong alliance during the Rushdie affair probably had to do with the existence of a strong common goal or enemy (Elgvin 2023b). In the absence of such a common goal later on, it would be more difficult to build bridges across lines of division.

After some time, the activities of the Defence Council seemed to die down. They lost the battle in court and were not able to stop the publication of Rushdie's novel. In my interview with Linstad, he made it clear that things did not transpire as he had hoped after the affair. Things went back to a certain normality in the mosques. They did not concern themselves much with activism in the public sphere, but rather took care of internal communal life, just like they had done before the Rushdie affair. For Linstad, this was a source of grief:

> During the Rushdie affair, I had hoped that something would change. But people withdrew back to their mosques. They conducted their activities in their own mosques. If one approached them and tried to get them out on the street again, they were hesitant. "We all need to be nice", that kind of stuff. Some of the dynamics had disappeared.
>
> OE: What do you mean by "we all need to be nice"?
>
> It was very important to them that the Norwegian public should cuddle them on their heads. The Church should be our friend, etc. That is a good thing in itself, of course. But who defines that dialogue? Who has power in that relationship? That is the Norwegian public. Or the Church. Mainstream society. Take one of the mosques that I used to have contact with. They invited Sonja, the queen of Norway, to visit them. So, the queen visits, and everybody was very happy. That's how it became.
>
> Interview with TROND ALI LINSTAD, 10.05.2018

This indicates that the kind of activity and organisation that the Defence Council had instigated could not be sustained for a prolonged period of time, and the mosques went back to normal. A similar story was told by two other activists who were active during the Rushdie affair, who would also get involved with IRN in the early years, and who did not want to make public their involvement during the Rushdie affair. Their version of the events is similar to Linstad's. At some point, the activity in the Islamic Defence Council largely faded away, they said. They had lost the battle in court, and most of those who had been active in the Council wanted to go back to normal: "The energy just wasn't there anymore", one actor told me, although he did not want to talk publicly about his activity in the Defence Council (interview with K, 2017–2019).

OVERCOMING THE CHALLENGE OF MULTIPOLARITY

In 1991 there were reports in the media that there were internal conflicts in the Defence Council, and the organisation seemed to be in trouble (Stanghelle 1991). When Rushdie visited Norway in August 1992, there was no mention of the Defence Council in the national press, suggesting that the organisation either had ceased to exist or lay dormant. Three mosque leaders protested publicly, including the sheikh from the Shi'a Anjuman e Hussaini mosque who had been a part of the leadership in the Defence Council, but they did so in their own name and in the names of their mosques, not in the name of the Defence Council (NTB 1992). The other leaders from the old Defence Council were notably silent, suggesting a change of approach. The Ahl-e-Sunnat mosque – the CJAS – which had dominated the mobilization against Rushdie in 1989, even came out publicly against these imams, and said that the imams were only speaking for themselves (Engelstad 2013, 54–55). This was a remarkable development. CJAS had led the Defence Council just a few years earlier, but now they distanced themselves from such protests – which were milder and softer than the protests which had taken place earlier.

One reason for this may have been that a new chapter in the institutional history of Islam in Norway was about to be written just around the time of Rushdie's visit: The IRN was about to be founded, because of an invitation letter from the Church of Norway.

2.6   The External Impetus: the Initiative from the Church

The initiative the led to the creation of the IRN was external and hailed from the church of Norway in 1992. It is impossible to know whether IRN would have materialized as an organisation without such an external impetus. What seems very probable, however, is that it would not have happened at this point in time. As will be shown in the following sections, there did not seem to be a strong demand for collective organisation in the Norwegian mosques in the early 1990s. It is of course possible that the mosques would have created such an organisation later. The decisive event happened in early 1992. The MKR – the *Council* on *Ecumenical and International Relations* in the Church of Norway, more or less functioning as a kind of ministry of foreign affairs in the church – sent a letter to all the Islamic congregations it could locate in Norway, and invited them to a meeting with the goal of establishing "formalized contact" (Bakkevig and Tveit 1992a).

Some background may be necessary to understand the context for this invitation. By the early 1990s, Muslims had become a more established part of the Norwegian societal landscape. Like in other Western European countries,

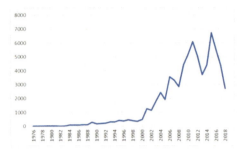

FIGURE 1 Mentions of 'Islam' in Norwegian print media
SOURCE: RETRIEVER/ATEKST, THE NORWEGIAN MEDIA ARCHIVE

Muslims moved to Norway with post-war labour migration, and the numbers subsequently increased with refugee and family migration. This resulted in a public and political debate where the presence Islam and Muslims increasingly became an issue, even though it still received less focus than it would later do. Figure 1 includes the mentions of the word Islam in Norwegian print media. Norway maintains an encompassing searchable media archive, where almost all Norwegian media can be searched all the way back to 1945 (https://www.retrievergroup.com/no/product-mediearkivet-atekst). As can be seen, the largest uptick happened after the attacks on 9/11 in 2001. But in the 1980s, there was a rising number of mentions of Islam and Muslims in the Norwegian media, with a particularly noted increase during the Rushdie affair in 1989.

This tendency can be easier to understand if we compare the mentions of "Muslims" "Pakistanis" and "immigrants" – three categories that could be used to refer to the same people. At the turn of the 1980s, Pakistanis constituted the largest group by far among the immigrants in Norway, and an overwhelming majority of the Pakistanis were Muslim. Figure 2 contains the annual mentions of Muslims, Pakistanis and immigrants in Norwegian print media, from 1970 to 1995. The timeline goes from 1970 – the year before the first major wave of Pakistani migrants arrived in Norway – and 1994, the year after the founding of the IRN.

In the 1970s, there was almost *no* mention of Muslims in Norwegian media, whereas Pakistanis, and subsequently immigrants, were mentioned. At the end of the decade, this began to change. From the early 80s and onwards, immigrants were the dominant category for a time. The mention of Muslims, however, was also increasing, and the shift seems to have started in 1979 – the year of the revolution in Iran and the Soviet invasion of Afghanistan. Muslims were mentioned with increasing frequency throughout the 1980s, until it

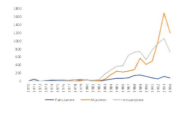

FIGURE 2
Mentions of "Muslims", "Pakistanis" and "Immigrants" in Norwegian print media, 1970–1994
SOURCE: RETRIEVER/ATEKST, THE NORWEGIAN MEDIA ARCHIVE

surpassed immigrants as the most mentioned topic in 1992. Some of these mentions did not have to do with Muslims in Norway, though. It is likely that Pakistanis and immigrants would usually be used to refer to persons in Norway, whereas Muslims could also denote Muslim groups who were involved in developments abroad. The increased use of "Muslims" throughout the 1980s and early 1990s nevertheless indicates that there was a stronger focus on Muslims and Islam in the Norwegian public sphere – as in in other countries in Europe (Brubaker 2013).

The political environment in Norway during these years also resembles the environment in other countries in Western Europe. A political culture which may be described as *soft multiculturalism* gradually gave way to a more critical discourse in immigration, Islam and multicultural society. There has been some debate among Norwegian scholars as to whether Norway has ever had a policy that can be labelled *multiculturalist* – where some aspects of cultural difference are promoted and celebrated, and minorities enjoy certain rights as groups (Bygnes 2013; Djuve 2016; Gripsrud 2018; Hagelund 2003; Simonnes 2013). It is safe to say that Norway has never had a formal multiculturalist policy that awarded group rights to immigrants or that doubled down strongly on celebrating diversity. But it can still be argued that there was a stronger discourse in the late 1970s and the first part of the 1980s empasising that one needed to meet migrants with understanding, and that migrants should be allowed to keep some of their norms and customs. We may label this *soft multiculturalism*.

But this began to change towards the end of the decade. The discourse of soft multiculturalism was challenged by a new political discourse that aspired to place harder demands on the migrants, and also by a sub-discourse of outright racism and Islamophobia. In the mid-1980s there were several violent attacks by Norwegian neo-Nazis which received much attention in the press, including an attack on an Ahmadiyya mosque in 1985. The far right also started to gain political influence for the first time. Before the municipal elections in 1987, the leader of the Norwegian populist far-right Progress Party Carl I. Hagen claimed to have received a letter from a Muslim man called Mohammad Mustafa, which warned that Islam would "gain victory in Norway too", and that "the infidel cross in the flag shall go away". The letter was soon revealed to be a fabrication, and the alleged sender of the letter – who was in fact a real person, located at the very address which was stated in the letter – took Hagen to court. Hagen claimed that he was not aware that it was a fabrication and apologised for having publicized it. It nevertheless created a stir, and the Progress Party went on to have their best election ever shortly thereafter, after a boost in the polls following the episode (Jupskås 2015, 85).

Such events led to a concern about racism and discrimination, and in the next decade there would be several academic and political debates revolving around immigrants and racism in Norwegian society (Eriksen 1995; Midtbøen 2017). In Norway, this situation led to an interest in interfaith and intercultural dialogue as a remedy against discrimination. Norway witnessed several high-profile dialogue projects in the late 1980s and the beginning of the 90s involving secular humanists, Muslims, Christians and Jews. These projects were carried out under the auspices of *Nansenskolen*, "The Nansen academy" – a humanist educational institution that had pioneered several influential dialogue projects in Norway in the 1980s and early 1990s (Eidsvåg 1993). Many of the actors who later became active in organised interfaith dialogue had their first encounter with inter-religious dialogue through Nansenskolen.

The Church of Norway also became a part of this trend. The Church of Norway is probably the oldest existing organisation in Norwegian society, going back all the way to the Reformation and the creation of a Danish/Norwegian protestant kingdom in 1536. In the 1990s, it was still a state church. The bishops were appointed by the government. Fundamentally, the leadership in the Church had to operate within the norms that were seen as somewhat appropriate within Norwegian society, even though it also aspired to maintain some independence towards the authorities and had at times been at odds with the influential labour movement (Haugen 2015). The prevailing ideology in parts of the church was that of a "folk church": A church which was not only for the few faithful, but for large segments of society, including those who only went to church occasionally (Hegstad 1999, 22–27). Many in the church felt responsible not only for saving souls, but also for the general welfare of Norwegian society. Activists in the church were also influenced by a more general preoccupation with interfaith dialogue within Western Christianity, in which people in the Church of Norway took part.

The very first records in Leirvik's archive have to do with international initiatives for inter-religious dialogue. In 1984 and 1985, several meetings took place in the Lutheran World Federation on the topic of dialogue between religions. These meetings called for the member churches to engage in dialogue with people from other religions. In Norway, this led the MKR – the *Council* on

Ecumenical and International Relations in the Church of Norway, more or less functioning as a kind of ministry of foreign affairs for the church – to establish a working group that was tasked with working on the "relationship to other religions in Norway" (Seim 1986). The MKR had previously written a report on how the Church could deal with the arrival of refugees in Norway. The previous report had been focused on issues of welfare and integration, while this new working group were to work on questions dealing with theology and identity. This work culminated in a book published in 1991 with the title *Når tro møter tro* – "When belief meets belief" (Nordhaug 1991). An overriding concern in these publications is that religious minorities are discriminated against – and that interfaith dialogue can be of benefit to society and the minorities themselves.

In 1991, the Church of Norway then took steps to formalize dialogue with Muslims in Norway on its own behalf. The MKR decided to take the initiative to arrange a "formalized contact" with Muslims in Norway – deliberately keeping the wording vague, as they didn't want to take for granted what form this formalized contact should have (Mellomkirkelig råd 1991). In order to get the "formalized contact" with the Muslims up and running the MKR enlisted the support of the theologian and priest Oddbjørn Leirvik. Leirvik had been one of the earliest clergymen in Norway to heed the call to have dialogue with people from other faiths, and had a broad contact network among Muslims and Muslim congregations.

Leirvik went to work and penned a draft of a letter, which contained an invitation to a meeting which was to be held in April. This letter was later sent out to all the mosques he became aware of on 20 January 1992, signed by the leaders of MKR (Bakkevig and Tveit 1992a). The invitation was also sent to several Christian organisations and to representatives from the authorities and other civil society organisations. The letter was formulated in an open-ended manner and avoided any mention of controversial topics. This open-ended strategy seems to have worked. In Leirvik's archive, one finds several positive responses from different mosques. No mosques declined the invitation formally.

But there does appear to have been some reluctance on the part of some mosques, as several mosques, including some of the largest, did not send a response, and some made it clear that they were not available on that date. Because of this, it was not possible to hold the meeting in April as planned. What happened instead was that several of the mosques tried to regain control over how to organise themselves – and created an umbrella organisation prior to the meeting with the church.

On 20.08.92, MKR received a letter dated 18 August 1992, which stated that some of the mosques had pre-empted the process: They had held a meeting among themselves, and it also emerged that they had created what they referred to as the "Islamic Council". The letter reads as follows:

> With reference to your letter from the 20/01/1992, where 1–2 persons from every Muslim organisation and congregation in Norway was invited to a meeting on the 26.04.1992. As you already know, this meeting was cancelled from our side, and you expressed that this meeting could take place at a later occasion.
>
> Later on, all Muslim organisations and congregations in Norway have come together and taken the decision that we will name an official delegation which will meet you, and which will represent all Muslim organisations and congregations in Norway. This in order to facilitate the communication between us.
>
> With this, we thank you again for your invitation, and we are looking forward to getting a suggestion for a meeting date from you. A response to this letter can be sent to this address.
>
> Regards,
> Zahid Mukhtar
> Secretary of Islamic Council
> MUKHTAR 1992a

It is not clear from the sources what kind of organisation this was – if they had a formal leadership and membership, etc. But the meeting between the mosques had at least led to the creation of a proto-organisation which was to function as their representative.

2.7   The Internal Response: the Wish to Represent Islam

The fact that the mosques organised between themselves prior to the meeting with the MKR and created an Islamic Council without input from the MKR, underlines how Muslim representation in Norway was the result of a double search for representation, from both the inside and the outside.

In August, a proto-IRN seemed to have been founded. What had happened? The sources from the period indicate that important issues had to with internal struggles about orthodoxy and correct representation: Who were proper Muslims and who were not? Who had the right to speak in the name of Islam? The MKR received a letter in April from the Ahl-e-Sunnat mosque. It was written in English and is reproduced verbatim below.

Contact between the Church of Norway and Muslim organisations in Norway

Your letter dated 20.01.92 & 05.03.92

We acknowledge with thanks for your above two letters. But regret to say that we cannot contact you well in time, due to Ramdan our holy month's engagements.

We have come to know that your church has invited all the muslim org. and religious muslim org. in Norway.

For your information, we mention that in muslim world the under-noted two named are not treated as muslim org:

1. Ahmediya Menighet, Frogner Oslo
2. Taloo-e Islam, Oslo

Therefore, they are not entitled to take part on behalf of muslims in Norway.

The detail has already discussed on telephone.

Thanking you again.

Yours faithfully,
Mohammed Ashraf
President

ASHRAF 1992

This letter, from the largest mosque in Norway, makes clear what boundaries they wished to set – for what Islam is, and who should count as a Muslim. The first name is a reference to the Ahmadiyya – the Muslim movement originating from Pakistan which defines itself as Muslim, but which is not accepted as such by most other Muslim organisations. Somewhat more surprising is the mention in the letter of the group Taloo-e Islam, more commonly spelled Tolu-e-Islam. This is a modern rationalist Muslim group, which was founded by the Pakistani scholar and activist Ghulam Ahmed Parvez (1903–1986) (Reetz 2010, 316). In the early 90s they had around a couple hundred adherents in Norway. Tolu-e-Islam espouse a rationalist interpretation of Islam in which the Quran reigns supreme, and most of the hadiths are discarded. The hadiths are sayings and stories from the prophet Muhammad and his companions, which were collected and written down some hundred years after the death of the prophet. In most traditional interpretations of Islamic theology, the hadiths have traditionally constituted a normative source on a par with the Quran. Some of the most famous Islamic commandments, such as the commandment to pray five times daily, can only be found in the hadiths. But the hadiths are also the source of some of the most controversial parts of traditional Islamic teachings, such as capital punishment for apostasy. There has therefore been a tendency among modern reformist Islamic groups to place more emphasis on the Quran, and less on the hadiths. Tolu-e-Islam goes quite far, in that they explicitly say that most of the hadiths are false. But they uphold that Muhammed is the final messenger of God, and the Quran is the word of God. While Islamic groups in Pakistan have put much focus on Ahmadiyya, there has not – to my knowledge – been a similar focus on Tolu-e-Islam. The fact that it was mentioned by Ahl-e-Sunnat at this time does nevertheless indicate that Tolu-e-Islam was also regarded as controversial, probably because of their stand regarding the veracity of the hadiths.

There are other indications as well that it was a preoccupation at this early stage to determine who should have the right to properly represent Islam, and particularly to avoid including heterodox Muslim groups. Olav Fykse Tveit, who was an advisor at the MKR and in charge of organising the planned meeting, wrote an internal memo to the MKR after the meeting which can be found in Leirvik's archive. He provided the following assessment in an internal report written some months later:

> In the process around the cancellation [of the first meeting], we received information that several Muslim organisations were considering how they should respond to the invitation and how they should conduct themselves. As far as I understand, the Islamic Council was created around this time. Their secretary, Zahid Mukhtar, contacted me in order to acquaint himself to me and in order to ensure that the meeting would be between MKR and the Islamic Council. As far as I could understand it was a strong wish from some of the largest Muslim organisations that that the Muslims should conduct themselves collectively when meeting with us, and to avoid that representatives from Ahmadiyya would participate at the meeting.
>
> TVEIT 1993

In their letter to the MKR, the Ahl-e-Sunnat mosque therefore wanted to lay down the limits of Islam – in terms of whom could and should be allowed to represent Muslims in Norway. Both the Ahmadiyya and the Tolu-e-Islam were deemed to be outside the fold.

The initial meeting between the interested parties among the Muslims was held on the premises of the Ahl-e-Sunnat mosque, according to several interviewees. There were also other kinds of organisations for migrants and migrant workers who came to the meeting, and who wanted to have a seat at the table, according to interviewees who were present at the meeting. In the 1970s and

1980s, the mosques were not the only important organisations for migrants in Norway – welfare unions and worker unions had also been important (Korbøl and Midtbøen 2018, 269–303). When it became a question of representing Muslims, should these older organisations have a seat at the table as well? Zahid Mukhtar, the first secretary of IRN, recalled it in the following way in our interview:

> We called in these organisations to the meeting, and there were more than 100 organisations there. Literally everybody. Among them was, for example, Pakistan Welfare Union. So, we discussed whether they should come along as well. But we made the point that MKR was a religious organisation, they want to meet about religious, theological stuff, so the welfare organisations do not have anything to do with that. Then it was decided that the mosques should go on with the process alone. So, we had two or three more meetings with the mosques. Some mosques stopped coming to the meetings as well. They did not have any particular interest in it. But some mosques continued, and that in time became the IRN.
>
> Interview with ZAHID MUKHTAR, 24.10.2018

Two other interviewees put the numbers of organisations attending the meeting as being respectively in the 40s and the 50s, so the number of organisations that attended is uncertain. The letter from the Church and this meeting nevertheless marks a turning point in the organisation of Muslim migrants in Norway. The welfare unions, which had for a long time been important, were now being sidelined and the mosques would go on to become central vehicles for representation vis-à-vis mainstream society.

It is not clear – neither from the written sources in Leirvik's archive, nor from the interviews – when the mosques took the ultimate decision to form the Islamic Council. What is clear is that by 18 August, when Zahid Mukhtar sent the letter to the MKR, a proto-IRN had come into being, even though it was still a nascent organisation without any statutes. This was accepted and recognized by the MKR. In a new letter of invitation dated 28.10, they once again invited to a meeting, this time on 15 December, acknowledging that the last meeting had to be cancelled. They upheld their original list of invitees, but also said that the new Islamic Council was "specially invited" (Bakkevig and Tveit 1992b).

The Islamic Council nevertheless responded positively to this new invitation, in a letter dated 4 December. They also stated that their delegation would consist of 19 people, and provided their names in a list (Mukhtar 1992b). When doing it this way, these mosques took back ownership of the process. They could decide who to include, and who not to include. This way, they were not only acted upon through the invitation MKR – they became proactive actors who shaped their own trajectory.

According to those I interviewed who were present at the meeting on 15 December, the meeting was deemed to be a success. It was attended by close to 50 people. The IRN sent their delegation of 19 people. Two other mosques who were not represented through the IRN also sent representatives. From the Christian side there was a comparable number of participants, ranging from the MKR to the bishop of Oslo, missionary organisations and the major theological institutions in Norway. There were also other observers present. There were journalists from many of the major newspapers, a representative from a government ministry, and Inge Eidsvåg, who was the head of the aforementioned dialogue-initiator Nansen Academy. Jan Opsal, an academic and scholar of Islam who was present at the meeting, emphasized later that this broad presence gave the initial meeting strong institutional weight (Opsal 2013, 24–25). It was decided that the MKR and the Islamic Council should continue with discussions on how to proceed with contact and dialogue. After this meeting it also appears that the IRN decided to form a proper organisation with statutes and a board.

After that initial meeting, the nascent organisation would become narrower in scope. At some point – the exact time is unclear – a committee was appointed which was to write statutes for the organisation, two of the interviewees told me. According to several interviewees, they took inspiration from a similar Swedish organisation, which had been founded a few years earlier – perhaps the Muslim Council of Sweden, which was founded in 1990 (Sorgenfrei 2018, 122). The committee then worked to harmonize the statutes from the Swedish organisation to the Norwegian context. On 22 October 1993, these statutes were signed, during the first annual plenary meeting of the IRN. Whereas it had called itself *Islamsk Råd* – "Islamic Council" – in the initial contact with MKR, it now called itself *Islamsk Råd Norge*, "The Islamic Council of Norway". These statutes were signed by only five mosques:

1. Ahl-e-Sunnat (Pakistani Barelwi)
2. The Rabita mosque (Arab/international post-Islamist)
3. The Islamic Cultural Centre Union (Turkish Süleymanci)
4. Tanzeem ul Muslimun (Pakistani Tabligh)
5. The Moroccan Cultural Centre (Moroccan traditionalist)

The MKR had invited over 40 Muslim organisations and congregations in January 1992, and the meeting at Paulus in December 1992 had attracted at least ten. Now they were now down to five.

2.8 Overcoming Multipolarity: Idealistic Entrepreneurs and Post-Islamists

At this early stage IRN was not in fact representative of most of the mosques and Islamic organisations in Norway. At the meeting on 15 December 1992, there were mosques that sent their own representatives, who apparently did not feel represented through the proto version of IRN. The data material I uncovered implies that the difficulty in uniting during this time had to do with both multipolarity – competition between centres of power – and diversity and differences.

The names of those who were not part of the official IRN delegation are preserved in Leirvik's archive. I was able to identify four of these people as belonging to two Pakistani Barelwi mosques: Ghousia Muslim society, and the Minhaj ul-Quran. The Ghousia mosque broke away from World Islamic Mission in 1989, which had in turn broken away from the Ahl-e-Sunnat mosque in 1984. The Norwegian branch of Minhaj ul-Quran, created by the Pakistani cleric Taher ul-Qadri was also created around the same time, in 1990. When the IRN was founded formally in October 1993, other mosques who had been represented at the meeting in December 1992 were not present anymore.

According to a couple of my interviewees, the disagreements during this period were not so much about theological profile, but simply about competition between mosques who often had a similar profile. This was most clearly the case in the Pakistani Barelwi community. One of the interviewees described the rivalry between the Barelwi mosques at the time in this way:

> All of these prejudices against each other ... These organisations were created because of personal conflicts and personal grudges, you know. It is not religious, theological stuff. They stand for the same thing! They are the same! Theologically they are exactly alike. But still, they are different organisations.
>
> OE: So, it has been personal conflicts which made it to be ... [interviewee interrupts]
>
> There were personal conflicts they had, yes. These old men. That is why they broke off from each other. You know, World Islamic Mission, everyone who created that mosque had been some of the most important people in the Ahl-e-Sunnat mosque. The same with the Ghousia mosque. They were in World Islamic Mission and broke away. That's why cooperation was difficult.
>
> Interview with K, 2017–2019

Given the fact that the Ahl-e-Sunnat mosque was the initial driving factor in the early stage of the organisation, one interpretation is that the other Barelwi mosques were sceptical. In our interview, Zahid Mukhtar also indicated that there could be distrust between the mosques:

> I remember some of the mosques being sceptical when I tried to get them to come along. They were looking at me like, 'this Zahid Mukhtar guy who runs around being so active. But whose project is this really'?
>
> Interview with ZAHID MUKHTAR, 24.10.2018

This does indicate a certain rivalry between some of the mosques. When Mukhtar tried to get the other mosques on board with the project, it was interpreted as being the project of *someone* – of somebody trying to gain something through the IRN project. At this point in time, some of the mosques which were close competitors – meaning that they competed over the same pool of potential sympathizers and members, and therefore had conflicts of interest – seemed to have been locked into a pattern of competition.

But there were also processes of exclusion that had to do with sectarian differences and theology. The archival record makes clear that this at least applied to the heterodox Ahmadiyya and the Tolu-e-Islam, as was discussed earlier. Even if they were interested, they would not have been let into the fold by the orthodox mosques. Among the Turkish mosques, the Sufi-oriented Süleymanci movement that was in opposition to the Turkish state took part, but not the state-connected Diyanet.

What about the Shia? They had been important players during the Rushdie affair, and they were part of the IRN's delegation to the meeting with the MKR in December 1992. But they did not sign the statutes in 1993 and would not take part in the work of the IRN in the years to come. A couple of the interviewees alluded to simmering conflicts between Sunni and Shia Muslims in the early 90s. This is also in line with Kari Vogt's assessment. She mentions that there had been debates on whether to include the Shia or not in the IRN (Vogt 2008, 216). She also mentions that the IRN decided not to exclude the Shia. But although there was no formal exclusion of the Shias, the fact that their later admission was controversial indicates that there was some scepticism towards the Shia among some of those who were active in the IRN. This may have led the Shia to feel they were not particularly welcome, even though they were formally allowed to participate.

A key difference from the mobilization during the Rushdie affair seems to have been that the perceived need for collective mobilization was much lower in 1992/1993. At this point, the potential reward for taking part in the IRN project was uncertain: Would the IRN become successful? Would it provide any benefits to those involved? Would the organisation reach their goals? Responding to a letter and showing up at a meeting – like the IRN project entailed in the very beginning after the invitation from the MKR – is comparatively easy. To spend one's time and resources building a new organisation is more demanding.

One of the activists from the early years of IRN was clear that most of the mosques did not see any reason to take part initially:

> In the beginning there was zero interest for IRN in most of the mosques. They laughed at us! Really, there was zero interest. I think the reason is that it didn't provide them with any reward. Muslim organisations need to, you know, they have to kind of see a value in it for themselves.
>
> But when IRN really became something and people got to read about it in the paper, they got to know that the authorities wanted to engage with the IRN, that we met the prime minister ... that was like honey for these organisations. It attracted them. Suddenly IRN had value for them. Then, one by one, they wanted to become a member.
>
> Interview with K, 2017–2019

The key to getting the organisation off the ground in these early years, was the presence a few highly devoted and idealistic organisational entrepreneurs. For them, the perception of a Muslim interest was the deciding factor, according to several interviewees. They simply thought that they had a duty to defend the interests of Muslims in a non-Muslim country. They therefore spent a lot of time and resources in making that happen. In this process it was particularly actors with a post-Islamist orientation from the Rabita mosque who became dominant, alongside some actors from other mosques who report to have been driven by a strong sense of idealism and duty.

When the proto-IRN started up in 1992, the Barelwi Ahl-e-Sunnat mosque had been dominant. Zahid Mukhtar, the first secretary of IRN, came from that mosque, and the very first meetings among the mosques where they discussed whether to form the IRN took place on the premises of Ahl-e-Sunnat. But Ahl-e-Sunnat soon became less influential and did not become the most dominating force in IRN. Zahid Mukhtar continued to be active in the IRN for the years to come. But he did so completely on his own, and told me that he did not receive any support from the mosque. He spent time being active in the IRN because it just seemed important to him that someone should do it:

I think I just wanted to contribute. I spent a lot of my spare time and my own money on going to these meetings. I was driven by the fact that I should contribute with what I could do. I could write good Norwegian, could write minutes from the meetings, could keep the meeting activity going, could hold things in place. The secretariat was in a way driven by me.

Interview with ZAHID MUKHTAR, 24.10.2018

Other important actors in the early years who may have been driven by a similar kind of motivation include Abdullah Tanatar, who was Turkish and represented the Süleymanci mosque, and Kebba Secka, who was from Gambia and represented the Gambian mosque. Both of them would fill important roles in the IRN in the years to come, and they have been mentioned by several interviewees as being important in the early phase (I was unable to conduct interviews with them myself). The records show that these actors were more or less the only representatives from their mosques throughout the next decade. That may indicate that they were driven by a personal belief that the work in the IRN was important, more than by pressure from their organisations.

Mukhtar provides an illustrative example of how the work was done in the early years:

In the start we had absolutely no funding. There was no membership fee from the start. But we needed some money to run an office. Most of it came from our own pockets. We bought coffee and biscuits out of our own pocket. The travel expenses were never covered! At this time, we had a small office in Trondheimsveien [a street in downtown Oslo]. One small room. I remember that it was often cold there. There was a toilet in the hall and a small kitchenette. That's how it was. One bought a printer, the other bought paper. No organisations gave us any money. We had to repeatedly collect money to pay the rent. One guy donated the carpet. These guys, [Mohamed] Bouras and Abdullah [Tanatar], they painted the walls of the office themselves.

Interview with ZAHID MUKHTAR, 24.10.2018

It is a reasonable interpretation that this kind of activity requires a fair share of idealism. To spend one's own money on a project like this, to spend one's free time, up to the point of paying for office expenses and spending time painting the walls, requires quite a lot of commitment and devotion to the cause.

The only mosque which seemed strongly devoted to the IRN in the very beginning was Arab-dominated Rabita mosque. Even though it did not sign the foundational statutes, the Pakistani Islamic Cultural Centre also became an important supporter of the organisation soon thereafter. Both in the foundation phase and in the years to come these two mosques would wield more influence in IRN than any other groupings. In the first couple of years, Rabita would be most influential by far. The two first leaders of the IRN, and several other activists in the IRN, belonged to that mosque.

The first leader of the IRN was Abdelmounim Elamin. He was a man of Sudanese origin who had come to Norway in 1973. I interviewed him over skype, and he confirmed that he wanted out of the organisation as soon as there were others who could take over:

> You know, I never wanted to have any of those positions. I had been the secretary of the Rabita mosque in the late 1980s. I didn't want that position either! But some people pressed me to take that position [as secretary in Rabita], because they needed somebody to do it. Then when the IRN came, people wanted me to be the leader of that organisation. I said no at first, but they insisted. So, I accepted, because I thought it was important that somebody did it. But as soon as there were others who could take over, I said that I didn't want to do it anymore.
>
> Interview with ABDELMOUNIM ELAMIN, 17.04.2019

It is difficult to know whether Elamin's recollections of his motivations are accurate, given that almost 30 years have passed. What his recollection does indicate, however, is that people from the Rabita mosque quickly became influential in the IRN, and that there had been people – presumably in the Rabita environment – who had asked him to be the leader. When Elamin stepped down in 1994, the next leader became Mohamed Bouras, who also came from Rabita. He served as the leader of the organisation until 1998. Other activists from Rabita also played important roles in the organisation in those early years.

Why did the Rabita mosque become so influential? It is reasonable to see this in light of the larger pattern of Muslim activism in European countries. Activists, mosques and organisations with a similar post-Islamist orientation have been hugely influential in many countries, far beyond what the numerical membership in their organisations should imply, not least when it comes to contact with authorities and other organisations in civil society. In an internal memo that Oddbjørn Leirvik wrote in 2003, in which he summarized the preceding decade of dialogue between the Church and the IRN, this very pattern was noted: "Those we have contact with are for the most part 'Islamists' of a moderate or relatively liberal kind, who stand for Islamic more than national-religious interests. This is otherwise a typical pattern in all organised Christian-Muslim dialogue, internationally as well" [quotation marks and italics in the original] (Leirvik 2003).

By "Islamists", Leirvik was probably referring to Rabita and to the Pakistani mosque, Islamic Cultural Centre, which would also become influential early on. As mentioned previously, this mosque had ties to the Islamist party Jameat Islami in Pakistan in the early years, and the founders were inspired by the Islamist scholar Mawdudi. Throughout the 90s, this mosque maintained a steady presence in the IRN. As Leirvik notes, this has also been seen internationally. Mosques and organisations with a post-Islamist orientation have been active in many different umbrella organisations (Khan 2013, 216–19). One reason may be their ideological and organisational heritage: Social activism and responsibility for society was encouraged and was been seen as a worthwhile ideal. While some mosques may have been content with tending to the communal life in the mosques, activists within the post-Islamist lineage may have wanted to set their mark on the broader society of which they were a part. When I interviewed activists from the post-Islamist camp, several of the interviewees volunteered an explanation along these lines, without being prodded. One leading activist identified himself in our interview as "very much a reformist":

> I have always been against Islamist politics. Always! Take Jameat Islami in Pakistan for example. It is just so completely backwards. And it is not only me. Even the people I know have been positive to the Jameat Islami in our mosque have said that it was more like that back in the day, that they do not support them that much now.
>
> That does not mean that I reject our heritage. I get inspiration from Mawdudi [the intellectual father of Pakistani Islamism] as to being engaged in society. For what is politics, you know? Politics is to care about society, isn't it? I need to care about whether that road is maintained, about how the kindergarten in my neighbourhood functions, about how things are in society. The alternative is to just lock yourself in and only have the vertical relationship [to God]. But that will not take you very far. It is about making society better for everyone, not just for the Islamist party ... I am very much against them.
>
> Interview with C, 2017–2019

This quotation indicates that this activist interprets the legacy of Mawdudi and political Islamism as being about a certain mode of being Muslim in society, rather than about adhering to specific policies or opinions that Mawdudi or the Jameat Islami might have held. He still held Mawdudi in high regard, but seemingly interpreted him in a way that is compatible with his scepticism towards political Islamism.

Another interpretation of why the post-Islamists became so central in the IRN can be found in a contemporaneous assessment that Oddbjørn Leirvik made in 2003. He wrote in an internal report that the Islamists or post-Islamists were ideologically more concerned with representing Muslims or Islam as such – they had a stronger pan-Islamic ideology (Leirvik 2003). Other mosques may have had identities which were more particularistic, and more oriented towards their own movement.

When looking back on the early phase of dialogue between the MKR and the IRN, this was also the impression that had stuck with Olav Fykse Tveit, who worked in the MKR in that period. His perception in our interview was that some mosques were interested in participation, while others simply were not interested:

> There was some narrowing in IRN very early on. Some mosques wanted to participate. Others did not seem as interested. I am not completely sure why. It seems as if some had an interest in participating in the democratic process, you know, being a part of society. Others mostly wanted to do their own thing.
>
> Interview with OLAV FYKSE TVEIT, 24.08.2018

One interpretation of why the membership in the organisation became narrower following the initial meeting with the MKR is therefore that it may have been a question of commitment. To engage in the IRN at this point required quite a lot of investment. There were no paid positions, and almost all of those who were active in the IRN had demanding jobs on the side. Furthermore, the potential reward was uncertain: 1993. At this point, the potential reward for taking part in the IRN project was uncertain. The only ones who seemed to have had such a level of commitment to the cause of the IRN in the early phase were the post-Islamists in ICC and Rabita, and some idealistic and ideological individuals who belonged to other mosques.

The public record backs up elements in this story: Only five mosques signed the statutes in 1993. But in the years to come, the number of member mosques would start growing. Part of this pattern, at least, can probably be explained by the fact that IRN was an uncertain project in the early phase, and most of the mosques were not sure if it was worth the investment. In addition, the multipolarity on the Islamic scene and the competition between some of the mosques was a barrier to cooperation. To invest in the organisation during this early phase, one would have to be deeply convinced, ideologically, that it was a worthwhile endeavour.

The record thus shows that IRN was created due to a double search for representation. Externally there was a push for someone to represent Muslims. In the Norwegian case, this external actor was the Church of Norway when the organisation was founded. But there was also an internal push for representation. Idealist entrepreneurs and actors with post-Islamists orientations felt a duty to advance the interests of Muslims. Orthodox Muslims were also concerned that the wrong kind of Muslims would not end up representing them. This double search for representation, from above and below, led to the creation of the IRN. In the years to come, this kind of cross-pressure would be one of the most important challenges that the organisation had to handle.

CHAPTER 3

Dealing with Cross-Pressures: a New Organisation Finds Its Place (1993–2006)

The previous chapter detailed an internal challenge for the IRN – multipolarity. The next phase in the history of the organisation soon began. In this phase, the challenge was not only about internal challenges or diversity, but also about relations to the external world. Throughout the next years, the IRN had to balance pressures and demands from both the inside and the outside. For understanding this predicament, I use the concept *cross-pressures*, adapted from voting research in political science.

This chapter surveys how the organisation attempted to balance these different demands during the first 13 years of its existence, from its foundation in 1993 until the cartoon controversy in 2006. Whereas the earliest discourse of IRN had an exclusionary bent to it, the organisation soon adapted to a discourse which was softer and more inclusive and aligned its goals to the political reality it faced. Throughout these years, the organisation sought to find balancing solutions: To avoid external conflict, while keeping their member organisations satisfied with the work of the organisation.

3.1 A Muslim Umbrella Organisation under Pressure

What kind of organisation was the IRN? When the organisation was formally founded, it was structured as an umbrella organisation. Within the sociology of organisations, such organisations have sometimes been called *meta-organisations*, following influential publications by Göran Ahrne and Nils Brunsson (Ahrne and Brunsson 2005, 2008). Their rationale for using the concept meta-organisation is that it directs our attention to one of the most important facets of such organisations: its members are not individual human beings, but other organisations. In this book, however, I will simply use the more common concept umbrella organisation, given that I think it works just as well. Ahrne and Brunsson's theorizing on meta-organisations, however, is highly useful for understanding some inherent challenges for the IRN project.

As Ahrne and Brunsson point out, organisations are often more goal-directed than individuals. Individuals have goals as well, of course, and organisations do not always operate in a very goal-directed manner. But

© OLAV ELGVIN, 2025 | DOI:10.1163/9789004701144_004
This is an open access chapter distributed under the terms of the CC BY-NC-ND 4.0 license.

goal-direction is nevertheless more pronounced in organisations (Aldrich 2008, 4). This means that the problem of collective action may be even more pronounced in a meta-organisation than in an individual-based organisation. In organisations where the members are individuals, the members can usually be moulded and socialized into some dominant norms or ways of thinking. This is less likely in a meta-organisation. The member-organisations have their own goals and will probably be less malleable than individual persons. They also have their own survival as an organisation to think about. If there is a conflict between the interests of the meta-organisation and their own interests as organisations, the member-organisations of a meta-organisation will usually prioritize their own interests. In order to overcome this challenge, meta/ umbrella organisations often have a structure which grants substantial autonomy and leeway to the member organisations.

The organisational set-up of the IRN fits neatly with the Ahrne and Brunsson's theory. The statutes emphasized that the organisation would not encroach on the autonomy of the member organisations. The IRN would not interfere too much in the internal life of the members, and the members were to keep their autonomy in many matters. This principle was laid down in the statutes: "IRN's statutes do not limit the sovereignty and independence of the member organisations in their work. The members can, within the limits of the statutes, work independently and have contact with the authorities and organisations in Norway and abroad" [sic].

When I interviewed Mohamed Bouras, the second leader of the IRN, this was one of the few topics he mentioned concerning how the IRN was organised in the early phase:

> Of course, we had our discussions. But if we quarrelled, we did it between ourselves. We don't go to the public with it. In that way we kept the respect for each other. Everybody had to follow and respect the laws of Norway, of course, but otherwise we tried to accept our diversity.
>
> Interview with MOHAMED BOURAS, 20.01.2018

Ahrne and Brunsson also hypothesized that meta-organisations may find it difficult to deal with conflicts (Ahrne and Brunsson 2005, 441). Meta-organisations often have weak hierarchies, given that they depend to a large degree on their members. This makes it difficult to solve conflicts by authority or managerial decree. When conflicts cannot be solved by authority or decree, they must be solved between the members themselves. This makes it essential to be able to reach consensus within the organisation.

The challenge for IRN, however, was that it would soon be asked to take a stand on many different issues. From the very beginning the IRN was experiencing various conflicting demands from above and below – from their members, and from actors in society at large. The pressure from the media, in particular, could at times be rather intense. Whereas multipolarity had been a challenge when setting up the organisation, the main challenge in the first period revolved around balancing the various demands the organisation was facing. In the interviews I did with actors who were active in IRN in the 1990s and the early 2000s, none of them mentioned internal multipolarity as a major challenge for the organisation during this period. Most of them described the experience of the 1990s, in particular, as a period when they had a sense that they were working towards the same goal. To the degree that they perceived challenges and difficulties for the organisation in the 1990s and early 2000s, it was about how to deal with different constituencies and stakeholders. Key actors perceived that the IRN consistently had to balance different demands and interests against each other, both among Muslims and between Muslims and mainstream society. The later deputy leader of IRN Asghar Ali – who became active in IRN at a later stage, in the 2000s – expressed this in clear terms in our interview:

> IRN is kind of in a squeeze. We are in a double bind. We are squeezed in between Muslims and mainstream society. Muslims, that includes everyone from persons who say that they don't believe in Islam, but nevertheless want to claim the Muslim identity hat in debates on TV, to those who say "we need to kill all the non-believers", or who'll call me an apostate because I'm on good terms with some politicians. I'm joking and exaggerating here of course, but I'm just trying to get the point across. This diversity is enormous! And all these people from the Muslim side look to the Islamic Council of Norway and want us to do what they want. Because we are the most authoritative organisation. And then you also have mainstream society, with politicians and the media, who also want us to do what they want.
>
> So, what to do? It's not always easy. Sometimes, you know, if you see that large groups of Muslims are angry, maybe it's better to give people a way to blow off steam ... but in a constructive way which will be understandable to people in mainstream society. But maybe such a demonstration will back-fire, if there are people there who will not act peacefully? That could give Islam a really bad name. One needs to weigh those things. Basically, it is about advancing the interest of Muslims in

Norway. That's the heart of it. But what is the best way of doing that in specific situations? It's not easy.

Interview with ASGHAR ALI, 25.04.2019

These different expectations were there from the very beginning. IRN faced some expectations from its members, other expectations from its dialogue partners in MKR, and other expectations from the media and policymakers. There are different ways of making theoretical and conceptual sense of this predicament. In organisational theory and the sociology of organisations, the term *multiple institutional logics* has gained prominence in the past couple of decades (Kraatz and Block 2008; Pache and Santos 2010; Thornton, Ocasio, and Lounsbury 2015). This term emphasizes that an organisation like the IRN simultaneously needs to operate within several institutional spheres – the world of the Norwegian mosques, transnational Islamic organisations, contact with the authorities, relationships with other faith-based organisations, contact with the media etc. Each of these spheres contain different logics concerning the appropriate modes of behaviour – the rules of the game differ (Kraatz and Block 2008, 243). The term institutional logic makes it clear that this is about more than expectations that certain actors hold. It is also about norms of behaviour which may be more or less formalized. The problem with this concept is that it is complicated and difficult to understand if one is not initiated into organisational theory.

A more intuitive way of making sense of this predicament is to use the term cross-pressures. This term was introduced in political science in the 1940s. The concept was introduced in 1948, when Paul Lazarsfeld and his associates published a study of the American presidential election in 1940 (Lazarsfeld, Berelson, and Gaudet 1948). Their idea was simple: People usually belong to more than one social group, and these different social groups or identities may draw them in different directions. In 1940, Protestants tended to vote for the Republicans, and Catholics for the Democrats. Likewise, richer people tended to vote Republican, and poorer people tended to vote for the Democrats. But what about those who were rich and Catholic at the same time? These voters were said to experience cross-pressure. According to Lazarsfeld et al., this would result in a tendency to abstain from voting, since there would be some unease connected to choosing either choice over the other. In recent years, several studies have confirmed the prediction of the theory (Belanger and Eagles 2007; Mutz 2002; Therriault, Tucker, and Brader 2011). In sociology, a similar kind of phenomenon has been accounted for through the notion of role conflict developed by modern classics in sociology such as Talcott Parsons (Goffman 1959; Merton 1957; Parsons 2005). This notion does not focus on the inner convictions, values or opinions of a person, but rather on the behaviour

DEALING WITH CROSS-PRESSURES

one is expected to display towards others. The idea is simple: In daily life – at work, in family and with friends – people assume different roles. Each of these roles carry with them certain expectations from people in the surroundings. Sometimes, these roles come into conflict with each other. When using the notion of cross-pressures in this book, I am understanding it in a rather common-sensical way: That different actors and environments placed different demands on the actors in the IRN.

This experience of facing cross-pressures and competing demands both internally and externally led the IRN to a search for compromise – finding balancing solutions which hopefully could make everyone somewhat happy. This approach may remind of the organisational strategy the sociologist Kerstin Rosenow-Williams called *adaptation* in her book on Islamic peak-organisations in Germany. Rosenow-Williams used the terms *adaptation, decoupling* and *protest* for describing the strategies these organisations engaged in (Rosenow-Williams 2014, 762–64). This conceptualization was inspired by a seminal work on organisational strategy by Christine Oliver (Oliver 1991). By adaptation she meant a broad range of actions which accommodate the demands of society at large. Organisations could also respond to pressure from the outside by *decoupling* – which meant that they tried to continue business as usual by creating a buffer between the core activity of the organisation and the external demands. *Protest* means direct confrontation with the external environment – clear resistance to the expectations of the external institutions.

One limitation of this conceptualization, though, is that organisational strategies are conceptualized as occurring between the organisation and *one* set of external demands, typically from the authorities and society at large. But an organisation like IRN faces cross-pressures and operates within multiple institutional logics. It deals with several conflicting demands at once – from member organisations, from unaffiliated Muslim actors in the Islamic field, from the media, from authorities, from partner organisations, and perhaps from international and transnational Muslim actors. Here I will therefore instead draw on an influential account by the organisational theorists Matthew Kraatz and Emily Block (2008), who explicitly dealt with how organisations react to multiple institutional logics. They proposed four different strategies through which organisations can try to deal with competing demands or logics. Adapting their framework somewhat for the case at hand, I propose that IRN throughout its history attempted to deal with conflicting pressures in four fundamental ways: *balancing – decoupling – withdrawal – independence*.

Balancing means to balance the different demands, by finding solutions all parties can live with. Decoupling means to compartmentalize the demands, by decoupling some of the demands from the activity of the organisation, for example saying one thing externally, and another internally. Withdrawal means to avoid having to deal with some demands in the first place, for example by staying out of the media spotlight. Kraatz and Block conceptualized withdrawal strategies as being part of a larger pattern of *resistance* or *defiance* strategies, where an organisation tries to resist one or more of the demands it faces. Due to the fundamental power imbalance between IRN and society at large, however, overt defiance has rarely been seen through its history. I will therefore focus mainly on withdrawal as the preferred strategy for resisting certain demands. Finally, an organisation like the IRN may try to achieve independence, by acquiring enough resources and power to be able to withstand demands from the outside.

Figure 3 shows how these different strategies relate to each other, from least to most accommodation of the various conflicting demands:

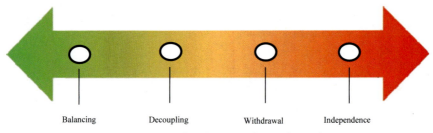

FIGURE 3   Organisational strategies when facing conflicting demands

These categories are abstractions, of course, and real organisational strategies may not always conform easily to a continuum like this. Throughout most of IRN's history, there were elements of all of these strategies. Even on the occasions when IRN pursued a strategy motivated by a wish for independence, it nevertheless tried to balance different demands to a certain degree. This categorization can nevertheless serve as a useful typology for understanding the kinds of strategies a meta-organisation like the IRN decided to pursue.

3.2   The Rushdie Case Once Again: Early External Pressure

The cross-pressure the IRN was facing was evident from the very beginning. On the exact same week that the organisation was founded in the end of October 1993, the organisation found itself under fire. The controversy was once again connected to the Rushdie case. A couple of weeks before the founding of the IRN, there had been an attempted assassination on William Nygaard, Salman Rushdie's Norwegian publisher and the editor-at-large of Aschehoug, one of the oldest and most prestigious Norwegian publishing houses. Aschehoug had been one of the first foreign publishing houses to translate Rushdie's novel, and

DEALING WITH CROSS-PRESSURES

was the first to publish a cheaper pocket version of the book (Engelstad 2013, 27). Nygaard was shot outside his house on the 11 October by an unknown shooter, who managed to flee and was never caught.

Nygaard was only one out of several people associated with the Rushdie novel who had been attacked. The Italian translator of the book only barely survived a knife attack in July 1991. The Japanese translator of the novel was stabbed to death in another attack only a week later. In June 1993, a hotel in the Turkish town of Sivas was torched by a mob because the Turkish translator of the novel was staying there. The Turkish translator survived, but 37 other people died. Then, some months later, in October, Nygaard was attacked. The identity of the attacker has never been determined, even though several of the journalists who have covered the case have claimed that signs point to involvement by Iran (Isungset 2010, 2018).

It was only natural that this would create public debate in Norway. Nygaard had become a famous figure in Norway, and Norway had witnessed a large mobilization against Rushdie's novel only a few years earlier, during the hey-day of the Islamic Defence Council. At this juncture, however, the IRN did not want to have that much to do with the Rushdie affair. This was evident in the opening speech that a representative from the proto-IRN delivered at the initial meeting with the Church of Norway December 1992. He emphasized that Islam should not be confused with various social ills, and "last but not least – Khomeini's death penalty over Salman Rushdie" (Qureishi 1992).

In spite of this reticence, it was the Rushdie affair that prompted IRN's first public appearance. The publisher Nygaard had been shot on 11 October. On October 20, two days prior to the formal founding of IRN on October 22, the still very young Zahid Mukhtar had been invited to participate in a discussion on the TV channel TVNorge and it was mentioned in the debate that he was the secretary of the IRN. In that debate, Mukhtar apparently made statements which were equivocal. I have not been able to find a recording of the debate itself. Some commentators, however, got the impression that he did not condemn the attack on Nygaard (Harket 1993). Mukhtar immediately sought to rectify this impression, and issued a communiqué the next day clarifying that he did not support the attack on Nygaard. In this communiqué, he notably did not sign as secretary of the IRN, even though he had been presented as such in the debate.

> What Mukhtar said on the program was that Nygaard could expect such a reaction after publishing Satanic Verses.
> – We are sorry for what has happened to Nygaard, Mukhtar says, who is the information secretary of the mosque in Urtegata in Oslo.
>
> VG 1993

The fact that Mukhtar did not sign this communiqué as secretary of the IRN may indicate that other actors in the IRN did not want to associate themselves with the Rushdie affair. When the IRN – through Mukhtar – and the MKR started discussing a joint meeting some weeks later, Mukhtar let it be known that they preferred not to discuss the Rushdie affair. This issue also indicated to the IRN that the relationship with the media and society at large would not necessarily be easy.

3.3 Choosing Moderation and Dialogue: from Early Discourse to Educational Policies

As the organisation began its work in the fall of 1993, it nevertheless became clear that the organisation attempted to find balancing solutions and strategies, and that they chose moderation and dialogue over confrontation.

From the statutes, it was not immediately clear what the organisation should do. The statutes outlined goals and activities which were rather general, such as to "represent Norwegian Muslim organisations in relations with Norwegian authorities and institutions", "help and give advice to the member organisations". The statutes also made clear what the aims of the organisation were. Most of the aims had do with the Muslim *ummah*, the imagined Muslim community, and have a clear defensive ring to them:

3.1. To unite all Muslims living in Norway in an Islamic community/union/ society ["samhold" in Norwegian]

3.2. To promote, protect, maintain and strengthen our Islamic identity.

3.3. To create external conditions which enable Muslims to live in accordance with Islamic teachings.

3.4. To spread knowledge about Islam in Norway by information activity.

3.5. To meet and respond to all attacks on Islam such as distortions/ propaganda or attempts at making Muslim life and culture difficult.

3.6. To strive to strengthen the ties of brotherhood and solidarity with the Ummah of the Muslim world.

3.7. To maintain the language of Al-Quran and its key position as the best means of maintaining the Muslim religious, cultural and political unity by offering all Muslims in Norway the possibility to acquire a fundamental knowledge of Arabic.

3.8. To give all Muslim children in Norway a thorough education in Islamic belief, doctrine, history and culture.

These aims are clearly marked by the Islamist or post-Islamist ideals that were present among some of the founders at the time. Muslims were construed as

DEALING WITH CROSS-PRESSURES

a distinct community, apart from Norwegians. It is noteworthy that these aims contain nothing about Norwegian society at large.

The only other source I have come across which contains clues to the early discourse in IRN circles is the speech that was preserved in Leirvik's archive. It was delivered at the meeting between the proto-version of IRN and representatives from the Church on December 15th in 1992, prior to the formal foundation of IRN in 1993. This speech was given by Tanveer ul-Islam Qureishi, a representative from the *Tanzeem Ul Muslimun* mosque, which was part of the Quraishi Tabligh movement. The impression that stands out in the speech is that Muslims was discriminated against, and that Islam was a misunderstood religion. When Islamophobia or scepticism against Muslims are discussed today, they are sometimes attributed to the development after 9/11. But Qureishi's opening speech in 1992 indicates that Muslim activists felt singled out as Muslims already back then:

> In times where political events happen in a so-called Muslim country, the individual Muslim can often feel attacked or being held responsible for what happens. It can be the Iran/Iraq war, the events in Algeria or the Gulf war. During the Gulf war we could read in the media about direct threats to Norwegian Muslims. During this time many people were stopped on the street and other public places by the police, who ordered them to show their passport. These were often Pakistanis who had been living in Norway many years. Such things scare the Muslims and we know that many women and kids were afraid to go out during the Gulf war. [...]
>
> When Muslims in Norwegian cities want to have mosques where they can perform the prayer together with fellow believers, they are met with much scepticism. We feel the fear from many Norwegians. It is the fear that Muslims will be too well established in the country. We think this is a great shame. Islam means peace. I believe in more information in order to increase our knowledge of each other, promote openness and tolerance and de-escalate images of the enemy.
>
> QUREISHI 1992

The only hint towards potentially conflictual issues is that he wants to work together with the Church to contribute towards what he labelled as "raising morals: The defence of values". Qureishi said that "we see that the limits of what is morally acceptable are continuously moved. We regard this as a grave threat".

This speech was clearly designed to reach a specific audience – the representatives from the Church and mainstream society who were present at the meeting. The image of Islam that is painted is therefore one which emphasized universal issues like human rights and tolerance. The most interesting aspect now, almost 30 years later, is that it shows how activists in the IRN, from the very beginning, had a sense of being in a defensive position. Their religion was misunderstood, they thought, and Muslims were discriminated against. This perception also found its way into the first statutes, which devoted much space to the defence of Islam and Muslims.

But the IRN would quite soon choose a route of action that was different from what these statutes and the earliest discourse could imply. The written sources indicate that there were few issues that engaged activists in the IRN more in the early phase than the issue of schooling and religious education. The importance of education was evident from the very start, in the statutes that were adopted in October 1993. The only formal requirement on activity that the member organisations had to comply with was that "the organisation must run a Quranic school [instruction in the Quran] for children and adults", even though the board could provide dispensation from this point.

The importance of the education issue was also evident in the first contact between IRN and MKR. Following the formal foundation of the IRN in October 1993, there was contact between Zahid Mukhtar from IRN and Olav Fykse Tveit from MKR. IRN had no formal contact with the authorities, and they still had only a small membership. The contact with MKR was therefore one of the most important pillars in their organisational life. In my interviews with the actors who were active in IRN in these years, all the informants mentioned the dialogue with the MKR as being central.

The first meeting between IRN and MKR was held on the premises of the Ahl-e-Sunnat mosque on 22 January 1994. In an internal memo which he wrote prior to the meeting, Olav Fykse Tveit wrote about his discussions with Mukhtar. He mentioned that he had suggested to Mukhtar that they should talk about education, which was "well received". In a later formal invitation to the meeting, Mukhtar mentions two topics they would like to discuss – international aid/relief, and an Islamic school (Mukhtar 1994). It appears from Mukhtar's letter that the IRN set the agenda for this first meeting. The agenda, which was attached to the letter, shows that a series of three introductory remarks were to be made by representatives for the IRN. The most prominent was an introduction by Trond Ali Linstad, the veteran from the Defence Council, on the topic of "an Islamic school in Norway". After the remarks, the IRN wanted MKR to provide comments, particularly on the topic of "an Islamic school in Norway".

At this early point, it may appear that the IRN were considering pursuing the idea of a separate school for Muslims. The Norwegian school system is largely public. But some groups have been granted the right to open private schools, if they want to give their pupils a programme of study based in either a different pedagogy or in a particular life-stance. Obtaining the right to open such a school is not easy, however, and the authorities have strict requirements before they will allow the school to open. In the 1990s, there were a good number of Christian private schools scattered around the country, but no Muslim private schools.

The project of a Muslim school had been pursued for some time by Linstad, more or less on his own. He had enlisted the help of other Muslims in Norway and sent an application to the ministry of education to gain approval for a Muslim primary school. Neither the IRN nor the largest mosques in Norway at the time – Ahl-e-Sunnat, Rabita, ICC or World Islamic Mission – had been formally involved in this project. There is no information in the sources, neither the written sources nor the interviews, as to whether the IRN were intending to lend their support to Linstad's school project. But it seems safe to assume that they were *considering* it, at least. If not, why would they invite Linstad to give introductory remarks on his project? The letter of invitation makes clear, though, that they were interested in hearing MKR's take on this idea. One interpretation is that they were gauging the level of the support such a project might receive. If the IRN threw their support behind the project, would they be able to enlist the support of the Church, a powerful institution in Norwegian society?

Leirvik's archive contains a summary that was written by an unnamed participant from the MKR after the meeting (Mellomkirkelig råd 1994). This summary mentions that the delegation from the MKR met among themselves prior to the meeting, in which they clearly expressed that they were sceptical of the idea of a Muslim school, because they feared that Muslims would isolate themselves. In the meeting with the IRN, they attempted to express this scepticism in constructive and positive terms: Would it be in the best interests of Muslims to have their own schools? Was there not a danger that this would let the authorities off the hook, so that they would not develop the public school in a way that could make it more palatable to Muslims? Leirvik's archive reveals that MKR continued to work proactively on the issue after this meeting. They were sceptical towards the idea of an Islamic school and wanted the IRN and the Muslim communities to engage pro-actively with the public-school system. They therefore attempted to provide the IRN with options on how to proceed.

At this time, in 1994, the future of religious instruction in the public-school system in Norway seemed open. There was uncertainty and unease among several political actors about how the education in religion was functioning in an increasingly multicultural and multi-religious society. MKR therefore suggested that they and the IRN should propose a solution together. For the IRN, this provided them with the option of providing input to the political process while piggybacking on the Church of Norway, a much more powerful actor. Even though the actors in MKR had some strategic interests, namely to avoid that Muslim private schools would lead to segregation, they also made a real effort to accommodate the IRN's concerns.

Leirvik proposed that the best solution was a model where there would be a core curriculum in religion and ethics that was compulsory for all, and separate instruction in Christianity and Islam (Leirvik and Birkedal 1994). IRN and MKR later agreed that they should send a common statement to the ministry of education, with an agreed-upon model for religious education in school, which was based on Leirvik's original proposal – one common subject, and separate subjects in Christianity and Islam.

One should not underestimate the importance of this decision on the part of the IRN. To commit to an Islamic subject in school was arguably a significant leap of faith for an organisation like the IRN. What would be the outcome for this subject? Would Islam be presented in a manner that is acceptable to the IRN? Who would control it – they, or the authorities? In addition, having a subject like this ran the risk that the mosques would lose out on an important source of funding. From 1986 and onwards, it had become possible for parents to ask for their children to get religious instruction from the congregation or religious community to which they belonged (Bakke-Lorentzen 2000, 45; KUF 1995, 46). Their congregation would then receive funding from the municipality, proportional to the number of children in the congregation that did not receive instruction in religion in the schools. For several mosques, this became a significant source of income. If Islam became a school subject, it was far from certain that this funding would continue. To advocate for an Islamic subject in public school was thus a large symbolic step towards integration – committing to common and public institutions, rather than defending their own turf. Given how short the IRN had been in existence, and that they were seemingly considering public backing for Islamic private schools only some months earlier, this was a remarkable development.

There seems to have been some disagreement on this issue within the IRN, however. Zaheed Mukhtar, the young secretary of the IRN, does not seem to have been fully on board with the idea initially. In an interview with the Christian daily, Vårt Land, he said that he was not principally opposed to the idea of an Islamic subject in school but that it was more important to solve other practical issues that Muslim pupils were facing (Guttormsen 1994). Nevertheless, on 9 July, the IRN had a meeting after this interview at which they discussed the matter, according to Leirvik's later memo (Leirvik 1995a). At

DEALING WITH CROSS-PRESSURES

that meeting, they decided to give their full backing to the idea of an Islamic school subject.

This moderate course could also be seen in the official statements of the organisation. In September 1994, they issued the first issue of what was planned to be a regular magazine for Muslims in Norway, published by the IRN (Veiviseren 1994). It was called *Veiviseren*, "Guideposts". Leirvik kept one copy of it in his archive. I have not been able to find other issues of the magazine, so it is unclear whether this was the only issue of the magazine that was published, or if there were other issues that have not been preserved in the archives.

The editor was Abdelmounim Elamin, the first leader of the IRN. He introduced the magazine with an article on the IRN in which he made clear what the most important goals would be for the organisation:

> One of the aims of the council is to improve the contact between the member organisations and Norwegian authorities. [...] There is a steady stream of information from Norwegian society. It is important that information reaches the Muslim organisations. IRN will work to facilitate this contact, at the same time as it will promote wishes from Muslims to Norwegian authorities. IRN will make sure that correct information goes both ways.
>
> The council will work to provide a correct image of Islam and the Muslims; their wishes, duties, needs and problems.
>
> IRN will work actively to make the integration of Muslims in Norway easier, and at the same time work so that Muslims will be able to keep their identity and religion.
>
> VEIVISEREN 1994, 2

If we compare this text with the statutes, we see clear differences. The word *integration* is not used at all in the statutes, but it is used in the text. The statutes do not mention that the IRN will try to help Norwegian authorities to reach Muslim groups with information. In the statutes, the focus is only on the IRN as a voice *for* the Muslim, while the focus in this text is on the IRN as an intermediary between the authorities and the Muslims. Furthermore, there are some topics which are conspicuously absent. There is no talk of uniting Muslims, or of creating solidarity with the larger Muslim ummah. This does not mean, of course, that the IRN or Elamin had stopped thinking that these issues were important, but it is indicative of the priorities of the IRN at the time. The main priority seems to have become the double aim of making the integration of Muslims easier, while allowing Muslims to "keep their identity and religion". This goal was not absent in the statutes, but it had become much clearer in the year that had passed since their signing.

The magazine also mentions that the IRN had been working with the topics of the instruction of Islam in the public-school system, and the general situation of Muslim pupils, which encountered many "practical problems" such as common/joint swimming, prayer areas, shower after gymnastics, hijab, sexual education, Muslim holidays, etc. (Veiviseren 1994, 3). What is notable about the language used in the text is the conciliatory nature of their wording. They do not make ultimatums or absolute demands, but rather suggestions. They are developing "a suggestion" for a curriculum. And they claim that the subject and curriculum should be developed "in cooperation with" Muslim experts, not "by" Muslim experts.

This suggests that the IRN, early on, had begun to understand their role within Norwegian society and the Norwegian state. They could make suggestions or demands but this only counted as input in a democratic process where their voice was one out of many. As we will see, however, the work they devoted to this issue did not bear fruit. Instead of an Islamic school subject that would exist alongside the subjects on Christianity and Life stances, all the pupils would be obliged to follow instruction in Christianity. In a paradoxical development, this led the IRN to become even less exclusivist in their approach.

3.4 New Allies and a New Direction: the Battle for the Public School

As was discussed in the previous chapter, the IRN had been founded in a period during which the public discourse on immigration and multiculturalism was in a period of flux. The first part of the 1980s had been marked by an official discourse which could be labelled *soft multiculturalism*. But towards the end of the decade, that soft multiculturalism was increasingly challenged by both the far-right Progress Party and by voices closer to the mainstream.

For various reasons, the 1990s and early 2000s saw a decisive end to what remained of the soft multiculturalism of the early 80s. The labour party in Oslo won the municipal elections in 1991 on a programme that promised to end what they called *snillisme*, literally meaning "kindism", a policy they described as being naïvely over-generous towards people who received welfare benefits (including immigrants) (Bakken 2010). One large policy shift was to stop teaching the mother tongue to the children of immigrants in the primary schools of Oslo. At the time, most teachers and pedagogues claimed that children of immigrants would have an easier time learning Norwegian if they had a good

DEALING WITH CROSS-PRESSURES

foundation in their mother tongue. But the ruling labour coalition wanted to prioritize instruction in Norwegian only.

There were other changes as well. In 1995, Norway followed Sweden in criminalizing female genital mutilation, with strict punishment for those who were found guilty of doing it. A few lone voices at the time claimed that criminalizing the practice could be counter-productive, and representatives of the Somali community were critical. But these voices did not resonate among the politicians and organisations in mainstream society that supported the law more or less unanimously (Bråten and Elgvin 2014, 112–14). Last but not least, the issue of education and the public-school system went through significant changes, with a stronger focus on a shared national identity and culture.

One of the thorniest issues in the emerging multicultural Norwegian society was the teaching of religion in the schools. How should religion be taught? Norway had a state church at the time and was a confessional state: the constitution stipulated that "the Evangelical-Lutheran religion remains the public religion of the state". This had implications for the school system, which had a formal aim of educating children as Christians. This principle had been watered down throughout the previous decades, however (KUF 1995, 9–17). With the advent of modernity in the 19th century an increasing number of Norwegians did not identify with the Lutheran-Evangelical state church. Some of them were not happy that the public-school system was tasked with turning their children into Lutheran-Evangelical Christians.

From 1936 and onwards, it was no longer obligatory for all pupils to be taught Christianity, if their parents were not members of the Church of Norway (Bakke-Lorentzen 2000, 36). Beginning in 1971, these parents could also ask for their children to be offered a school subject called *livssyn*, "life stances". This subject covered different religions, and also secular and non-religious life stances. It was to be explicitly neutral towards the different life stances or religions being taught. From 1986 and onwards, as I mentioned previously, it also became possible for parents to ask for their children to get religious instruction from the congregation or religious community to which they belonged.

In the early 1990s, a number of actors in Norwegian society were becoming increasingly uneasy about how this system was functioning. As an example, the social democrats in Oslo started to consider whether they should control the Islamic curriculum that was being taught to the children in the mosques, given that the mosques received public funding for this instruction. They also considered whether the municipality should provide teaching in Islam. I interviewed Bente Sandvig from the Norwegian Humanist Association (HEF), who worked with schooling issues at HEF at the time. According to Sandvig, part of the reason for this concern was that there were several schools in central Oslo where fewer students were enrolled in the official subject of Christianity than there were students enrolled in the alternative *Life stances* subject, or who received instruction in the mosques in the evenings. One school – *Ila* – had attempted to create one neutral subject for all students, but this was turned down by the government. This led to a political reaction, according to Sandvig:

> I think this situation was perceived as a threat by two different political factions, for different reasons. The social democrats perceived it as a threat to social cohesion and were afraid that pupils from different backgrounds would not develop a common identity based on what was perceived as a potentially divisive topic. The Christian democrats perceived it as a threat to the dominant position of Christianity in school. That is when they began talking about Christianity as a cultural heritage and as a school subject aimed at creating identity. The Christian Democrats then decided that they saw it as a goal to get more pupils to study the Christianity subject. These two political movements then joined forces.
>
> Interview with BENTE SANDVIG, 20.05.2019

The social democratic government appointed a governmental advisory commission in 1994 that was tasked with discussing the teaching of religion in school. Their report – delivered in May 1995 – proposed upending decades of educational policy with regards to religious minorities (KUF 1995). From now on, according to the working group, the teaching of Christianity would be compulsory for all pupils, with only limited rights to exemption. Their proposal was to broaden the existing subject and include ethics and other religions. But Christianity was to remain dominant and was to function as a normative framework aimed at equipping the pupils with a secure identity. In the first years of schooling, the pupils were to learn only about Christianity; only later were they to broach the issues of other religions and secular ethics. Later on, when the pupils got older, they would also learn about what working group sometimes referred to as "foreign religions". When the advisory committee unveiled their proposal, several interviewees described to me that that they were in a state of shock and disbelief. This led to a counter-reaction which few had expected. Elin Bakke-Lorentzen, in a comprehensive master's thesis on the inner workings of the advisory commission, cites one of the key actors in the commission describing what happened after the committee published their proposal: "all hell broke loose" (Bakke-Lorentzen 2000, 75).

DEALING WITH CROSS-PRESSURES

The most important actor in the emerging protests was the Norwegian Humanist Association (HEF), which was the most powerful and resource-rich actor among the minority life stance communities who felt affected. It had been established in 1956 and had a large and often resourceful membership base. In 1995, the Norwegian Humanist Association had 33 full time employees. The IRN had none, and the Jewish Community of Oslo (DMT) – which would play an important role in the protests as well – had one part-time employee (Bakke-Lorentzen 2000, 116).

Lars Gunnar Lingås, the leader of HEF at the time, told me that they quickly decided to form a broad alliance against the proposed compulsory school subject. When creating this alliance, HEF decided to tone down any wording which other actors in the coalition might find offensive. His story about the events is worth quoting in full:

> When the Pettersen working group came with their proposal, I and Levi [Fragell, a former leader of HEF] told each other: Well, now it is time to buckle up and do something here and get others on board! So, we took the initiative to form an action group we called ALIS ("action for life stance liberty in school"). We then made a T-shirt where there was a priest who was chasing an innocent pupil with a cross. It was really like that ... yeah [laughs]. After a while I started to calm down and thought that if we are to cooperate with others, we can't just think about ourselves and our own members. We came to an internal consensus that this T-shirt here, well, let's just say we'll shelve it and store it away in the archives.
>
> Then we got in touch with the group which had been part of the most recent dialogue project at the Nansen Academy. What should we do now, sort of. Oddbjørn Leirvik very soon came and said that he did not agree with what had been proposed. He was one of the most pronounced dialogue people in the Church, particularly with the Muslims. Then we called for a joint meeting and discussed the action group against the proposal of the Pettersen group – we should share the work between us, how we should lobby the politicians, how we should make a powerful organisation.
>
> Then I remember that we had an open meeting down at our premises. There was a panel, and on that panel sat the leader of the IRN at the time [Mohamed Bouras], the Jewish rabbi Michael Melchior, and Oddbjørn Leirvik. And me. And one from the Buddhist organisation. There was one thing I'll never forget. The Jew and the Muslim were talking on stage. And they called each other *brothers*. That made a deep impression on me.
>
> Interview with LARS GUNNAR LINGÅS, 03.05.2019

This version of events is confirmed in the written sources that I could find in the written archives of Bente Sandvig, who worked with schooling issues in HEF at the time, and who kept a comprehensive personal archive.

In a letter dated 29 August 1995, one of the secretaries in HEF sent a letter out to the secretaries in the local branches of the organisation, which revealed that the action group had become very broad and that the IRN was joined by organisations such as The Heathen Society (bold text in the original):

> As you may have noticed the action group has now reached a breadth in life stances and political affiliations which may be of great help. **The Jewish Community, The Islamic Council, The Buddhist Association, Alternative Network and The National School Association, and also the Free Democrats, International Socialists, Liberal Youth of Norway, Women Against Fundamentalism, The Heathen Society and others have joined the action group**, something that has created much press coverage.
>
> MATHIESEN 1995

The Islamic Council of Norway – which was run by conservative Muslim actors – suddenly found themselves in an alliance with very unexpected bedfellows. ALIS embarked on a prolonged campaign through which they asked people to sign postal cards that signalled protest. Some 25,000 postal cards were signed by people and handed to the minister of education Gudmund Hernes in September 1995. Their initial demand was to scrap completely the proposition of the Pettersen working group and start the process from scratch. As this demand was not heard, they tried to lobby the politicians and debate in the media, in order to influence what kind of subject the compulsory school subject would become. Sandvig's archive documents that representatives from the IRN met with the other organisations in ALIS all through the fall of 1995, and for quite some time in 1996 as well. Leaders from the IRN met with leaders from other organisations, often at the premises of HEF. The minutes from the meetings seem to indicate a friendly atmosphere.

The organisations in ALIS did not succeed in fundamentally changing the school subject, but they did succeed in influencing the new common school subject to a limited degree. The result was a somewhat more open subject than the initial proposal from the Petersen group. The IRN and the other organisations in ALIS then decided to follow two different tracks. They tried to influence the curriculum of the new subject at the same time as they fought for the right to full exemption for pupils. In 1998, both the IRN and the Humanist Association took the state to the court in two different cases. They argued that

DEALING WITH CROSS-PRESSURES

obligatory instruction in Christianity, with the chosen profile, represented a violation of their human rights.

Why did they not cooperate and launch a joint lawsuit? Bente Sandvig from HEF indicated to me that they discussed whether they should cooperate on the case but decided it would be better to pursue the matter in separate cases. The reason was that their arguments were somewhat different. Whereas HEF argued for the right of the children to shape their own identity without being forced into a certain religious tradition by the state, the IRN argued that the Muslim pupils should have the right to keep their identity as Muslims. There were differences of opinion within the ALIS coalition, even though they shared a common goal. But Sandvig emphasized that they cooperated all through the process and that HEF provided informal counsel to the IRN on how to proceed. In the end, both HEF and the IRN lost their court cases in 1999. The IRN could not afford to appeal, whereas HEF did. HEF went on to lose again in the Norwegian supreme court, but finally emerged victorious in the European Court of Human Rights in Strasbourg in 2007.

For the IRN, this cooperation signalled a new direction, and it arguably went further than before in adapting its discourse and goals to the realities of Norwegian society. In their initial positive response to the invitation from the MKR in 1992, key actors in the IRN had signalled that they thought they could find common ground with the MKR in their scepticism against moral relativism and the erosion of traditional values. Even though it is not stated in the written sources, it is reasonable to assume that atheism was not held in high regard in IRN circles in the mid-90s. When I did field work in the mosques of Oslo for my master's thesis in the years 2008–2011, I found that the key antagonists in the discourse in many mosques were not Christians or people belonging to other religions. The key antagonists were instead atheists or strong secularists. There is little reason to believe that the discourse was fundamentally different at the 90s. Key Islamic thinkers who were widely read in mosques like Rabita, such as Yusuf al-Qaradawi, wrote books presenting the main challenge for Muslims in Western societies as *godlessness*, not other religions such as Christianity or Judaism (Al-Qaradawi 2003, 22).

But when accepting to join this action group, the IRN joined forces with the secular Humanists, and became part of an ad hoc organisation that the Humanists had created. Equally significant was the cooperation with the Jewish community, and the fact that Jewish and Muslim leaders were actually able to call each other "brothers" publicly. The Palestine conflict had for many decades been one of the most important issues for Muslim activists all across the globe (Haddad 1992). In my interview with Trond Ali Linstad, he mentioned that the only issue on which he was able to get the mosques to engage in collective activism after the Rushdie affair was on the Palestine issue. There is every reason to believe that actors in IRN at the time had strong feelings about Israel and Palestine. The Jewish rabbi in Oslo, Michael Melchior, was not only a Jewish rabbi, he also held Israeli citizenship. Later on, he would be elected to the Israeli parliament as a representative for a moderate, left-wing religious party. It would not be unnatural to expect some animosity between Jewish and Muslim activists at the time, even though the Oslo accords had just been signed. But both Bouras and Melchior seemed to put whatever differences they had aside, joining forces for a common cause, and called each other brothers.

Was this seen as controversial inside the IRN at the time? The sources I have had access to for this period – the oral interviews and the written sources in Leirvik's and Sandvig's archives – are silent on this issue. In my interviews with Mohamed Bouras and Lena Larsen, who were IRN's main representatives in ALIS, I did not ask specifically on whether this tight cooperation was controversial. I did pose a general question, however, as to whether there were any decisions or questions that created internal controversy and disagreement in the IRN in the 90s. The informants mentioned several issues, but none of them mentioned the participation in ALIS. That may indicate that IRN's participation in this action group was not seen as very controversial internally – or at least that is not remembered as such today. Kari Vogt, however, does mention in her book that one mosque decided to leave the IRN in 1996 because of IRN's approach on the schooling issue (Vogt 2008, 219). This means that there must have been some debate on the IRN's choice of direction, even though only one mosque left the organisation. A broader tendency seems to have been that the IRN was backed by the mosques on this issue, beyond the membership of the IRN itself. Six mosques that were not members of the IRN gave the IRN authorization to take part in the ALIS committee on their behalf (Vogt 2008, 219). This may indicate that the struggle against the compulsory Christianity subject was seen as so important by many mosques that they were willing to accept the cooperation with the Jewish and Humanist communities that it entailed.

The joint undertaking in ALIS also seems to have influenced how the IRN approached the instruction in religion in schools. The minutes from the meetings show that ALIS – and in particular HEF – were very keen on encouraging the member organisations to provide written input to the government on how they wanted the school subject to be. The previous joint statement the IRN issued with MKR in 1994 had emphasized that they wanted a separate Islamic school subject, with an additional subject which was common to all and emphasized ethics and dialogue. But in their official comments on the proposed subject, the IRN now emphasized the need for a unified subject that would be common to all:

1. A common subject which has common norms and values as its starting point, not a particular religion/life stance to the detriment of other religions or life stances. The children must experience community through instruction in common, universal moral values; visit each other's religious communities/houses of worship, be present at each other's festivities when religious feasts occur.

2. All children in the lower classes should get instruction in their own religion/tradition to create the necessary foundation for their identity before going into dialogue with children from other religions or life stances.

Islamsk Råd Norge v/ Undervisnignskomiteen 1995

This was a marked departure from the language and the proposals the IRN had employed previously. They still said that children in the lower classes should familiarise themselves with their own religion *before* entering into dialogue with others. But they did not advocate a separate Islamic subject. Of note also is the fact that they emphasise "common, universal moral values". The tone here is strikingly different from the tone in the statutes from 1993, where the emphasis was on the separate and distinct identity of Muslims and defending Islam and Islamic identity against external attacks.

The fact that IRN provided such an official response to the request for comments on the proposed school subject (*høringssvar* in Norwegian) was highly symbolic in itself and an important milestone in the institutional incorporation of the IRN into the corporatist aspects of Norwegian society. Before the government of Norway proposes major amendments to parliament, it is customary to appoint a governmental advisory committee – like the Pettersen committee – and to task them with writing a proposal. This proposal is sent out on a consultation round to organisations and parties who may be affected. Based on this feedback, the government or the ministry usually take both the proposal and the feedback into account when making a formal proposal to parliament. When the IRN wrote a full response to the proposal from the Pettersen group, as a *høringssvar* or response to the request for comments, they had in many ways become full members of corporatist Norwegian democracy.

This cooperation between the actors who were involved in ALIS – secular humanists, Muslims, Jews and Buddhists – also had another, indirect and unanticipated result. It led to the creation of an organisation that would become heavily influential in Norway in the next decades, the Council for Religious and Life Stance Communities in Norway (STL). When the anthropologist Cora Alexa Døving wrote an article about the history and impact of STL in 2016, one of her informants – the former minister of education from the Socialist Left Party Bård Vegar Solhjell – was quoted as saying, "Where STL says that there is agreement, the road is short to it becoming Norwegian policy" (Døving 2016, 362). As Døving documents, STL would have a large influence on Norwegian policy in the 2000s. But it would also have an important impact on the trajectory of the IRN.

The idea of creating STL grew out of the ALIS network. Several of my sources – inside and outside the IRN – have indicated that it was Mohamed Bouras, the second leader of the IRN, who initially came up with the idea. After some discussions between the founders, it was formally founded in May 1996. STL adopted two goals: to work for equality for all life stances and religious communities in Norway, and to work for increased respect and understanding between life stance and religious communities (Døving 2016, 363). They chose an organisational model that emphasised consensus. Each and every life stance community was to have one vote, irrespective of their size. STL thus became a meta-organisation which partly had meta-organisations as members. The latter factor may have made it even more important to make decisions by consensus.

On the Muslim side, the IRN became the organisation that got the one vote. In addition, an important feature of the organisation was that the Church of Norway – represented by MKR – decided to join. This lent much weight to the consensus decisions of STL. When STL decided to support a cause, it meant that it was also supported by the Church, which had about 90 percent of the Norwegian population as members. Still, STL could make statements even though not all of its members agreed. They therefore developed a distinction between *strong* and *weak* statements. When a statement was strong, it meant that all the member organisations agreed, and the organisation would throw their full weight behind the statement. When a statement was weak, it meant that not all the members agreed, and STL would be more careful when promoting the statement. The quote from Solhjell reflects this: If the politicians heard a statement that the STL had thrown its full force behind, they would know that all of the life stance communities in Norway agreed on an issue, from the small Bahai to the Church of Norway.

In her article, Døving documents how STL proved important in the process that led to the formal separation between church and state being implemented in Norway on 2017. By committing to STL, the Church also committed to the

DEALING WITH CROSS-PRESSURES

rights-based and dialogue-based discourse that prevailed in the organisation, where minority rights were seen as paramount. STL provided central input to the policy-making process throughout the 2000s, which led the government to appoint a governmental working group in 2010 that wrote the proposal essentially ending the status of a state church in Norway (Døving 2016, 371). The annual reports of STL document that the leadership of the IRN frequently participated in joint activities with the STL, in addition to the dialogue they were engaged in with the MKR. Through STL, IRN became even more integrated into the corporatist structure of Norwegian society and democracy.

3.5   Internal Agreements on Contested Issues

Throughout these early years, it appears that the external compromises of the organisation did not endanger their internal cohesion. The organisation was able to deal with its internal multipolarity, and even managed to reach agreement on issues that were heavily contested among its member organisations. The most important achievement was an agreement which strengthened the symbolic ties between Muslims in Norway – the adoption of a shared lunar calendar for determining when the Islamic holidays should occur.

When visiting the old IRN website from 2001 through the Internet Archive, it becomes clear that the lunar calendar was an issue of great importance to the organisation. Prior to 2001 there are no captures. Kari Vogt mentions in her book that the website of the IRN – which had a different URL address when it was introduced in the 1990s – become dormant in the late 1990s (Vogt 2008, 309), so it may appear that the website was rebooted in 2000 or 2001. The website in 2001 did not contain much information. It had an entry on the organisation: what its aims were, what it worked with and what it wanted to achieve. It listed its members. It also had an entry presenting the dialogue/contact group with MKR. The only other main entry on the front page was an entry about the *hilal committee*, which was to determine when Islamic holidays should be celebrated. This pattern repeated itself throughout the early 00s: One of few recurring topics on IRN's website were postings about the hilal committee, and when it had decided that the celebration of the Eid holidays would take place.

This indicates that the question about when the holidays should occur was of deep importance to the IRN and the Islamic field in Norway. Curiously, however, there is almost no research on this topic, neither in Europe nor abroad. Kari Vogt devoted three pages to the issue in her book (Vogt 2008, 187–90), and mentioned that there was a contentious topic in an encyclopaedia entry on

Eid al-Fitr, the holiday which marks the end of the Ramadan fast (Vogt 2019). The disputes over when to celebrate Eid have also attracted some newspaper coverage in Western media during recent years, as the disputes have become more public (AP 2019; Khoury 2019). Nevertheless, a thorough search on google scholar turned up only two articles focusing specifically on the discussions and disagreements over the lunar calendar and when to celebrate Eid (Moosa 1998; Vahed and Waetjen 2014). It is difficult to know for sure what the reasons are for this scholarly neglect, but one possibility is that the calendar controversy has been mostly an *internal* problem for Muslims up until now – and therefore has not generated any interest from the outside world.

The challenge for Muslims, in brief, is twofold: it is about both theology and social/political power. The Islamic calendar, like the Jewish calendar, is a lunar calendar. A lunar year is eleven days shorter than a solar year, which means that the lunar months will "move" from one year to another. For this reason, all Muslim countries except Saudi Arabia have adopted the Gregorian calendar for administrative purposes, as it makes it easier to plan ahead. The Islamic calendar has been retained for religious purposes and for determining holidays, which thus move every year, compared to the Gregorian calendar. In addition, the determination of when a new month occurs, coinciding with when the holidays take place, has been a thorny issue. The traditional theological requirement is that the new month starts when the new moon – *hilal* in Arabic – can be observed with the naked eye by a qualified observer (there are some additional requirements as well).

In premodern times, before modern science and before the globalization of Islam, this was not a problem. The religious authorities in each country or region determined when the new moon had been sighted, and when the holiday should take place. The problem occurred in modern times, for two reasons. Firstly, the development of scientific astronomy meant that there were ways of determining when the new moon occurred which were in principle more reliable than sighting by the naked eye. As modern science penetrated Muslim societies in the 19th and 20th centuries, people began asking themselves whether the requirement of sighting by the naked eye should be upheld, given that there were more robust scientific methods available. Another theological hurdle was what to do about those regions of the world which lay far north or far south, such as Norway and South Africa, where it was not always clear that the new moon could be observed according to the traditional requirements. Secondly, new information technology and the globalization of Islam and the Muslim populations meant that lines of authority became blurred. A South African Muslim of Indian origin might hear from relatives in India through telegraph or telephone that the religious authorities in India had decided that

Eid should take place one day, whereas the religious authorities in South Africa had decided that it was to take place the next day. Should he then celebrate Eid with his fellow Muslims in South Africa, or rather celebrate with his relatives back home?

In addition, this was turned into a political problem. As there were few practical religious issues more important for Muslims than when to celebrate their main religious holidays, several countries and religious bodies fought over the right to decide when this should occur, as the right to determine this issue conferred great symbolic power. Saudi Arabia, for example, developed its own method for calculating the lunar calendar, which it attempted to get other countries to follow. In 2019, Saudi Arabia unexpectedly announced that the moon had been sighted after Ramadan on a day which surprised most observers. Some analysts assumed that they did not want its announcement to coincide with the Eid announcement of its political arch-rival Iran (Khoury 2019).

Particularly among Muslim groups in non-Muslim countries, this has created difficulties and challenges. Some reformist groups claimed that one should adopt a scientific method for determining when the new moon occurs, but most groups opted to follow one authority or the other from the Muslim world. This meant that different Muslim groups often celebrated Eid on different days. There were also many activists – in Norway and other countries – who felt sorrow for this state of affairs, and thought that it would be difficult to achieve the long sought-after goal of uniting Muslims as long as they continued to celebrate their main holiday on different days. Both the media reports that exist and the sparse scholarly literature indicate that this has often created challenges and difficulties for Muslims. Vogt relates in her book about an episode from the year 2000. The ICC mosque had at that time opted to follow Saudi Arabia's announcement. That year, most people had assumed that Eid ul-Fitr after the fast would take place on 8 January. On 6 January, however, ICC received a fax from Saudi Arabia which stated that Eid would take place the 7th, i.e. the next day, "to the great despair of all the housewives" (Vogt 2008, 189). The South African historians Goolam Vahed and Thembisa Waetjen also tell about several cases from South African history when this debate created significant difficulties for poor Muslims in South Africa, who sometimes prepared Eid food only to see it go to waste if Eid did not occur as planned (Vahed and Waetjen 2014, 57).

In many ways, this was another instance of a collective action problem. For the large majority of Muslims worldwide, it would solve many practical problems if one could follow one jointly approved calendar for religious holidays. But given the vested interests of some parties on the multipolar Islamic field, this has proven difficult to achieve.

Given these difficulties and challenges, it was no small feat that many of the mosques in the IRN managed to agree upon a shared lunar calendar late in the year 2000. Once again, the solution which was agreed upon was an attempt at balancing different interests. Fundamentally, there were three different approaches Muslims could take to the issue. One approach was that sighting with the naked eye was the only legitimate method. Another approach was to rely only on astronomical calculations. A third approach was to rely on some combination, for example to accept sightings only when it was scientifically possible that the new moon could be seen.

In a document which was agreed upon 17 November 2000, twelve of the largest mosques in Norway agreed on a method for calendar calculation that was closest to the third approach (Hilalkomiteen 2000). This method relied on a complicated calculation which was gaining some steam among different Islamic organisations in the late 1990s and which relied on astronomical calculations for determining a common start for Eid for Muslims worldwide. Crucially, however, the proponents of this method did not say that the sighting method was *invalid* – but they claimed that the new method was a reasonable approximation of when the moon could in principle be expected to be seen. In addition, the calendar committee in IRN had agreed upon a further requirement: The calendar committee of IRN could never say that Eid had occurred before at least one Muslim country had done the same. In this way, IRN and the Muslims in Norway would avoid having to deal with the controversy that might be entailed by being the first to determine that Eid had begun. Prior to the implementation of the agreement in 2000, however, the mosques decided that they would follow Saudi Arabia's decision on Eid ul-Adha, the other main Islamic holiday a couple of months after Ramadan, for that particular year. Once again, this displayed how IRN attempted to take different interests among the members into account when arriving at balanced decisions.

IRN was actually among the first national Islamic umbrella organisations to decide that Islamic holidays should be decided nationally, in accordance with astronomical principles. In the US, for example, it was not until 2006 that the *Fiqh Council of North America* – a body of American Islamic religious scholars – decided to follow the same approach. When this happened, a British Islamic scholar called this a "very courageous decision", given that the Islamic Council of Britain had not yet been able to arrive on a similar decision (Masood 2006).

When the major mosques in IRN adopted this calendar, it took a significant step towards reaching one of its aims: more unity among Muslims and mosques in Norway. Although it did not get any attention in the media or from scholars besides Kari Vogt, this agreement also signalled an accommodation to

DEALING WITH CROSS-PRESSURES

life in Norwegian society: IRN decided that they would decide on this hugely symbolic issue between themselves, instead of depending on transnational or foreign Islamic authorities. It also showed that the organisation was able to deal with the internal multipolarity it was facing.

3.6   Limits to Compromise: Decoupling and Withdrawal

The sections above may give the impression that IRN adapted easily and smoothly to Norwegian society, without conflicts or fissures, or that balancing was the only approach the organisation chose. This, however, was not always the case. The first time the organisation chose not acquiesce fully to external demands occurred in 1995, one and a half year after their founding. This was occasioned by human rights abuses in Pakistan, which the Norwegian media showed an interest in. The case in question was a blasphemy case against a Pakistani Christian teenager, Salamat Masih. Over the previous decades, the policies of the Pakistani state had become increasingly hostile towards religious minorities (Ispahani 2017). One law which was often used to target minorities was the blasphemy law, which had become stricter under the reign of the Islamist-sympathizing general Zia ul-Haq in the late 1970s and the 1980s. In 1995, one particular case created a global outcry. Salamat Masih, a boy from a poor Christian family, was accused of having committed blasphemy when he was 12 years old, along with his father and uncle. According to the accusers, they had written blasphemous slogans on the wall of a mosque. But no evidence was presented, as the accusers claimed that they had erased the blasphemous graffiti right away when they saw it. During the trial, it emerged that Salamat Masih was illiterate and could not read or write. It also emerged that one of the accusers was illiterate as well, which made it somewhat mysterious in terms of how he had been able to understand what the accused three persons had allegedly written on the wall (Dahlburg 1995). Still, the case went to court. During court proceedings, Salamat Masih's father was shot and killed outside the courthouse. Salamat Masih and his uncle were initially sentenced to death at February 1995, when Salamat Masih was 14 years old. Some weeks later they would be acquitted in the high court of Lahore.

This created a stir in many Western countries, including Norway. Some journalists had travelled to Pakistan to cover the case in detail, which was uncommon at the time. Norwegian politicians condemned the verdict in harsh terms. Carl I. Hagen, the leader of the far-right Progress party, proposed that all development aid to Pakistan should be halted immediately. It is difficult to say why this particular case created such a stir. After all, there is no shortage of human rights abuses or discrimination of religious minorities in the world. Possible reasons may have included that this happened only a short time after the Rushdie affair, which meant that Western publics were sensitive to issues that had to do with blasphemy and Islam. It may also have played a role that the accused in this case was Christian, and that Christian groups in Western countries were mobilizing in solidarity. In any case, this was a case that was much talked about in Norway, and the IRN could not avoid being drawn in.

The IRN started receiving questions about the case after it emerged that two large Norwegian mosques publicly supported the capital punishment verdict against Salamat Masih and his uncle. The imam of the Ahl-e-Sunnat mosque, Nehmet Ali Shah, stated in an interview that he supported the blasphemy law in principle and that he did not think it made a difference that Salamat Masih was only 12 years old when he allegedly committed his act of blasphemy (VG 1995). Shah said that he could not comment on this specific case, as he did not know the details, but he seemed supportive of the verdict. This was not insignificant, as Ahl-e-Sunnat was still the largest mosque in Norway, and it was also a member of the IRN. From the interview, though, it would seem that the journalists were the ones who had sought out comments from the imam, rather than the imam reaching out to the newspaper to offer commentary. But representatives from another mosque actively tried to make it known that they supported capital punishment in the case. This was the *Turkish Islamic Union* in Oslo, a mosque connected with the Milli Görus movement in Turkey. This was one of the largest Turkish mosques in Norway, even though they were not part of the IRN. They sent out a press release stating the following:

> We wish to make it known to the Norwegian people that the Turkish Islamic Union shows understanding for Pakistan's death penalty towards a 14-year-old boy and thus supports it. This is on the condition that the court which has treated the case is independent.
>
> SOLØY 1995

Why would a mosque voluntarily put itself in the spotlight in this way, with a statement that it knew would be harshly received and judged by most actors in Norwegian society? A couple of the leaders in the mosque were interviewed in Aftenposten and explained their reasoning. They stated that their dispute was mainly with the actions of Norwegian politicians, and in particular the call to halt development aid to Pakistan from the Progress party. It seems like they wanted to double down on the case, in order to show the Norwegian

DEALING WITH CROSS-PRESSURES

politicians that they would not bow down to the criticism (Soløy 1995). It emerged a couple of weeks later, however, that this was a controversial matter internally in the mosque. *Aftenposten* reported that many of the other leaders in the mosque were highly critical of their statements. Other leaders in the mosque claimed that these statements had not been cleared with the board of the mosque, and some were even trying to get the secretary of the mosque fired (Brudevold 1995).

Given that representatives from two of the largest mosques in Norway had publicly supported the verdict, or at least supported Pakistan's right to issue such a verdict against a 14-year-old boy, there was increasing pressure on the IRN to make a statement. In an internal memo to MKR from 21 February, Leirvik mentions that he had been in touch with some actors in the IRN. He wrote that:

> According to what I've heard, they were going to discuss the issue on 17 February. According to the signals I have received, there are several in the council who wish to distance themselves from what the two mosques have stated.
>
> LEIRVIK 1995b

Leirvik made it clear in the memo that he was very unhappy with what the mosque representatives had said, and that he sincerely hoped that the IRN would come out with other statements. On the same day that Leirvik signed his memo, 21 February, the IRN called for a press conference. They had asked Leirvik and Tveit from MKR to be present at the press conference, "probably to signal a dialogue-oriented and moderate profile", as Leirvik wrote in a later memo (Leirvik 1995c).

Before the press conference, Leirvik and Tveit had an "open conversation" with them, according to Leirvik's memo. The message IRN gave at the press conference was somewhat vague, and not altogether easy to decipher. On the one hand, they said that the capital punishment against the boy was not "according to the Quran", given that Islamic law required that a person had to be able to take responsibility for his actions in order to be held accountable by a court – and this was not the case with such a young boy. But at the same time, they specifically did not condemn the ruling in this particular case. The reason they gave was that the IRN could only provide general opinions on Islamic law, so they did not have the right to weigh in on cases where they did not know all the details. This mixed message led to a mixed newspaper coverage as well. The Christian daily, *Vårt Land*, wrote about the press conference with the title "Death penalty is against the Quran" (Navestad 1995), while *Aftenposten*, the newspaper of record, wrote an article with the title "The Islamic Council does not dare to condemn death penalty" (Stokke 1995).

Overall, it is fair to say that IRN's message was perceived in a negative way by most commentators in the media. One example is an op-ed by Asbjørn Kristoffersen, a respected veteran commentator in the liberal-conservative newspaper *Bergens Tidende*, who had not been known for writing critical commentary on Muslims or migrant groups. After this press conference he wrote a scathing op-ed, where he chided the IRN for giving fodder to those who wanted to promote fear of Muslims. His op-ed ended with these harsh words: "The Islamic Council of Norway has let all of us down" (Kristoffersen 1995). The IRN was also criticized by their dialogue partners in the Church. In the internal memo on the press conference, Leirvik wrote that

> we have told them that we appreciate their wish to make moderate statements, that we understand their problem with internal disagreements, but that we nevertheless would have wanted clearer words than what they have expressed.
>
> LEIRVIK 1995C

This also became a topic at the next meeting in the contact group between the MKR and the IRN on 19 April, according to the minutes from the meeting (Steinsland 1995). Jan Opsal, a scholar of religion and a member of the contact group, gave an introduction on the topic. The minutes from the meeting indicate that some of the representatives from the IRN seemed on the defensive and claim that they would have liked to do more in cases like these, but that it is a "question of resources". The only Pakistani representative in the meeting, from ICC, went on the offensive, and said that he knew for a fact that there were no problems between Muslims and Christians in Pakistan. But the overall message was that IRN did not have the capacity to engage in issues which were not related to Norwegian issues, a response that the MKR representatives do not seem to have found convincing. Leirvik's response seems to have been fairly blunt, even as it is preserved in the dry language of the minutes from the meeting: "If you have the resources, it would be a good thing if you showed some engagement [on such issues]". Internally, at least, the IRN was facing pressure and disapproval from its closest ally.

Why was it so difficult for the IRN to condemn the death penalty in Pakistan more forcefully? The rationale they gave for not weighing in is not particularly convincing. The facts of the case were widely reported, and could be available by picking up any contemporary newspaper: the accused boy had been 12 years old when the alleged blasphemy case took place, he could not read or write, and one of the witnesses could not read. The appeal court in Lahore easily came to the same conclusion some weeks later. It would have been possible for the IRN to issue a mildly-worded statement saying that the information provided in the press about the case gave them cause for concern, for example. Such a response was more or less what the Rabita mosque – the dominant mosque in IRN – gave on its own some weeks later, around the time the high court of Lahore acquitted the accused.

For the IRN as an umbrella organisation, however, who had to keep all of its members reasonably happy, it was apparently difficult to provide such a response. Several of the mosques that were members of the IRN at this point were fairly conservative, and occasionally frustrated with society at large. If the leadership in IRN wanted to keep their standing with these mosques, there were limits to how far they could go in accommodating demands from the outside.

A few months after this affair, the newspaper VG published an article which gives some hints about the landscape the IRN operated within. It was an article about the 30 largest mosques in Oslo, to find out who these mosques were and what they were about (Schmidt and Hansen 1995). Out of the 30 mosques VG contacted, almost a third declined to answer or said that they did not want to have anything to do with the media. Of those that answered, several provided answers which appeared antagonistic towards the media. If VG's article is indicative of the state of mind among mosque leaders at the time, this would obviously present the leadership of the IRN with a dilemma. They had a stated goal of uniting the mosques and the Muslims in Norway. But they also had a goal of engaging with the authorities, with the media and with external organisations. How then were they to deal with the fact that a large number of the mosques in Norway were sceptical of dealing with the media or with actors in mainstream society?

The IRN leadership seemed to follow a balancing approach, where different demands could be met through compromise. But among its members, the approach of *withdrawal* seems to have been more prominent. This is evidenced by the fact that many mosques sought to stay completely out of the media spotlight and did not want to talk with VG when the newspaper approached them. In her brief treatment of IRN, Kari Vogt also mentions that the criticism the IRN received internally was that it was "too Norwegian" (Vogt 2008, 219). During this early period, it does appear that the pressure from the membership was towards more caution and withdrawal, not towards more balancing and external engagement. The IRN thus had certain organisational constraints on how far they could go along with the demands that external stakeholders placed on them.

This double bind first came to the fore with the blasphemy case in 1995. But it would continue to be a challenge for the IRN. The next mediatized controversy occurred five years later, in 2000, revolving around female genital mutilation (FGM). At the time, FGM had been criminalized in Norway for five years. But no cases had been prosecuted, and the authorities did not prioritize working with the affected communities once the ban was in place (Bråten and Elgvin 2014, 114–15). The IRN had not been much involved in the issue and had not been asked by the media to comment on issues relating to FGM.

In 2000, all of this changed. A TV crew did a hidden camera documentary on the advice Norwegian imams and Muslim leaders would give to a young woman who came to them and said that her mother wanted her to get circumcised. The Norwegian TV channel TV2 employed the young Somali woman Kadra Noor as an undercover investigator. She went to several mosques in Oslo and asked them for advice. According to the story she presented to them, her mother wanted her to go Somalia to undergo female genital mutilation, and she was not sure what she should do. One of the mosques she contacted was the Gambian mosque in Oslo, which was an active member of the IRN. She had talks with the imam, Ebrahim Saydi, who had also been involved in the IRN. Saydi said in his conversation with Kadra that FGM was not obligatory in Islam, and that it could create difficulties. He said it was better if she could avoid doing it. He said his wife was not circumcised and that he would not circumcise his own daughter. He also said that he had never heard of any Gambian girls growing up in Norway who went abroad to get circumcised. Nevertheless, he said that if a decision to disobey her mom would lead to Kadra losing contact with her family, it would be better to do what her mom said.

In the documentary that was aired on TV, TV2 left out the part where he said that it would be better not to get circumcised, and only included his advice to not disobey her mom. Still, Saidy assumed full responsibility for his statements, said that he had given them in good faith, and apologized for what he had said. A charitable interpretation of his advice is that he thought that losing contact with her family would be a bigger evil than becoming circumcised. Still, what he did was actually a punishable offense, as he condoned an action that was illegal according to Norwegian law. He later said that he did not know that it was illegal to get circumcised outside of Norway.

But the largest scandal was the interview in the program with Kebba Secka, who had been chosen as the leader of IRN in 1999. Secka was a highly respected leader of the Gambian community in Norway who was active in the same mosque as imam Saidy. He had been active in the IRN almost since the beginning and was often perceived by people outside the IRN as one of the most progressive actors in the IRN. He had for example been appointed as the deputy leader of the *value commission*, a government advisory commission which the government appointed in 1998, with the task of starting a national conversation on values and social cohesion. Leirvik's archive reveals that this

DEALING WITH CROSS-PRESSURES

appointment probably happened as a result of a recommendation by Leirvik himself, who had penned a recommendation letter for Secka to the prime minister's office (Leirvik 1998).

As far as actors in IRN go, Secka was probably one of the more well-liked and respected in external circles. My interviews with actors who were active in IRN around this time also indicate that Secka commanded a high degree of respect internally. In 1999 Secka was chosen to be the leader of the IRN, as the first leader who did not have a background in the Rabita mosque. But then the TV documentary appeared. In the parts that were shown on TV, Secka was seen as advising Kadra not to disobey her mom and to get circumcised. When the full transcript was released somewhat later, it emerged that the conversation between Secka and the woman had been more complex. The transcript is actually somewhat confusing, and it is not completely clear what Secka is trying to say. He does say that he thinks it is better for a woman not to get circumcised. A theme he keeps returning to is finding out what Kadra wants or thinks herself. The parts of the conversation TV2 aired were the ones where he said that it is important to avoid ruptures with one's family, and where he seemingly gives her the advice to obey her mom. But he also says repeatedly that it is Kadra who must make the choice herself, and that he will give her his full support whatever she ends up doing.

Secka's case is still puzzling. I spoke to several independent sources in the Gambian community, and they are adamant that Secka had spoken out against FGM internally in the Gambian community in the years prior to the Kadra affair. It is a possibility, of course, that he was speaking with two tongues, and secretly was open to FGM in private – or thought it was a lesser evil than disobeying one's parents – while being against it publicly. At the very minimum, he is shown advising a young woman to prioritize relations with her mother over maintaining her bodily integrity, in the choice between two evils. But Secka has to this day maintained that it was all a misunderstanding. His claim is that he early on became suspicious of Kadra's story, because it did not seem convincing to him, an experienced youth worker. He was not sure what it was about. He thought that she was not telling the truth, and that she was hiding something from him. Secka then started to wonder if she had experienced sexual assault. According to him, he therefore just tried to talk with her, to go along and build trust, in order for her to open more up. According to Secka, he also tried to provoke her in order to get her to reveal what was really on her mind.

What may strengthen Secka's version is that the transcript shows that he repeatedly asks about what Kadra wanted herself – what was her motivation, her thoughts? It does seem from the transcript that he is inquiring about what she is on to, since he tries to remain as vague as possible in his answers. There is no way of knowing definitively what the truth of the matter was. Secka was either caught up in a misunderstanding that toppled his life, or he was indeed caught advising a young woman to circumcise herself so as not to rupture her family ties. Whatever the truth of the matter is, this scandal led to a fall from grace of enormous proportions for Secka. From being a highly respected professional, IRN leader and deputy leader of a governmental commission, he became a persona non grata almost overnight. He reportedly became clinically depressed and was not able to continue working. When I approached him, almost 20 years later, he did not want to be interviewed for this research project, citing that he was not able to trust outside professionals anymore. In addition to Secka's personal fall from grace, this episode created a breach in trust for the IRN among many of IRN's partners.

In the trajectory of the IRN, the Secka case also marked a turning point when strategies of decoupling and withdrawal also became apparent, meaning that actors in the organisation either tried to "talk the talk" without engaging in internal change, or attempted to stay out of the spotlight altogether. Up until then, the IRN had mostly attempt to find balancing solutions, without trying to decouple of withdraw. In my interviews with activists from the IRN around 2016–2018, it was clear that Secka's case still resonated with them. Nobody thought that what happened to him was *right*. Everybody who was involved, from the most reformist-minded to the most conservative, thought that he had been the victim of a grave injustice, and that it was a misunderstanding that cost him his professional life. Nevertheless, the IRN did not take this fight to the public. Secka had stepped down and did not want to put up a public fight. In its press release on the matter, the IRN said that it was critical of the methods used in the programme, and that the press had acted as a *pillory* (IRN 2000). But it also reaffirmed that it was against FGM, and that it had mostly been a non-issue up to that point in time, given that the vast majority of the Muslims who were represented in IRN came from countries where FGM was not practised. The IRN also made the point that it had engaged in dialogue for many years with the Church of Norway and with the authorities and was a member of STL. In this way, the organisation was seemingly trying to uphold its reputation. In the data I have had access to, this is the first occurrence in IRN's history where there developed a clear gap between what key actors thought and believed internally, and what they said to the external world. Internally, they all felt that a grave injustice had been committed against their previous leader Secka. Externally, the organisation was attempting to rebuild trust through other kinds of statements.

A similar occurrence happened a few years later, in 2004. Zahid Mukhtar, one of the veterans of IRN, was at the time the spokesperson of the organisation.

DEALING WITH CROSS-PRESSURES

He participated in a debate on TV following the assassination of the Dutch filmmaker Theo van Gogh. In that debate, he was asked whether he could understand that some Muslims became so provoked by blasphemy that they committed murder. He answered, "I can understand it, although there is no justification for it". This created a public outcry. The leaders of the two largest political parties in Norway both demanded that the IRN should denounce Mukhtar's statements, which they thought were too lenient towards those who committed murder in the name of Islam. The IRN did not denounce Mukhtar's statements. But key actors in the organisation did not lend him their support publicly. As a result, Mukhtar subsequently decided to opt out of the organisation. Like others who left the organisation during this period, he told me in our interview that he left the organisation with mixed feelings.

In my interviews with IRN actors in recent years, some of them brought up this episode as an example of pragmatism. None of them perceived that Mukthar had actually said anything wrong. One previous board member of IRN said it like this:

> Mukhtar did not actually say anything wrong. Or, you know, he didn't find the best words, because Norwegian is not his mother tongue. But in terms of what he said, he was extremely clear in his condemnation of the attack. But still, we thought that the best option was that he didn't continue representing the organisation. It was about pragmatism and not taking unnecessary fights.
>
> Interview with C, 2017–2019

Once again, this demonstrates a gap between what actors in the organisation thought internally, and their external public actions.

The 2000s also saw the birth of another phenomenon: The gradual withdrawal of key actors from the organisation and the public sphere, due to the personal toll of being a public Muslim. Some people also began to become involved in IRN in secret, because they feared what public involvement would do to their career, according to two interviewees (interviews with T and M, 2017–2019). One of those who withdrew was Lena Larsen, who was elected as the new leader of the IRN after Kebba Secka withdrew. It is worthwhile to quote her at length, as this quote provides a vivid illustration of how some activists in IRN began to feel (she also described some of these experiences in an essay in the weekly newspaper *Morgenbladet* in 2009 (Larsen 2009)).

> In the beginning I was seen as a fresh breath of air in the media. As I said, the Muslims had for the first time done something which was politically

correct, completely by accident, and elected a woman as their leader. I had a portrait interview in one of the major newspapers. This honeymoon period lasted about one week, I think. Then I was immediately cast as a religious bogeyman, a conservative figure who was a threat to others. You know, I was wearing the hijab, and that probably played a role as well.

And then I remember I got my first real hit in the media. There was a debate about forced marriage. I said something along the lines that forced marriage was unacceptable but that we can't forbid arranged marriages. What we can do is to ensure exit opportunities, to work for the autonomy of women and young girls, etc. But that was not enough for some, and you know how the media dynamics work. You have three roles, basically: The victim, the perpetrator and the expert. Suddenly I was cast in the role of the perpetrator. I had assumed that my background, as a native convert with an academic education, would allow me to build bridges between mainstream society and the Muslim communities. But that was not how it turned out.

And it continued like that. It was just swimming against the stream, again and again and again. When I look at pictures of myself from that time, I look terribly serious. I am on the defensive. I am tired. You can see it in my body language. So, at the first opportunity, after my first period ended, I stepped down. That night, when I had quit, I went home and cried. I cried when I was elected, and I cried when I stepped down.

I was broken down mentally, and it took me about ten years to really get back together. You know, if you go on the subway you need to have a ticket. Normal people just need to have a ticket. And then you are fine, you can go on the subway if you want to. But for me, representing a Muslim organisation, I felt like ... not only did I need a ticket to be accepted onto the subway, I needed to wave it constantly, up and down. Hey, look at me, I have a ticket. Here is my ticket! That feeling, of having to wave my ticket constantly, to prove myself for Norwegian society ... That feeling of continuously being under suspicion does something to you.

It was academic life that became my safe haven. I was finally admitted to a doctoral programme in 2006, where I was to investigate the issuing of fatwas on women's issues in the European context. I had dreamt about that for a long time. And I just cherished the freedom of going to conferences, to write articles as myself, to represent only me and nobody else ... I have vowed that I will never again represent a Muslim organisation publicly.

Interview with LENA LARSEN, 22.01.2018

DEALING WITH CROSS-PRESSURES

Similar feelings and experiences were expressed to me by another former activist in the IRN, who preferred to stay anonymous. Just like Larsen and Secka, he also went into a period which was mentally challenging after leaving the organisation and had isolated himself from other people. He claimed that the 90s had been fine, even though "it wasn't a walk in the park", but that the 2000s had been difficult. After our interview had formally ended, we began talking about Norwegian politics. The conversation turned specifically to the woes that the Social Democratic party was experiencing at the time, as both of us had friends and acquaintances who were active in that party. We discussed whether there were any politicians who would be able to rise to the top and become party leader once the current leader stepped down. I mentioned that one candidate could be Hadia Tajik, a talented and articulated politician who was the deputy leader at the time, whose parents were migrants from Pakistan and who identified as a Muslim. Tajik had often taken vocal stands against fundamentalism and conservative interpretations of Islam. The former IRN activist then paused, looked me straight in the eye and said with emphasis:

> Do you really think they will ever let somebody like us become prime minster? A Muslim? No, that is never going to happen.
>
> Interview with v, 2017–2019

I had known this activist as somebody who was seemingly well at ease in Norwegian society. And yet, all of these years of contact with actors in mainstream society had left him with the impression that "they" would never let a Muslim become prime minister, even a Muslim as liberal and progressive as Tajik. As will be seen later, these experiences and perceptions – of being unfairly treated and singled out as Muslims – would have an impact on the organisational development of the IRN.

3.7 Redefining the Muslim Interest: towards a Norwegian-Muslim Identity

But these tendencies towards a withdrawal approach coincided with a continued process of accommodation and balancing towards Norwegian society, where key actors subtly redefined what it involved to advance the Muslim interest. Even though there were tendencies towards decoupling and withdrawal, the main tendency in the organisation was an attempt at continuing the balancing process – to find a way to compromise that the different parties could live with.

This period also saw a larger presence in the organisation of young second-generation Muslims who had grown up in Norway. These activists came of age during the 1990s and early 2000s, and were influenced by transnational Islamic intellectuals of the period who emphasised that Muslims needed to develop what may be labelled *hybrid identities* – being good Muslims, but also full-fledged citizens of the countries they lived in. Chief among these intellectuals was probably Tariq Ramadan, a charismatic Swiss Islamic theologian and public intellectual. I did an informal interview in 2009 with Imran Mushtaq, one of the key second generation activists in IRN at the time. In that interview, he explicitly mentioned that Ramadan's first book – "To be a European Muslim" (Ramadan 1999) – had been a source of inspiration for him. The impact of Ramadan is confirmed by the anthropologist Christine Jacobsen, who did thorough fieldwork among young Muslims in Oslo in the 1990s and 2000s and published the results in a book in Norwegian for the general reader and later in an academic monography (Jacobsen 2002, 2010). Writing on the 1990s and 2000s, respectively, Jacobsen attested to Ramadan's importance, particularly as mediated through local elites:

> Although their writings [Ramadan and others] were unfamiliar to most of my interlocutors in the late 1990s, their material addressed to 'Muslim youth' had a certain impact as their ideas were read, transmitted and made relevant to the Norwegian context by local figures of religious authority who acted as 'brokers' within the Muslim communities in Norway. [...]
>
> Tariq Ramadan was already familiar to some in the late 1990s and during the last decade he has visited Norway several times, giving talks, among other things, addressing Muslim youth in particular. Although Ramadan is highly controversial among non-Muslims as well as Muslims, his ideas have become increasingly known and mediated in Norway in the last few years.
>
> JACOBSEN 2010, 79, 126

In recent years Ramadan has fallen from grace, both among Muslims and in the general public. He has been accused by several persons of sexual harassment and rape, a behaviour which according to the accusations goes back many years. Even though Ramadan has forcefully denied the rape accusations, he has acknowledged sexual relations with several of the accusers. At the very minimum he led a double life, having several extra-marital affairs with young Muslim women whom he met as a public speaker, all the while praising the virtues of marriage and pre-marital chastity. While this behaviour is hardly unheard of among powerful men, he nevertheless lost the backing of some of his previous supporters when it became public.

But in the early 2000s, none of this was publicly known. He was surrounded by controversy then as well, but more so in terms of his ideological leanings than about his personal life. Some pundits accused him of being an Islamist in disguise. When reading his books, these accusations seem far-fetched. A reasonable interpretation of Ramadan's writing is that he championed a hybrid type of Islamic identity, in which young Muslims were to feel fully Muslim and fully Norwegian/French/British. What he encouraged was a conservative Islamic piety in the personal sphere, combined with a kind of leftist-oriented political activism for global social justice, and a respect for the fundamentally liberal and secular nature of the states in Western Europe (March 2007, 2011).

The influx of young Muslims who were influenced by Ramadan probably had an impact on the direction of the IRN, which can be seen in two subsequent revisions of the statutes. These statutes were not meant for public use – in fact, I had some difficulty finding copies of them – and they are therefore indicative of genuine processes inside the organisation. The first revision came in 2002, and there were further revisions in 2005/2006 (there were only minor revisions in 2006 compared to 2005). I will call them the *first edition*, *second edition* and *third edition* of the statutes (they are all reproduced in the appendix). The new statutes from 2002 and 2005/2006 reveal several interesting differences compared with the original statutes from 1993. These statutes are generally formulated in a more precise and concise manner; the language is better, and it is easier to understand what the organisation is about. The language is also less exclusionary, and there is an increasing emphasis that the IRN and Muslims form an integral part of Norwegian society.

The revision from 2002 was mainly an update of the first statutes. The structure and organisation from the first edition was kept, but the wording was different. The third edition, on the other hand, was a fundamental restructuring and rewriting of the statutes. In the first statutes, the IRN's relationship to Norwegian society was expressed in this cumbersome and almost inexplicable way: "IRN is a voluntary, religious and democratic association, to the degree that this distinction can be transferred to a society and is in accordance with the laws of Norway". In the second and third edition, it was presented in this simplified manner: "IRN shall be a voluntary, religious, democratic and politically independent organisation whose activity is in line with the laws of Norway".

A change along similar lines was made to the statute which laid out that the IRN was to follow Islamic doctrine. In the first edition it was as follows: "IRN has no right whatsoever to take decisions which are against the Al-Quran and the Sunnah". In the second and third edition, it does not say that IRN has no right to take decisions *against* the Quran or the Sunnah. After all, this requirement creates an immediate need for interpretation: Who is to say whether a certain decision is against the Quran or the Sunnah? Was it against the Quran and the Sunnah when the IRN got a woman as its leader, or was this in line with the Quran and the Sunnah? In the second and third edition, it is simpler: "IRN's decisions shall be in line with the Quran and the prophet Muhammed's (peace be upon him) sunnah".

Additional differences from the first edition of the statutes can be seen in the aims. In the first version of the statutes, the list of aims was quite long, and had a clear tendency to prioritize the internal Muslim community. In the second edition, there were some revisions. Much of the intent from the first edition was kept, but with a different wording. In the third edition from 2005/2006, these sections had been thoroughly and fundamentally simplified. Now, the IRN only stated three basic aims:

1. Work towards the goal that Muslims can live in accordance with Islamic doctrine in Norwegian society and contribute to building up a Norwegian-Muslim identity.
2. Promote unity among Muslims in Norway and work for the interests and rights of the member organisations.
3. Be a bridgebuilder and dialogue partner who creates understanding and respect among Muslims and non-Muslims in Norway, with regards to religion, culture and moral values.

These aims are strikingly different from the aims in the first two editions, partly in tone and partly in content. Some important aims are kept and maintained: To ensure that Muslims can live according to Islamic doctrine in Norwegian society, to create unity among Muslims, and to work for the interests of the member organisations. But the wording is now very different. The term "Islamic identity" is not used, but instead the term "Norwegian-Muslim identity". Two further terms were added: Bridgebuilder and dialogue partner. Furthermore, one aim is strikingly absent: There is no talk of Norwegian Muslims being part of global Muslim ummah. The focus throughout is on Norway and the Norwegian context.

Why did the discourse of the IRN change in this way? Based on the language used in the third edition, one interpretation is that the discourse changed as a result of the influx of a younger generation, who were influenced by Tariq Ramadan's ideas about a "Norwegian-Muslim" identity. The aims in the third edition emphasize precisely what Ramadan often spoke about: Being Muslim *and* being Norwegian, being a bridgebuilder and engaging in dialogue. The IRN still attempted to advance Muslim interests, but it construed this in a different way: It was to be achieved *together* with other actors, through a Norwegian society where different groups respected each other.

CHAPTER 4

Unstable Institutionalisation: New Responsibilities and New Divisions (2006–2012)

The next period in the history of the organisation would end with a split and a public fall for grace. The period started with increased public recognition. During the Cartoon Crisis in 2006 and 2007, the organisation played a role as a bridge-builder which Norwegian policy makers appreciated. As a result, the organisation received public funding for the first time and increased in visibility and standing. Conflicts emerged in the early 2010s, however, when new persons joined the leadership of the IRN. They had new ideas about how the organisation should be run. Whereas the IRN had long sought to reach many of their goals through external dialogue and soft means, the organisation increasingly sought a more independent profile. The IRN sought independence from state funding by relying on income from halal certification, and began to voice more criticism towards external actors. This created opposition on the part of the old leadership in IRN.

The chapter builds on the preceding chapters, and shows that the heart of the conflict was a disagreement about how to respond to cross-pressures and competing demands. This can lead to different organisational strategies: To deal with conflicting external demands by a balancing approach, or to seek independence by building strength from within. The chapter also introduces the final analytical building block, which is the importance of internal and external institutionalisation. I argue that the institutionalisation of the IRN was inherently unstable. Internally, the organisation took on new responsibilities and new funding with an unstable organisational structure. Externally, the environment the organisation operated within was unstable and unpredictable. This instability made it more likely that conflicts and disagreements could emerge.

4.1 On the Importance of institutionalisation and the External Environment

In organisational theory among sociologists and political scientists, scholars have long recognized the importance of institutionalisation for stability in organisations. Institutionalisation is a concept that has been used by scholars

© OLAV ELGVIN, 2025 | DOI:10.1163/9789004701144_005

This is an open access chapter distributed under the terms of the CC BY-NC-ND 4.0 license.

in different ways. When I write about institutionalisation here, I have in mind a process which the sociologists Leonard Broom and Philip Selznick defined as "the development of orderly, stable, socially integrating forms and structures out of unstable, loosely patterned, or merely technical types of action" (Selznick and Broom 1977, 222). An important part of such processes has to do formal rules and regulations. At a work place, for example, institutionalisation of the relationship between the manager and the workers occurs if it is written down that the manager has to have formal talks about work with his employees once or twice a year, as opposed to having such talks whenever or if he sees fit. In an organisation like the IRN, institutionalisation can mean that rules and regulations come in place for various procedures: How and when to elect leaders or board members, procedures for dealing with conflict, rules about what happens if an employee quits, et cetera. Philip Selznick, one of the most influential sociologists of organisations of the 20th century, emphasized that institutionalisation in organisations is also about what he called "character": Certain ways of dealing with issues, beyond what is written down in rules and regulations (Selznick 1996, 271). If an organisation behaves in a similar way over time in response to various challenges, even if it is not written down as a rule, the organisation may also be said to have become more institutionalised.

The external environment of an organisation can also be more or less institutionalised. For an organisation like the IRN, for example, the external environment would be institutionalised if their relationships with other actors take place within formal structures: Annual meetings with partners, formal expectations from the authorities, and more. In organisational research, internal institutionalisation and institutionalisation or predictability in the external environment has been extensively studies. A key finding across many studies is that internal institutionalisation and centralisation in an organisation leads to stability (Fleck 2007; Larson 2009; Zucker 1977). In management studies, this has sometimes even been framed as a bad thing: institutionalisation may hinder innovation and the ability to respond to challenges in new and creative ways, the argument goes (Fleck 2007). As to the external environment, results are less clear-cut. This may be because it is difficult to measure and operationalize institutionalisation in the external environment. Some scholars have talked about stable versus unstable environments, others have talked about changing vs unchanging environments, others about predictable vs. non-predictable environments (Aldrich 2008; Jurkovich 1974). Here I will talk about institutionalisation of the external environment. By that I mean that the external relations of the organisation take place within an environment that is regulated by formal rules and regulations. Conversely, the external environment lacks institutionalisation if it is not regulated by rules and regulations, and is more unpredictable.

My argument in this chapter is that the IRN experienced institutionalisation from 2007 onwards. This institutionalisation was inherently unstable, however, both internally and in the institutional environment. This made it more likely that conflicts would arise, and also made it more difficult to solve the conflicts once they had occurred.

4.2   Becoming a Trusted Partner: the Cartoon Affair

The event that led to the increased institutionalisation of the IRN was the cartoon affair in late 2005 and early 2006. The outcome of this affair gave the IRN external recognition and public funding. The basic facts of the affair are fairly well known by now – see for example the seminal work by Jytte Klausen (Klausen 2009). The editor Flemming Rose in the Danish newspaper Jyllandsposten invited different cartoonists in Denmark to make cartoons of the prophet Muhammad in 2005. He believed that freedom of expression was threatened, and that Westerners censored themselves with regards to Islam, and he wanted to challenge this tendency. Twelve cartoonists responded and created cartoons, five of which actually made fun of Jyllandposten and Rose himself. But there were some cartoons that explicitly mocked the prophet. The most famous of them was drawn by Kurt Westergaard and depicted the prophet Muhammad with a bomb in his turban. This created a stir among Danish Muslims, and also came to the attention of Muslims abroad.

The case reached global proportions when a delegation of imams and Muslim leaders from Denmark decided to take the case further. They travelled to the Middle East, where they implored governments and Muslim leaders to take diplomatic action. The imams had previously attempted to engage in dialogue with the Danish government, but did not even receive an answer to their invitation, and then took the case abroad. Eleven ambassadors from Muslim countries also asked then prime minister Anders Fogh Rasmussen for a meeting and were turned down. When the imams went to the Middle East, they took a dossier containing the cartoons with them, including a couple of cartoons that had nothing to do with Jyllandsposten, which were included to make the case appear even worse.

The result was an emerging global crisis. There were riots in many places and calls for a boycott of Denmark. In January 2006, the crisis spread to Norway. The newspapers Aftenposten and Dagbladet had printed small facsimiles of their cartoons in the autumn, without inciting notable reactions. What created a stir were the actions of the small Christian weekly magazine *Magazinet*, edited by Vebjørn Selbekk. It printed the cartoons in full format on the 10 January, with the explicit motivation to contend that Muslims in Europe were threatening

94   CHAPTER 4

freedom of speech. This created reactions from many Muslims in Norway. It became the IRN's big and defining moment in Norwegian political history: they stepped onto the stage and changed the outcome.

The events that transpired have already been written about elsewhere, both by some of the participants themselves (Hamdan 2006; Horsfjord 2013; Kobilica 2006; Leirvik 2006b; Selbekk 2006), as well as by outside observers (Austena 2011; Engelstad 2013; Klausen 2009; Malik 2010; Steien 2008). According to Vebjørn Horsfjord, who was the assistant secretary general of MKR at the time, nobody had expected that the cartoon crisis would blow up in Norway as well, even after the publication of the cartoons in Magazinet (Horsfjord 2013, 409). When Magazinet published the cartoons, several Christian leaders immediately made it known that they were against the publication. MKR and IRN met on 19 January 2006, only nine days after the publication of the cartoons by Magazinet. On this meeting, MKR suggested that MKR and IRN should publish a joint statement. But participants from the IRN were skeptical and were afraid that condemning the cartoons would mean playing the game according to the rules set by Magazinet. They made it clear that they were indeed offended by the cartoons, but preferred to let the affair blow over by itself, and did not want to respond in the way they thought Magazinet expected them to, by condemning the publication (Horsfjord 2013, 409). MKR and IRN therefore made a very bare-boned statement:

> Freedom of speech is a fundamental right which must be upheld, but this freedom also involves big responsibility.
> The cartoons published in Jyllandsposten and Magazinet offend religious feelings
> Speech acts must not be met with violence and threats. We disapprove of threats against those make such speech acts.
>
> Kontaktgruppen mellom Islamsk Råd Norge og Mellomkirkelig råd 2006

It is notable that this statement – rather remarkably – does not outright condemn the publication of the cartoons by Magazinet. According to Horsfjord's account, this was due to reticence from the IRN, not from the MKR. The board of the IRN, at this time, consciously avoided a combative approach. They preferred working *with* friendly actors in society, rather than working *against* actors such as Magazinet.

Following this meeting and this statement, there were developments which made it mandatory for IRN and MKR to respond in a more forceful manner. Media outlets in several Muslim countries reported on the cartoons and Magazinet's publication, and there was a growing perception that this was the beginning of an anti-Islamic campaign by Western countries (Austena 2011, 157). There were calls for boycotts of Norway and Denmark, and violent riots erupted in several Muslim countries. On the 3 February, persons from MKR, IRN and the Christian Council of Norway (NKR) – a Christian umbrella organisation – therefore convened at the house of the bishop of Oslo, Ole Christian Kvarme. NKR is an umbrella organisation or meta-organisation which includes not only the Church of Norway, but also the Catholic church and several independent Lutheran or Evangelical churches. This meeting therefore represented more or less all the Christian congregations in Norway, and all the Islamic congregations who were represented in the IRN. The participants at this meeting issued a joint statement, which went further than the previous statement from MKR and IRN. This statement said that they "disapprove of the publication of cartoons of the prophet Muhammad, as well as of the violent reactions the cartoons have caused" (Medlemmer og ledere i Islamsk råd i Norge, Norges kristne råd og Den norske kirke 2006). The statement also stressed that relations between Muslims and Christians in Norway were good and defended Norwegian humanitarian organisations who had a presence in Muslim countries. To a large degree, this statement seems oriented towards calming the emotions that were running high in several Muslim countries.

On the same day – Friday, 3 February – the leaders of the IRN also met with Jonas Gahr Støre, the foreign minister at the time. They proposed that a delegation from IRN, together with representatives from MKR, should travel to Muslim countries "in order to provide true and accurate information about the position of IRN and other religious leaders in Norway (in particular the Church of Norway)" (Hamdan 2006, 1). This meeting was followed up by a formal meeting with the Ministry of Foreign Affairs, where MKR also participated. The MFA was positive to the idea, and would provide funding, but emphasised that this delegation was not to have an official mandate from the Norwegian authorities. At the same time, the IRN also reached out to Selbekk and Magazinet through the media and asked him to apologize.

During the following week, the leader of the IRN – Mohamed Hamdan – would have a meeting with Magazinet's editor Vebjørn Selbekk. This meeting was not organised through MKR or the Church, but through people in the Christian Democratic Party (KrF). The leader of KrF at the time, Dagfinn Høybråten, hailed from the same part of the Christian landscape as Magazinet – the charismatic evangelical congregations. He therefore had good indirect connections to Magazinet and Selbekk. KrF also had one notable Muslim politician, Ali Khan, colloquially known as *KrF-Ali*. While people close to Høybråten worked to get Selbekk onboard, Khan worked with the IRN (Austena 2011, 167). Hamdan and Selbekk met, and Selbekk wrote a statement in which he stopped short of apologizing for publishing the cartoons, but nevertheless said that he was sorry that the feelings of Muslims had been hurt. On Friday, 10 February, Selbekk and Hamdan held a joint press conference. At the press conference, Selbekk offered a half-apology. Hamdan said that he accepted Selbekk's statement and said that no harm should come to Selbekk.

Later that same day, the IRN held a press conference of its own. Fourteen imams were present at this press conference (Stokke and Hegtun 2006). Never before had so many imams gathered together for a press conference of this type. This lent their statements considerable religious and institutional authority. At this press conference, the IRN and the imams specifically talked to Muslims in Norway and abroad and said that they now regarded the cartoon affair as over, as far as they were concerned, and that they had accepted Selbekk's apology. The IRN's leader was also interviewed directly on Al-Jazeera and Al-Arabiyya, the two largest Arabic satellite channels (Engelstad 2013, 81). Some days later, IRN would send delegations to the Middle East and Pakistan to ease tensions and act as goodwill ambassadors for Norway. The delegation to the Middle East consisted of Mohamed Hamdan and Olav Dag Hauge, who was the dean of the cathedral of Oslo, and the Pakistani imam Zulqarnain Sakander (Hamdan 2006, 1). The delegation to Pakistan consisted of Senaid Kobilica, the main imam of the Bosnian religious community in Norway and the deputy leader of IRN, imam Mehboob ur-Rehman from ICC who was the leader of the imam committee in IRN at the time, the two vicars Geir Valle and Knut Kittelsaa from the Church of Norway, and Arne Sæverås from Norwegian Church Aid (Kobilica 2006, 1). Both of these delegations met with highly influential figures in the countries they visited, ranging from religious figures to ambassadors and political leaders. The participants themselves, both the Muslims and the Christians, had the impression afterwards that these meetings had helped in easing tensions and bettering Norway's image in these countries (Egeberg 2006).

At the same time, this affair also showed that the IRN and the imams in the major mosques did not wield unlimited authority over Muslims in Norway. The day after the press conference of the IRN and Selbekk, a large peaceful demonstration was held in Oslo, in which 1500 Muslims demonstrated against the publication of the cartoons. This conference was organised by a loose group who called themselves *De frivillige*, "the volunteers". They did not hail predominantly from any of the established organisations or groups. Both the IRN and nearly all major mosques – with a couple of minor exceptions – actually warned against participating in the demonstration (Fosse 2006; Grimstad 2006). It is notable that most of the people who gave speeches during the demonstration, and who provided comments to the media, were unknown to the general public, and did not have particular institutional affiliations. This does indicate that the demonstration reflected a swell of frustration among ordinary Muslims in Norway, who wanted to make their voice heard, and who thought that the conciliatory approach of the organised Muslim leadership was not a sufficient answer. The only speaker with a known institutional affiliation was Fuad Ahmed Iman, who was the imam at the time in Masjid Bilal, a relatively small Arab mosque in Oslo. He spoke at the demonstration, and later claimed in an interview that the IRN "did not represent Muslims in Norway" (Geard 2006).

In the same interview, there were other voices as well who said that the IRN did not represent them, for example Saera Khan, a Muslim politician from the labour party. But whereas imam Iman seemed to criticize IRN for being too soft and dialogue-oriented, Khan claimed that IRN was more conservative than the average Norwegian Muslim. This foreshadowed a development that would continue in the following years: IRN was criticized by some for being too soft, and by others for being too conservative.

4.3 Funding with Strings Attached

In Norwegian public discourse, the role of the Norwegian government, the IRN and the Church during this crisis has been much criticized in recent years – for example the fact that the Norwegian delegation met with the controversial Islamic cleric Yusuf al-Qaradawi, or that the government chose to participate in the press conference with Hamdan and Selbekk, even though it had stated that the government did not interfere in such issues at all (Austena 2011, 227). Nevertheless, it is fair to say that the IRN put in quite a lot of effort into easing the tensions during the cartoon crisis; and that key actors from the IRN acted as goodwill ambassadors for Norway in the Muslim countries they visited. The affair also attested to the possible value of a unifying organisation such as the IRN: When called upon, the IRN was able to calm spirits and reach out to Muslims worldwide in the interest of both the Muslims in Norway and Norwegian society at large. This provided the IRN with much goodwill in political circles.

For IRN, this became a symbolic and strategic victory of an importance it is hard to overstate. They had managed to obtain something amounting to an apology for the publication of the cartoons, which gave them high standing across the Muslim world. Mohamed Hamdan, the leader of the IRN, was touring the Middle East and met a veritable who's who list of Arab and Muslim leaders. Secondly, they had been taken seriously by the Norwegian authorities as a legitimate power-broker and increased their symbolic standing with the government. Some months later, then foreign minister Jonas Gahr Støre – who later became leader of the Norwegian Labour Party and prime minister – visited the World Islamic Mission mosque in the multicultural quarter of Grønland in Oslo, where he gave a speech which became famous. This speech was highly symbolic: It was Støre's first visit to a mosque as a foreign minister. He was invited to speak just after the Friday prayer on 8 December, while the mosque was full to the brim with congregants who had come to pray and hear him speak. The speech itself was well-prepared and charged with symbolism. Støre chose this very occasion to introduce for the first time a term he would continue to use during the years to come, both as foreign minister and subsequently as party leader: That people in Norway needed to develop a "new, big, Norwegian we" (Berge 2013, 124). In his speech he also complimented the Muslims and mosques of Norway and said that they were important parts of the new Norwegian *we*. He specifically mentioned the cartoon crisis and the role of the IRN and the MKR:

> During the cartoon crisis it was the trust and the dialogue that helped us along. The IRN and MKR became important – even more important – both in domestic and foreign policy. Representatives for different communities made statements, and they did it together – about values and belief, about belonging and freedom of speech. This was decisively important.
>
> RODUM 2006

Next year, in 2007, IRN would also, for the first time, be mentioned in an official government document. As was mentioned in the previous chapter, STL – the Council for Religious and Life Stance Communities in Norway – had been mentioned in such government documents almost since its founding in 1996. It was not until now, 14 years after its founding, that the IRN was formally acknowledged by the government, in a parliamentary proposition on voluntary associations. Once again the cartoon crisis was specifically mentioned: "The council became particularly visible during the cartoon affair" (St.melding nr. 39 (2006–2007). Frivillighet for alle. 2007, 149). It seemed as though the IRN had finally accomplished the goal that was set out in the very first statutes from 1993: To "represent Norwegian Muslim organisations vis-a-vis Norwegian authorities and institutions".

This recognition from the Norwegian authorities was not only symbolic. When the government proposed their budget for 2007 in the fall of 2006, the IRN was included for the first time. I have not been able to ascertain exactly how the process unfolded. None of the interviewees remembered in detail how the process started. Several interviewees in the IRN told me that the question of funding had been there for a long time; they had been thinking about how to secure some basic level of funding. It was only now, in the aftermath of the cartoon crisis, that it came to fruition. The *Ministry of Church and Culture* – which has since been reorganised administratively – shared with me the application and the documents pertaining to the matter. The email that accompanied the application was written by board member Arshad Jamil, and referred to a prior conversation by telephone with one of the ministry's senior advisors (Islamsk Råd Norge 2006a, 2006b). This means that there must have been some contact between the IRN and the ministry before the application was sent. In a later interview, Jamil confirmed to me that they indeed received informal signals that an application would be viewed positively (interview with Arshad Jamil, 06.02.2023).

The IRN wrote a detailed application, containing a short application letter and a longer background document. In the application, the main point was that the IRN did not have sufficient resources to fulfil its assignments and obligations, neither vis-à-vis its Muslim member organisations nor vis-à-vis society at large. The IRN mentioned that all its work was done on a voluntary basis, in stark contrast with the situation of its "dialogue partners", who had several funded, full-time employees (Islamsk Råd Norge 2006a). One consequence of this was that the IRN could not participate in important meetings during daytime, for example, as most of them had other jobs they needed to attend to.

The most interesting aspect of the application and the response, however, is what the IRN applied for, and the answer they received. IRN applied for a substantial yearly sum – almost two million Norwegian kroner (NOK) – which was to cover a secretary general in a full position, an information/press secretary in a full position, and an office secretary in a part-time position. The aim was to better serve *both* its member organisations and the Muslim communities in general, and society at large. Even though this was a substantial sum, such a sum was not very large compared to what many other organisations in Norway of a similar size received from the state. In response, however, they were only granted a quarter of this sum, 500,000 NOK.

Furthermore, the ministry decided to support only one part of IRNS activities – the external and dialogue-oriented part. IRN had stated several aims in its application letter. It said that the aim of the organisation was to "ensure that Muslims can live in accordance with Islamic teachings in Norwegian society and contribute to building a Norwegian-Muslim identity. In addition, IRN shall build a community among the Muslims in Norway and work for the interests and rights of its member organisations. The IRN was also to be a bridgebuilder and dialogue-partner that creates mutual understanding and respect between Muslims and non-Muslims" (Islamsk Råd Norge 2006b). The letter from the department meanwhile stated that the aim of the funding was that the IRN could "be a bridgebuilder and dialogue-partner who creates mutual understanding and respect between Muslims and non-Muslims" (Kultur- og kirkedepartementet 2007). The department did not say expressly that they did *not* support the other internal aims, but it chose to highlight only one of IRNs stated aims as the specific area they were willing to fund and support.

This funding, as is customary with funding from the state in Norway, also came with several strings attached. The IRN needed to submit an annual report which clarified how the funding was spent, and it was made clear in the letter that the ministry had the right to control that the funding was spent according to how it was intended. Even though it was not stated in clear terms in the letter, this was a goodwill gesture from the government and the authorities, which could, in principle, be taken away.

When the IRN, in 2006, learned that they would receive funding from the state, there was a call for applications to the post of secretary general. It was decided by the board that the post would be on *åremål*; which means a fixed-term contract. The applicant chosen for the job was Shoaib Sultan, who had reportedly been approached by people on the board who wanted him to apply. He hailed from the ICC mosque, and had a dialogue-oriented profile the IRN board deemed suitable.

Sultan had grown up in Norway and was perceived by many of those I interviewed as a soft-spoken and intellectual type. Like many resourceful young persons of immigrant background, Sultan had studied «hard sciences» (economy and business administration in his case), even though his main interests lay elsewhere. After a brief stint working in business in the early 2000s, he began working as a freelance journalist and commentator, writing and commenting on various issues relating to Islam and integration. During the 2000s he had occasionally worked as an unpaid secretary for the IRN board. He had also worked for the European Council of Religious Leaders, a network of leaders from Islam, Christianity, Judaism, Hinduism, Buddhism, Sikhism and Zoroastrianism. This council was established in 2002 by Gunnar Stålsett, the bishop of Oslo at the time, and maintained a small office in Oslo for a period of time. The office employed Sultan, together with Vebjørn Horfsfjord, who would go on to work in MKR.

When Sultan was approached by people in the IRN, they had asked him whether he would be interested in applying: "They told me I had a profile that might suit the position", he told me in our interview. This indicates that the leadership of the IRN in 2006 were interested in employing someone who would give the IRN an open and dialogue-oriented profile, who could in that way secure their status as a trusted partner. One of the most important principles for Sultan was indeed to develop good relations to people in the media, he told me in our interview:

> It was important for me to develop a good network among people working in the media. If they called, I always tried to answer. There was a pronounced scepticism to the media among several of our communities. I always told them that it didn't help to just sit on the sidelines and be angry, if the media wrote something they didn't like. It was better to pick up the phone and explain why you think it was right or wrong.
>
> Interview with SHOAIB SULTAN, 12.09.2019

This open approach seemed to work. Sultan was able to command much respect, both internally in the Muslim milieus and in mainstream society, even from actors in the anti-Islamic camp. When I wrote my master's thesis in the late 2000s, I also did some interviews with high-profile activists or journalists who could be deemed as critical of Islam. Several of them mentioned that they were on good terms personally with Shoaib Sultan from the IRN. Sultan seems to have been able to develop a good relationship with actors one might have expected would be highly critical towards the IRN or himself. This indicated that IRN had indeed succeeded in becoming a trusted partner for large segments of society.

4.4 New Responsibilities and External Expectations

This new situation of being a trusted partner, having an employee and a regular source of funding, was something key actors in IRN had sought for a long time. At the same time, this situation brought with it new challenges. The experience of being between *in the squeeze* intensified. The new situation intensified the experience of facing cross-pressures and competing expectations. Its Muslim member organisations wanted the organisation to provide them with services and work for their interests. The authorities, meanwhile, from now on the main funder of the organisation, allocated money to the IRN only to work for external dialogue and bridgebuilding.

In the previous chapter I discussed the term *multiple institutional logics* (Kraatz and Block 2008; Pache and Santos 2010; Thornton, Ocasio, and Lounsbury 2015) This term emphasizes that the different spheres or fields the IRN operated within – the world of the mosques, transnational Islamic organisations, contact with the authorities, relationships with other faith-based organisations, contact with the media – contain different logics concerning the appropriate modes of behaviour. The rules of the game in each of these spheres differ from each other. The situation of having public funding and a paid employee seems to have made this situation more acute: On all sides, stakeholders and parties were expecting the IRN to deliver more than before. Muslim activists expected the IRN to do more than before, and politicians, public officials and dialogue partners had other expectations to the IRN.

One of the first indications that the IRN was facing increasing scrutiny was a controversy about homosexuality 2007. The deputy leader at the time, Asghar Ali, had participated in a public debate on homosexuality. He also held assignments in the Labour Party and worked in one of the largest labour unions of Norway. Ali had grown up in Norway, had a master's degree in political science, and was perceived by persons in the organisation as an articulate and intelligent person. IRN then received an invitation to join a debate on homosexuality and Islam. He volunteered to go, he told me in our interview, because he thought that someone should go – and that it should be somebody who was prepared to take the heat. He was asked during the debate whether he could condemn the death penalty for homosexuality in Iran. He said that he did not support the death penalty but would not outright condemn it either. It was a "theological question" (Kumano-Ensby 2007).

This led to a huge debate: Did the IRN support capital punishment for homosexuality? A government minister, Manuela Ramin-Osmundsen, condemned Ali' statements in harsh terms. Shoaib Sultan, the new secretary general, attempted to diffuse tensions and tone down the issue, and said that he was personally against capital punishment as a general principle, even though he regarded homosexuality as a sin (Gran 2007). This did not appease many critics, however. Politicians and journalists in the media wanted to know what the IRN as an organisation thought about the issue: Did it condemn capital punishment for homosexuality, wherever it occurred, yes or no?

This was a tricky issue for the organisation and its representatives. The view among many orthodox Islamic theologians, up until recently, has been that acts of anal penetration between men in fact should indeed be punishable by death (El-Rouayheb 2009, 6). Throughout most of pre-modern history, however, many Muslim countries in fact had a thriving culture of sex between consenting men, as well as pederasty (sexual relations between adult men and teenage boys), which was tacitly accepted by large segments of society (Bauer 2011; El-Rouayheb 2009; Lapidus 2014, 1429–31; Mujtaba et al. 1997). Part of the reason for this was that religious Islamic law prescribed that the act of penetration needed to be witnessed as it occurred by four witnesses to be adjudicated in court. This seldom happens, of course. This requirement made it a largely dormant law, which could not be applied in practice. Actual cases of prosecution of men for homosexual relations were therefore rare all across the pre-modern Muslim world. What was probably not accepted – or even assumed as a possibility – was *being homosexual*, as an exclusive public identity. Sex between men was something which was assumed to co-exist with marriage between men and women and the rearing of children. Some scholars have assumed that this pattern changed with the onset of modernity, when Muslim countries were colonized and affected by the more restrictive Victorian European laws and discourses regarding sexual relations (Lapidus 2014, 1429–31). Still, modern anthropologists have noted that sex between men has apparently been relatively common in Muslim countries from Morocco to Pakistan up until today (Mujtaba et al. 1997; Rebucini 2013). At the same time, there is no doubt that many modern Muslim countries have instituted harsher policies regarding homosexuality in recent decades, arguably retaining the letter but not the spirit of earlier Islamic laws.

The IRN, when facing the issue, was asked to comment explicitly on the issue of capital punishment – yes or no? For modern moral sensibilities in Norway, it is not sufficient to say that homosexuality (or anal penetration) in *principle* should be punishable by death, but not in practice, as the evidentiary requirements are so difficult to attain. But if IRN said that it was against capital punishment for homosexuality as a matter of principle, it would intrude on an issue which is still hotly theologically debated in Muslim countries. When Tariq Ramadan attempted to create social change on these issues, for example, he called for a "moratorium" on corporal punishment in Muslim countries, as he thought this would be easier to attain than an outright theological or political ban (Ramadan 2005, 2009). But even this requirement was largely rejected by most theological bodies in Muslim countries (Ramadan 2009). Among IRN's members, it is likely that a substantial number were not ready to say publicly that capital punishment for homosexuality was categorically *wrong* – particularly given that IRN and the member mosques did not have any time to process or discuss the issue. In our interview, Ali stated that he simply did not think he had the theological stature to weigh in this question, which was so hotly debated among theologians.

The IRN attempted to solve or bypass the problem by sending a letter to the European Fatwa council, headed by Yusuf Al-Qaradawi, to ask for counsel. In many ways, this was a withdrawal approach: By sending the problem to another theological body, they hoped to avoid having to deal with the issue. They did not receive an answer, though. Asghar Ali subsequently lost all his positions in the Labour party but retained his job in the labour union and his position in IRN. This controversy would continue to dog the IRN in the years to come. As a result of the controversy, politicians in various parties began talking about taking away the public funding of the organisation (Utrop 2007).

At the same time, the interfaith dialogue the IRN was involved in became more encompassing than ever, according to several of those involved (Horsfjord 2013, 413). In the last couple of years before the cartoon crisis, documents from the MKR show that the dialogue activities between the MKR and the IRN had been declining (Horsfjord 2005b, 2005a). The internal documents from MKR do not indicate that the lack of dialogue meetings was due to ill will on the part of the IRN. Before the cartoon crisis, the last meeting IRN had with the MKR occurred on 30 November 2004. Throughout 2005, no meetings were held. Horfsfjord and others in the MKR seemed to attribute this to a certain lack of organisation in the IRN – not to a lack of will.

After the cartoon crisis, the dialogue activities with the MKR picked up steam. The number of meetings increased, and they seemed to have increased in status and importance. The main outcome of the dialogue activities that occurred during these years were three joint statements from the IRN and MKR, concerning contested theological and political issues. These statements were significant steps for the IRN, where they weighed in on controversial issues which were contested internally. The first statement was issued in 2007. It stated that all people, irrespective of their faith, had the right to convert to another religion (IRN and MKR 2007). In Muslim circles, this was not – and is not – uncontroversial. In premodern times, all the four Sunni law schools as well as the main Shia law school, stated that apostasy away from Islam was forbidden according to Islam, and should be punishable in a proper Islamic society (Peters and De Vries 1976; Saeed 2017). Some Islamic scholars claimed that the punishment should unequivocally be death, while others advocated milder punishments, or the possibility of repentance for the apostate. With the advent of modernity, influential Islamic scholars claimed that this view had originated from a misinterpretation of the Islamic sources. The punishable offence, according to these scholars, was not apostasy in itself, but only rebellion against the state or the community, and this was what the sources had in mind when they condemned apostasy (Alibasic 2016; Peters and De Vries 1976, 14–18). The traditional view that apostasy was a capital offence continued to prevail in other theological circles, however. It was not until the 2010s that important Islamic theological institutions, such as al-Azhar in Egypt, began to endorse the reformist opinion (Pellegrino 2017; al-Tayyeb 2012).

Nevertheless, the IRN ended up taking a clear stand on a question that was disputed and controversial in Muslim countries and in conservative Muslim circles in Europe. Leirvik's archive indicates that the process leading up to the joint declaration started with an initiative from him, at a meeting between IRN and MKR in May 2006 (Leirvik 2006a). There were actors in IRN, however, who were also interested in working on this issue, and Leirvik's initiative was well received. The joint statement was made on 22 August one year later, after a process which anchored the statement in the organisations.

Following this joint declaration, the contact group between IRN and the MKR soon began working on a new joint declaration. Once again it was on a contested issue, on gender-based violence. The initiative to this seems to have originated with the theologian Anne-Hege Grung, one of the participants from the MKR. She had been engaged in interfaith dialogue for a long time and had focused on women's rights within religious communities. Back in 2000, she and Lena Larsen had published a book together which documented the experiences of women who were engaged in interfaith dialogue (Grung and Larsen 2000). She started raising the issue at one of the meetings between MKR and IRN in May 2007.

At a meeting between the IRN and MKR in March 2008 it was decided that a small working group would work on a draft on gender-based violence (MKR 2008). This working group worked on the draft throughout 2008 and planned publication in 2009. It was finally made public at a press conference on the 9 November 2009 (IRN and MKR 2009). Just like with apostasy, this issue is not uncontroversial among Muslims. In the writings on this issue in the orthodox juridical Islamic tradition before modernity – which have been looked into by the scholar Ayesha Chaudhry – the common view was that men had a right to discipline their wife physically, if she was disobedient (Ayesha S. Chaudhry 2013; Ayesha Siddiqua Chaudhry 2009). The recommendation was to do it in a "non-extreme" way (Ayesha S. Chaudhry 2013, 82). However, men did not face any penalty according to Islamic law if they did not follow this recommendation – only beatings which resulted in broken bones or death were punishable offenses (Ayesha S. Chaudhry 2013, 89). The actual legal practice may have been different, and works in the genre of philosophical Islamic ethics also contain other recommendations. In the 20th century there was also an increasing number of traditionalist theologians who argued that one needed to reinterpret the idea that men had a right to physically discipline their wives.

But Shoaib Sultan, the secretary general who was in charge of adopting the declaration in IRN, said in our interview that the declaration on gender violence received zero pushback internally:

> SS: I actually can't remember that I heard anything negative on that declaration at all. Nobody contacted me to voice their disaffection, and I didn't pick up any resistance from any of the mosques. I think I would

have remembered it if anybody contacted me, and I don't think anybody did. I really perceived this declaration as very non-controversial.
OE: Why?
SS: Well, it is very hard to vocally make the case that a man actually has
a right to beat his wife, you know. I would say that the norms against
that in the different Muslim communities in Norway have become
pretty firm by now. Sure, it happens, like in many places, but it is not
something that anybody will stand up and *defend*. Even for the small
minority that might think theologically that men have this right, it is
not ... it is just not something they will say out loud.

Interview with SHOAIB SULTAN, 12.09.2019

Following this declaration, representatives from the IRN and the MKR decided
to go on their first joint study trip abroad, to the Balkans, which was well
received among all of the participants. They also issued a final joint declaration in 2011, against religious extremism, which was relatively uncontroversial
(Den norske kirke 2011).

4.5 Internal Tensions

At the same time, the IRN began getting pressure internally, from other actors
in the Islamic field and from members who had previously not held much
influence in the organisation. As was detailed in chapter 2, the IRN had been
dominated by the post-Islamists in Rabita and ICC ever since the beginning.
In the 2000s there was also an increasing presence from the Bosnian mosques.

One example of this dominance can be found in the domain of halal food,
which was of huge importance and concern to most devout Muslims in Norway.
IRN instituted a halal committee in the 1990s, which was tasked with coordinating and overseeing the issue of halal meat in Norway (Vogt 2008, 220). Halal
slaughter is a hugely controversial topic among Muslims: What kind of meat is
actually *halal*, i.e. allowed, for Muslims? The traditional requirement for both
halal/Islamic and kosher/Jewish slaughter is killing through a cut to the throat
when the animal is conscious, while invoking the name of God/Allah. Animals
must be alive and healthy at the time of slaughter, and all blood must be
drained from the carcass. This, however, is not allowed under Norwegian law,
which stipulates that animals must be stunned before their throat can be cut.

The issue of stunning is contentious. Some Islamic groups are categorically
against it. Some support it, whereas others accept it, but do not regard it as
ideal. During the 90s and early 00s, the IRN had put their mark of acceptance

on this method of slaughter – stunning the animal first, then a cut to the throat, as long as the other requirements were met. When referring to the theological issue of stunning and halal slaughter on the IRN website in 2003, there were only two theological documents which were referenced: A classic work by Yusuf al-Qaradawi, and a report in Norwegian written by Nora Eggen for The Islamic Information Society (Al-Qaradawi 2013; Eggen 2000). Both of these works hailed from the wasatiyya or Islamist/post-Islamist tradition. More restrictive perspectives on stunning could also be found among the mosques, particularly among some of the Barelwis. But these perspectives were not referenced on the IRN website.

The summer months of 2007 would be the first time that actors in the Barelwi mosques began to challenge the primacy of the post-Islamists in the public sphere. During the spring of 2007, uncertainty was beginning to spread among some Muslims in Norway concerning whether the halal-marked chicken they bought was indeed halal. The reason was that the largest supplier of halal and non-halal chicken in Norway – Nortura – had changed their method of stunning fowl. Previously, they had relied on electric stunning. But increasingly, they had begun to stun chickens with gas. Some were concerned that the chicken would die directly from the stunning and would thereby not be halal for consumption.

Uneasiness about this among some Muslims was first reported in March, in the rural-oriented newspaper *Nationen*, which frequently writes about issues of interest for the farmers (Brandvol 2007). In June, the newspaper *Aftenposten* reported that IRN had asked the Norwegian food safety authorities to look into the slaughtering of chicken, in order to verify how many died after being stunned with gas. The food safety authorities promptly turned this request down, saying that their sole concern was animal welfare, not religious issues. If chicken indeed died from stunning it was not their concern (Engström 2007). Then, in the end of July, chaos erupted within the Muslim communities. The newspaper VG reported that IRN now wanted to boycott all Norwegian chicken. Apparently, an SMS was circulating and widely shared in several Muslim communities:

JOINT DECLARATION FROM ULEMA/IMAMS IN NORWAY!!
After a systematic and thorough investigation, all the Ulema and Imams in Norway have concluded that chicken which are being sold in Norway or on the border to Sweden, ARE NOT HALAL!!
Buying and selling of these is not allowed according to Islamic law, even though it reads HALAL on them. All Muslims are encouraged to avoid eating these.

Sign:

THE ISLAMIC COUNCIL OF NORWAY

AHLE-SUNNAT IMAM COUNCIL

JAMIAT ULAMA-E NORWAY

For more information you may contact those mentioned above. PS! Send this to all the Muslims you know

KIRKNES AND WIDERØE 2007

In VG's article, the representative who articulated this demand was Ghulam Sarwar, who was the administrative leader of the Ahl-e-Sunnat mosque and did not sit on the IRN board. The only problem, it would soon emerge, was that it was actually not the case that "all the ulema/imams" in Norway had agreed to this, and it was unclear whether this was something that the board of IRN really wanted. Aftenposten reported two days later that there were several important mosques who had not signed the declaration. Islamic Cultural Centre – which had been important in the IRN – had not signed it. Neither had Idara Minhaj ul-Quran, an important Barelwi/Sufi mosque (Riaz 2007b, 2007a). According to sources I spoke to in 2018 and 2019, neither had the Bosnian imams or the Rabita mosque. This meant that most of the mosques which were dominant in IRN at the time were against the declaration.

Furthermore, the imam network which had signed the boycott declaration was actually not formally connected to the IRN. For a long time, the IRN had an imam committee, where the imams in the member mosques could meet to discuss theological issues. But alongside this imam committee, a different imam council existed in Norway, which mostly stayed out of the media spotlight. To my knowledge, this committee has never been written about by researchers or journalists in Norway. It was called the *Ahle-sunnat Imam council* at the time and convened imams from mosques in the Barelwi tradition. It is reportedly a council where the members meet between themselves to discuss issues of common interest. For many years they mostly stayed out of the spotlight, until they changed their name to *Norges imam råd* ("The Norwegian imam council") in 2018, and created a public Facebook page in 2019 (Norges Imam Råd 2019). The halal controversy in 2007 was the first instance when they took a clear public stance on a contested issue.

This controversy caused substantial insecurity among Norwegian Muslims: Was it ok to eat Norwegian halal chicken, or not? It created problems for several Muslim restaurants that relied on halal chicken for their business. It was a provocation for Nortura, which up until then had cooperated well with the IRN and now risked losing many customers. It also created a headache for the IRN board. By putting their name on this declaration, they were actually empowering a network of imams which were operating outside the confines of the IRN. Furthermore, the drastic move of boycotting all halal chicken in Norway had happened without the approval of several of the most important mosques.

What had happened? When I conducted interviews on this in 2018 and 2019, there was much confusion among my interviewees concerning what had actually transpired. It does seem as though Shoaib Sultan did sign the boycott declaration on behalf of the IRN, but it seemed unclear to many actors in IRN why he did so. Some interviewees attributed this to Sultan's style of working: He was relational and attempted to balance different demands, even though he did not always follow organisational protocol. Because many of the board members in the IRN were on vacation, it was also difficult to communicate and agree on what to do. Some of these board members claim that they never agreed that the IRN should sign the declaration, and that there was never a formal vote about it.

Although there was much internal disagreement and confusion in the IRN board, the organisation did not officially retract their support for the chicken boycott. In November, for example, Aftenposten wrote a new article on the issue, and the journalist stated that "the leader of the IRN, together with 25 imams, has signed a declaration that the chicken in Norway and Sweden are not slaughtered in an Islamic way. A minority of imams have not signed the declaration. They think it is ok to eat chicken" (Riaz 2007a). This makes it somewhat ambiguous what IRN actually thought about the declaration – a perception of ambiguity that seems to have been shared by key actors inside IRN.

About one year later, in September 2008, the IRN finally announced that they had reached an agreement with the chicken producer Nortura (IRN 2008b). In the agreement, IRN essentially accepted the slaughter method some of the mosques had temporarily objected to from the summer of 2007 and onwards. Nortura would still use gas to stun the chicken before killing them. According to an article from Aftenposten, what had convinced the IRN to accept this was that Nortura promised to employ more people in their slaughterhouses to shorten the waiting period between the stunning and the slaughter (Riaz 2008).

This episode revealed that an important development had taken place. Most of the Barelwi mosques had begun to cooperate among themselves and began to assume a larger role in the IRN and on the Islamic field in general. The Barelwis constituted the largest group among Pakistanis by far and, together, amounted to the largest denominational group among Muslims in Norway. But as was mentioned in chapter 2, the Barelwis had seen significant competition between themselves in the 80s and 90s. This competition seems to have hindered any collective action. They could seemingly not enter the IRN together, it was only the Ahl-e-Sunnat mosque that became a part of the IRN in the early years. But in 2007, at least, it appears as if their internal competitive relationship had transformed itself into a pattern of *coopetition*. They still competed among themselves but could also come together to advance some common interests, such as a more restrictive approach to halal slaughter. The development during this controversy indicated that the Barelwis were still not speaking with one voice. The Minhaj ul-Quran mosque, for example, did not agree with the statement that the Norwegian chicken was not halal. However, the fact that many Barelwi mosques had overcome their divisions and had begun to cooperate in an imam council that was independent of the imam committee in IRN, was significant.

The halal controversy was not the only internal controversy, where the IRN received pressure from actors on the Muslim field. Among Muslim youth, tension arose during war in Gaza in late 2008 and early 2009. This led to huge demonstrations in which both far-left activists and Muslim youth – leftist or otherwise – participated. Between 8 and 10 January 2009, there were riots in the streets, with widespread destruction of store fronts and property. According to several interviewees, many Muslim youths had said to the IRN that they perceived them as too meek and careful in their response to the war.

In 2010, tensions mounted once again following a somewhat bizarre episode in Norwegian media history. *Dagbladet*, the second biggest tabloid in Norway, published a large caricature of the prophet Muhammad as a pig on the front page, seemingly for no reason at all. The occasion was that it had been contacted by Arfan Bhatti, who would later become one of the most infamous jihadist entrepreneurs in Norway. He was a former violent criminal who had gone on to become a devout and radical Muslim, and had been indicted for shooting at the Jewish synagogue in Oslo in September 2006. He probably had delusions of grandeur as well, as he apparently had plans to become a symbolic leader for Muslims in Norway (Rasch 2010). Bhatti sometimes engaged in debates on Facebook with non-Muslims, and one of the forums he used for these debates was the public Facebook page of the Norwegian secret police, which saw much public debate from actors who had no connection to the secret police at all. In one of these debates, another Facebook user had posted a caricature of the prophet Muhammad made out to be a pig. Bhatti contacted Dagbladet, and told them that the secret police would not remove such caricatures from discussions on their Facebook page (Hultgreen 2010). Dagbladet wrote an article which claimed that the secret police allowed racism and Islamophobia on their Facebook page. But at the same time, Dagbladet chose to put the caricature of the prophet as a pig on their front page, thereby angering Muslims in Norway far more than the Islamophobic Facebook users on the page of the secret police had ever been able to do.

This led to large-scale protests. Many Muslim owners of shops and kiosks refused to sell Dagbladet that day, and many hundreds of Muslim taxi owners went on strike and parked their taxis the following weekend. Furthermore, Bhatti and some of his associates took the initiative for a large demonstration against the caricature, allowing Bhatti to take the role as a leader for young Muslims. This led to accusations from others that Dagbladet had been played by Bhatti for his own gain (Saum 2010). Internally among Muslims, IRN warned strongly against the demonstration – particularly because it was spearheaded by Bhatti, and other young Muslims they suspected of sympathizing with radical interpretations of Islam. Asghar Ali, still the deputy leader at the time, told me that IRN actively tried to dissuade the protestors from going through with the demonstration.

> We did not want to have a situation that would get out of control in Norway. We felt that it was unpredictable. This was only a few years after the big demonstrations against the Danish cartoons, and right after the Gaza demonstrations. We also didn't know the persons in charge. Now Bhatti and Mohyeldeen have become famous, but back then we still weren't sure what they were about, whether Bhatti had changed his ways etc. So, we didn't know what to expect; but we had a bad hunch, if I remember correctly.
>
> The second aspect concerned what we thought the prophet would have done. If we go along with this and call for a demonstration in the name of Islam, and it gets out of control and property is destroyed, or something like that – we will give Islam a bad name. We need to present Islam in the best light possible. So, we thought that our job as Muslims was to stop that from happening.
>
> Interview with ASGHAR ALI, 25.04.2019

But despite IRN's warnings, the demonstration proceeded. It was well-attended, attracting 3000 participants. The demonstration also marked one the first major public displays of radical Salafi-jihadism in Norway. One of the speakers at the demonstration was Mohyeldeed Muhammad, a young man who had grown up in a small town in Southern Norway as the son of an imam. He gave an impassioned speech, in which he gave some words which became famous in Norway: "If this [caricatures and discrimination against Muslims] is allowed to continue it will in the end be too late. Then we will have 11 September and 7 June on Norwegian soil. This is not a threat; it is a warning" (Granbo 2010).

This statement was widely condemned, including by some of the other organisers of the demonstration. But the episode demonstrated something for the leadership in IRN: There was a large group of Muslim youth in Norway who felt disaffected, and who could react strongly when something like this happened. This left key actors in IRN with a lingering question: Had they chosen the right approach? Would it perhaps have been wiser to do *something*, in order to give the youth a possibility to vent their frustration in a controlled and less aggressive manner?

4.6 Diverging Approaches: the Dialogue Path vs the Community Path

The situation the IRN found itself in in the late 2000s was thus one where they faced ever stronger cross-pressures – both from society at large and from their own Muslim member organisations and constituencies. For a long time, the overall pattern was that IRN attempted to meet these competing expectations with an ever clearer focus on dialogue and bridge-building. It engaged in external dialogue and attempted to find compromise with external demands from society, but also sought to keep its internal Muslim constituents reasonably satisfied.

As was detailed in the section on the homosexuality controversy, this balancing act did not involve acquiescing to all of the demands from external society. Such an approach would effectively have jeopardized IRN's internal standing among the member mosques and the larger Islamic field. Throughout these years, IRN nevertheless attempted to reach many of its goal as an organisation in a mild-mannered way, through dialogue and external alliances. IRN attempted to achieve their goals by employing a rhetoric which struck a balance between talking about Islamophobia, and taking a pro-active, positive role. I will label this approach as the *dialogue path*. The key goals of those who championed the dialogue path was that the organisation should function as a bridge-builder, and that they should reach their goals through building alliances with external partners. This made it important to engage in dialogue, balancing acts and public outreach. Such an approach can also be labelled as *respectability politics* – a concept which has been used for describing the process in which members "of marginalized groups comply with dominant social norms to advance their group's condition" (Dazey 2021a, 2021b). Given the centrality of dialogue for this approach in Norway, however, I will rather use the term *dialogue path*.

Both the oral and written sources indicate that this was a discourse they sometimes struggled to maintain. In 2010, for example, the Socialist Left party was briefly considering banning the wearing of the hijab in primary schools. For the Socialist Left party – usually considered as a party with a *soft multiculturalist* approach – this would have been a substantial departure from their earlier positions. Ultimately, they decided against pursuing the policy. But the very fact that they considered it was something that people in the IRN took notice of. In a meeting with their dialogue partners in the Church of Norway, one representative from the IRN is quoted as follows:

> This proposal is frustrating. Particularly because of all the youth who thinks that society is against them. We in the IRN try to argue that Muslims are not discriminated against in Norway today, but we find it increasingly difficult to defend this position in relations with young people in light of what the politicians are saying.
>
> MKR 2010

The idea seems to be that the Muslims should not perceive or present themselves as victims, but rather take an active role. The minutes from this meeting do not go into detail about what this meant: Was it something that the MKR and the IRN had discussed on their meetings? This statement does indicate two things, however: there were youth outside the IRN who may have wanted IRN to argue more forcefully against discrimination. It also indicates that there was an idea in elite circles, in IRN and MKR, that it was better to be "constructive" than to play the victim card, and – rather remarkably – that Muslims were in fact not discriminated against.

Even though the dialogue path was the dominant approach of the leadership in the organisation during these years, there were already signs that some actors in the organisation thought that other tasks were equally important for the organisation. If we are to put a label on this other approach, we may say that it was about building the Muslim community – so I will label it the *community path*. In early 2008, for example, an internal strategy document circulated among some of the key actors in the organisation and was shared with me by a former board member (Anonymous 2008). This document was never adopted by the board of IRN, and it is unclear who wrote it originally, but it was discussed among some of the IRN activists, at least. As such, it offers a glimpse into the internal discussions at the IRN at the time. The document discusses what it mentions as "possible and necessary projects" for the organisation in the decade ahead. It does not go into detail on most of the projects it mentions – the idea seems to be to brainstorm different projects that IRN could pursue in the years ahead. The document does mention "cooperation with important actors in society", and "close cooperation with political parties and authorities". But the main focus in the document is on various internal challenges in the organisation, among the mosques and in the Muslim communities in general. It mentions, for example, "independence from public funding", and adds: "it is an eternal discussion about the funding of the IRN". The document also mentions certification of halal food, developing a joint fund which could help congregations build mosques, imams in prisons and hospitals, legal aids to Muslims, and more. The emphasis in several of the projects mentioned is on *services*. For the proponents of the dialogue path, the most important job of the IRN was to advance common interests through a soft dialogue-centric approach. For other actors in the organisation, it was equally important that the organisation should provide services to its members and the Muslim communities at large.

Furthermore, 2008 saw the birth of another project which would become even more important in the 2010s. This initiative was called *Safe Muslim* and was initiated by Irfan Mushtaq. He was the younger brother of Imran Mushtaq, who had been central in the initiative for a joint holiday calendar in the late 1990s and in the revision of the statutes in the early 2000s. Irfan Mushtaq would go on to become a key person on the board of the IRN in the 2010s. In the late 2000s, he mainly provided input to other people in the organisation, and one of his suggestions was the Safe Muslim initiative. In April 2008, IRN made the following announcement on their website:

> IRN has the pleasure of introducing a unique service for Muslims in Norway – *Safe Muslim*.
>
> Your Safety, joint responsibility
>
> The Islamic Council of Norway has created a security service, Safe Muslim, for Muslims in Norway. This has been done in order to safeguard the rights of Muslims according to Norwegian law. With Safe Muslim in the Islamic Council of Norway, a unique network will have your back – no matter when you are discriminated against as a Muslim. The Islamic Council of Norway is an interest organisation for Muslims in Norway.
>
> With Safe Muslim you can be sure that we will engage those who are best qualified to support your case. You will get a network of competent persons to follow up on your case. You will always know that you have a solid and resourceful organisation to follow up on your case. But this requires that you as a Muslim contribute to strengthening this work.

UNSTABLE INSTITUTIONALISATION 115

This will not happen to me ...

It is a fact that Muslims are unjustly labelled as terrorists. Because of this, many are bullied or discriminated against in society. The Islamic Council of Norway will work so that you as an individual, with an Islamic life stance, will not be bullied or discriminated against because of your religion. No matter whether this should happen with a/an:

Employer
Educational institution
Hospital
The state
The police
Anybody else
In addition, we will promote causes like:
– Halal food
– Circumcision of Muslim boys in public hospitals
– Islamic banking

You may have heard the story about the king who had three sons who fought between themselves about who should inherit the throne after their sick father. The king first gave them a pen each and asked them to break it in two. This was easy to do. The king asked them to do it again, but this time with three pens each. This was more difficult.

The moral of this story is that we are stronger together.

The IRN is dependent on your contribution to take care of your and other Muslim's rights. Therefore, contact us today to make an agreement how you can contribute to strengthening the Muslim community in Norway.

Show solidarity and get into the Safe Muslim arrangement to secure that you yourself, your family, friends and coming Muslim generations will have your rights secured according to Norwegian laws.

IRN 2008a

The message in the text is that Muslims are discriminated against in Norwegian society, and that the solution lies in creating stronger intra-Muslim solidarity. What is not mentioned is a reference to potentially non-Muslim allies, for example. It is interesting to compare the sentiment in this text with the sentiment which was expressed in the meeting between MKR and IRN and in 2010, that was discussed above. In that meeting, the IRN representative said that "we in IRN try to argue that Muslims are not discriminated against in Norway today, but we find it increasingly difficult to defend this position in relations with young people [...]", as was mentioned earlier. This statement stands in direct opposition to parts of the text on the Safe Muslim initiative, which claim without qualification that "many Muslims are bullied or discriminated against in society".

It therefore seems likely that there were several ideas or discourses in the organisation at this time. The dominant discourse was about dialogue and seeking allies, and to find a balance between pointing out discrimination and being a positive and constructive partner. But there were also undercurrents in the organisation that emphasised primarily that Muslims were discriminated against, needed to stand together and build a community. According to several interviewees, Mushtaq's Safe Muslim initiative was well received by most people in the organisation, even though not much came out of it initially and it lay dormant for a while. One key actor framed it as follows:

> When Irfan introduced that Safe Muslim initiative around 2009 or so, I also thought it was a cool concept. It was about creating a fund for Muslims; they were to get help from lawyers. But that is the attitude which really created problems for the IRN, if you ask me. I think today that the IRN should never have supported that kind of initiative, that if somebody is discriminated against, then *we* must be there to help them. Our job should instead be to work so that nobody gets discriminated against. And then somebody else can help those who is discriminated against. There is a substantial difference in vision.
>
> Interview with C, 2017–2019

This indicates that key actors in the organisation did not perceive these approaches – focusing on dialogue or focusing on community building and services – as being in conflict with each other at the time. It was only later that this kind of initiative, which Mushtaq proposed, would be perceived as being opposed to dialogue and outreach.

4.7 Unstable Institutionalisation and a Shift in Personnel

It is fairly likely that these divergent approaches within the organisation could have been handled without ending up in a deepened conflict and a split. As will be detailed in this and the subsequent chapters, the organisation was not able to reach such an outcome. One reason was the relative lack of internal institutionalisation in the organisation. When the organisation hired a secretary general in 2007, it retained the organisational structure and organisational culture of the voluntary umbrella organisation it had been up until then, where everything happened on a voluntary basis. The statutes of the organisation were mostly concerned with relations between the member organisations and the central umbrella organisation. The statutes did not say much, however, about the relationship between employees of the organisation and the central organisation. Several questions were thus left unsettled: What would happen in the case of an organisational conflict, involving an employee? Should the organisation want to fire the secretary general, were they allowed to do so – and who in the organisation had the right to do it? What mechanisms were in place for dealing with interpersonal conflict? As long as everything went smoothly, nobody in the organisation gave much thought to these issues. But as soon as disagreements and conflicts broke out, the lack of institutionalisation in the organisation became clear.

The major shift in the organisation occurred through a shift in personnel. At some point in late 2010, Shoaib Sultan decided to step down as secretary general (Brandvold 2010). Over the next year, several new persons became part of the IRN leadership and would set their mark on the development of the organisation. The new secretary general was Mehtab Afsar. For many years he had been active in the *Minhaj ul-Quran* mosque in central Oslo and had served as their spokesperson prior to joining the IRN. This mosque was part of the transnational Minhaj ul-Quran network, a Barelwi and Sufi movement founded by the Pakistani Islamic leader Tahir ul-Qadri. Qadri gained international fame in 2010 when he published a 600-page fatwa against terrorism and suicide bombing (Casciani 2010), but he had long been well known in Pakistan. In Pakistan and South Asia, Qadri and Minhaj ul-Quran have been regarded as fairly traditionalist, even though they have developed from hard-line *sufi-Islamists* into softer *post-Islamists* in the last couple of decades (Philippon 2014, 54–58). In the Norwegian context Minhaj ul-Quran has for many years been known as one of the most progressive and dialogue-oriented mosques. It has been heavily involved in external outreach, and it is one of the few mosques in Norway where men and women share a common prayer space, only separated by a curtain.

Afsar himself was well-acquainted with Norwegian society when he began working in IRN. He had grown up in Norway, moving to Norway from Pakistan with his parents when he was only a toddler. He was educated as a dental technician but had spent most of his working life doing other pursuits. He had been active in the socialist left party during the 2000s, and prior to joining the IRN, he had been the leader of the Norwegian cricket federation. He had also been an accomplished cricket player himself, even playing for a period on Norway's national cricket team. He was also interested in environmental issues and was a board member at the Norwegian association for electric cars.

People I spoke to in the hiring committee in the IRN who made the recommendation to hire Afsar, said that they did so under the assumption that he would continue in the mold of Sultan, i.e. creating contacts with actors in mainstream society, focusing on dialogue and generally striking a balance between placating the membership of IRN and placating mainstream society. This was also how he was perceived in the beginning. He was portrayed in the weekly paper Morgenbladet under the heading "A rock n' roll spokesperson". Alongside a photo of him with long flowing hair and displaying a big smile, he was quoted as saying that he did not think it was anybody's business to tell homosexuals how to live: "I am not concerned with whether somebody is gay or not. My hairdresser is gay. It is up to each and everyone how they choose to live" (Morgenbladet 2010). His first public appearances were therefore more or less in line with what the hiring committee had expected. After some time, though, he also began to reveal a more combative public persona, which led to tension both internally and externally.

Another person who became important in IRN in the following years was Irfan Mushtaq, who was briefly mentioned in the last chapter as the prime mover of the Safe Muslim initiative. Mushtaq was elected to the board of the IRN in 2011 as responsible for IRN's finances, coinciding with when Afsar began in his job. Mushtaq was born in Norway and was educated as an economist. According to almost everybody I spoke with in the IRN, he was highly intelligent and disciplined, a *doer* type with a large working capacity. He already had a successful career in business when he joined the IRN; and wanted to see IRN move towards delivering professionalised services.

It would not be long before the new leadership in IRN became embroiled in controversies. In his very first acts as secretary general, however, Afsar acted in the conciliatory manner the hiring committee had expected of him. In January 2011, immediately after he started in the job, IRN was targeted by a one-person demonstration outside its gates – a protest that received some media coverage. The activist was Sara Azmeh-Rasmussen. She was a migrant from Syria, who had come to Norway to study, and who stayed on and became highly active and visible in Norwegian public life. She frequently wrote op-eds in the newspapers and received notoriety when she publicly burned a hijab on the international women's day in 2009. She identified as a lesbian, and subsequently as a Lesbian transperson, and campaigned for LGBTQ rights. On 29 January 2011, she started a protest outside the Rabita mosque, where the IRN office was located at this time. She sat on the pavement outside, with a sign that read, "Freedom and dignity for gay and transgender people ". On the third day of the protest, she even started a hunger strike. Her demand was that the IRN should clearly and unequivocally condemn capital punishment

UNSTABLE INSTITUTIONALISATION

for homosexuality, relating to the controversy about capital punishment from 2007 which had refused to go away.

Several media outlets reported that Rasmussen was harassed during the sit-in demonstration. When she was interviewed for the online Norwegian magazine/blog *Religioner.no*, the journalist remarked that it even happened during their interview. The journalist described it as follows: "Suddenly the interview takes an unexpected turn. A box with a fluid which looks like vomit is released from a window in IRN's building. The fluid hits its target, but also splashes over her belongings, and us standing nearby. It is probably leftovers from dinner, and you can see that it includes tomatoes, cabbage and eggshells" (Arnesen 2011). When the journalist interviewed one of the people who came out of the mosque, the mosque attendee said that the leadership in the mosque had implored people to be nice and polite to her – but this call was apparently not heeded by all the people who visited the mosque.

During this mediatized crisis for IRN, Afsar managed to strike a balance that made most people happy. Afsar met with Rasmussen several times and had a dialogue with her concerning whether they could reach a compromise. After five days, Rasmussen accepted IRN's offer. The IRN did not back down on its claim that homosexuality was wrong according to Islam, but they did emphasise in stronger terms than before that the organisation "neither wishes nor seeks capital punishment for homosexuals". It also made this statement:

> The parties have agreed that the most important thing in this situation is to stand together in order to ensure the rights of all Norwegian citizens. To achieve this, we must all contribute to working with values and opinions in order to fight against denigration, harassment and violence against homosexuals.
>
> NTB 2011

In her first public op-ed after the demonstration, some days later, Rasmussen was equivocal in her reaction, and stated that she had "met a simplistic religion where reflection was replaced by blind faith and pure repetition", even though she also emphasised that some Muslims in the Rabita mosque had given her perfume and food as signs of support (Rasmussen 2011). Some months later, though, she had changed her tune, and appreciated IRN's efforts. In the meantime, she had travelled to Dublin, to do a similar protest outside the premises of the *European fatwa council*. While she was there, she was not granted the right to talk to any representatives from the council at all, unlike with the IRN. She also experienced harassment of an altogether worse and different kind, with some people even going as far as threatening to kill her (Gran 2012). She wrote in an op-ed from October that she had an appointment with Afsar when she came back from Dublin. He had invited her to meet in his office and even told her that she was free to visit the prayer room of the mosque – an offer she did not expect and strongly appreciated (Rasmussen 2011). Some months later, she said that she had met a positive attitude in Afsar, and now had a different understanding of the organisation:

> I understand of course that the IRN cannot change Islamic theology with a decree. But if attitudes among Norwegian Muslims change, it may also lay the groundwork for IRN to become clearer in their attitudes.
>
> GRAN 2012, 20

One may argue Rasmussen here displayed an understanding of the fact that IRN was a meta-organisation facing cross-pressures: It could not simply change what its member organisations were thinking. Afsar had seemingly managed to approach Rasmussen in this conciliatory manner, without getting negative pushback from inside the IRN. According to people I spoke to who were active in the IRN, most people were happy with how he handled the situation. This controversy had dogged the IRN for four years by 2011, and Afsar's ability to cooperate with one of their strongest critics, without getting internal push-back, was no small win for him. It was textbook *balancing strategy*, namely to make some adjustment, in a way which can be acceptable to different parties with different interests.

4.8   Internal and External Tensions

This early win would soon be overshadowed in the public by other conflicts and issues. Quite soon, Afsar began to show a more combative side when responding to demands from the outside. This led to negative reactions among journalists and politicians as well as discontent among IRN's dialogue partners in MKR and STL. What seems particularly to have irked some of IRN's dialogue partners was an episode that had to with antisemitism in Oslo. In June 2011, the municipality of Oslo published a report on racism and antisemitism among pupils from the 8th through 10th grades in the schools of Oslo (Perduco 2011). The report had an explicit focus on antisemitism, more than on Islamophobia, but also looked into the experiences of Muslim pupils. Some of the context for the report – which was mentioned in the introduction – was that there had been several media reports focusing on antisemitism among Muslims. The report found that a full third of the Jewish pupils in Oslo had experienced neg- ative episodes every month relating to their religious affiliation, whereas only

UNSTABLE INSTITUTIONALISATION

5.3 per cent of the Muslim pupils experienced the same. An important caveat is that the report only had 36 respondents who identified as Jewish. But the report also showed that over a half of the respondents had heard "Jew" used negatively as a slur.

When the report was published, there was a discussion panel with comments from both Afsar and two representatives from the Jewish community (DMT). The discussion on this report seems to have become heated, and some comments from Afsar rattled some of the IRN's dialogue partners: "If there is a minority which really gets rough treatment, then it is Muslims, and it is about time that we got a report about discrimination against Muslims" (Sylte 2011).

The newspaper article did not go into the context – was this Afsar's first response to the report, or was it a response to something the other participants said? Whether there may have been a qualifying context or not, Afsar's statements were not well received by the Jewish community, STL or MKR, and not in the wider public sphere. The perception was that the IRN did not take antisemitism among Muslims seriously, and preferred to play the victim card.

This episode seems to signal a new development in IRN's relations to outside actors. Subsequent to this debate, there were other instances where Afsar did not want to accept publicly the premise that Muslims needed to work towards reform, but rather claimed publicly that Islamophobia was the *real* problem. In STL and MKR, which had been the most important external partners of the IRN, this attitude was increasingly perceived as a significant problem, according to several actors in these organisations. As I wrote in the introduction, I was appointed to the contact/dialogue group between the Church of Norway and the Jewish community in Norway in 2011, as a lay representative from the Church of Norway (I was appointed due to the fact that I spent several years of my childhood in Jerusalem, and speak Hebrew fluently). Due to stays abroad I was not able to attend many of the meetings, but I nevertheless met many actors in STL and MKR during early 2010s. I had an informal conversation on the developments in IRN with a representative from MKR in March 2012. Even though I did not study the IRN in particular at that time, I did do academic work on Islam in Norway. I wrote down the main points of the conversation in my field diary when I came home, because I was surprised by what the MKR representative had said. Before this conversation, I did not know that the relations between the IRN and the MKR had soured. The conversation started with the MKR person – called *MKR* below – asking me if I had any advice, as she/he perceived the situation with the IRN as challenging:

> MKR: Do you have any knowledge about what's going on over at IRN? Maybe you have any thoughts about what we can do ... the situation is difficult now.

OE: Oh, how so?

MKR: Well, things are challenging with the IRN. They don't seem that interested in dialogue anymore. We've been thinking about whether we did something wrong ...? But we're not sure what it might have been. And Mehtab ... do you have any ideas about how we may approach him?

OE: What do you mean?

MKR: I think he's made his fair share of mistakes by now. I mean when you start in a new job, we all know that you're allowed to do some missteps. That's how it is. But by now I think he's filled his quota ... I mean, we had built up something so good. It was working so well. I really think he has used up his quota.

OE: What do you think the main problem is?

MKR: For one, they don't answer emails, don't seem to want to have contact. But also, how Mehtab answers when journalists ask ... you can't always say that the answer is Islamophobia to every possible question. You know what I mean? Even though we have stood together against Islamophobia many times. ... You know, several people have actually reached out to them and said that we can help them if they need something concerning how to deal with the media. People from the Church, from the MKR, we have experience with the media. It's part of the job for most of us. But that didn't seem to work, either.

Conversation, March 2012, reconstructed from field notes

Seen in retrospect, this conversation and quotation says a lot about the situation between the IRN and external actors at the time. It reveals that the relationship between the MKR and IRN had already began to sour. But what it also reveals, though, is that some persons outside the IRN actually perceived that they had some ownership to developments in the IRN. They felt that they had stakes in what was going on. The person from MKR thought that they had invested a lot in IRN, and that it previously "was working so well", until now – and also thought that Afsar had "used up his quota".

When I did interviews with IRN activists, some of them also mentioned this, but from different perspectives. One of those who was at the IRN board during this time told me that they had received emails from the MKR, but that he had perceived them as very condescending:

Suddenly we started to receive emails from the MKR. They were like "you should do this", or "maybe you shouldn't say that". But who were they to tell us what to do! I really didn't like getting those emails.

Interview with R, Oslo, 2017–2019

UNSTABLE INSTITUTIONALISATION

Another person in the IRN, who would later have a fall-out with Afsar, also mentioned in our interview that the MKR were sending them some emails offering help. But for him, this was not an indication that the MKR were meddling in affairs they shouldn't meddle with, but rather that things were not functioning as they should in the IRN.

> At some point we began getting emails from our partners. Like in the Church. They were offering to help us, to use their expertise to guide us a bit ... What does this tell you? That they need to offer us such help? It means that things were not going so well with IRN, no?
>
> Interview with F, 2017–2019

From different perspectives, all of these interviews point to the same phenomenon: The IRN – represented by Afsar – had changed its rhetoric, adopting a more combative tone. This did not go down well with some of the IRN's dialogue partners. This probably also influenced how IRN was seen by other important actors in Norwegian society – authorities, politicians and journalists.

In addition to these external tensions, there were also mounting tensions internally, according to several interviewees. It got to the point where board members got up and left meetings in protest. One interviewee described an episode in this way:

> At one of the board meetings, I was actually afraid that it would turn into a physical fight. Two of the board members where shouting insults at each other. At the end one of them got up, all red in the face, and was raising his fists as if he was getting ready to hit the other. It was really dramatic. In the end nothing happened and they did not start to fight. But it was like that quite often. It was not a very pleasant atmosphere.
>
> Interview with C, 2017–2019

Some of the interviewees attributed this to the personalities and personal disagreements. Several of the board members from 2011 and onwards could become combative if conflict erupted. Many of them were persons who were not afraid to speak their mind and did not shy away from criticizing others publicly if they thought it was warranted. Some of the disagreements, however, were about organisational goals – disagreements about what goals and strategies the organisation should pursue.

Importantly, none of the interviewees said anything about such intense conflicts being dealt with through institutional channels or venues. Work places in Norway are often highly institutionalised. In many work places, such a quarrel – almost leading to a physical fight – would lead to some kind of intervention. The persons involved would be called to a meeting with a superior, or a mediator, and would attempt to work out their differences. Sometimes, one or the other will get a warning. But in the IRN, this did not happen. Instead of the conflicts being solved, the disagreements remained. The interviewee I referred to above, chose to leave the board, for example, as he did not want to deal with all those conflicts anymore.

4.9 Emergence of the Community Path: Halal Food and Muslim Solidarity

Little by little, the IRN did change its direction as an organisation, and began to focus on new activities and goals. In my original thesis, I had described this as choosing a new *strategy*. One key actor in the organisation, however, took issue with this description, and said that it was not a conscious choice between strategies:

> It was not a conscious choice about strategy. We didn't sit down and decide that we were going to take the organisation in another direction. At least I did not perceive it that way. It was more that we did one thing, and then that led to another thing, which again led to another thing. And suddenly we were at a different place, kind of.
>
> Personal communication by email from R, 12.12.2020

In this book, I will therefore refer to this as a new *approach*, not as a new strategy. In any case it is clear that some of the new actors who entered the organisation in the 2010s did have some new ideas about where to take the organisation. Irfan Mushtaq. for example, said in out interview that he had been sceptical towards how the dialogue work had been conducted until then:

> IM: I think that 'dialogue' had been kind of holy cow in the IRN. You could not ask questions about it! They were always talking about it – dialogue, dialogue, dialogue. But it was always an elite phenomenon.
>
> OE: So you were sceptical towards the dialogue activities?
>
> IM: No, I was sceptical to what one would get out of those dialogue meetings. Dialogue is always good, but you should have a goal with it. My understanding of dialogue is that the two of us meet, for example. We discuss Islam and Christianity. Next time we will bring a couple of friends along. Then we get to know each other, and hopefully we get wiser. That

UNSTABLE INSTITUTIONALISATION   125

> kind of contact between people is very important. And I was asking what
> do we get out of the kind of dialogue we've been having until now? Why is
> this dialogue group so closed? Why can't we enlarge it and include people
> from our two organisations? I was not sceptical to dialogue as such. I just
> wanted it to become more accessible to ordinary people. The way they
> had done it was only a closed, "holy" group.
>
> Interview with IRFAN MUSHTAQ, 03.05.2019

This critique of the dialogue activity was not entirely new. This concern had
in fact been voiced by people inside the dialogue groups themselves for many
years, even though many people also saw much value in this kind of high-level
dialogue between leaders (Brottveit, Gresaker, and Hoel 2015; Opsal 2013).
Nevertheless, the internal magnitude of Mushtaq's challenge to the existing
way of doing dialogue should not be underestimated. IRN's whole existence had
come about as a result of an initiative from the Church of Norway, who wanted
to have somebody to do dialogue with. The high-level dialogue with MKR – and
with other actors, such as STL – had in fact given IRN access to the corridors of
power, particularly after the cartoon crisis. This dialogue had probably helped
the careers of some of the individuals who were active in the dialogue group,
among both Christians and Muslims, as the previous dialogue participant and
academic Jan Opsal noted in his description of the dialogue group (Opsal 2013,
208). Arguably, the larger elite network which emerged as a result of the
dialogue had also helped IRN reach some of their goals as an organisation.
Norway retained a fairly liberal policy towards Muslims and Islamic communities, compared to several other European countries, and this probably had a
lot to do with the dialogue work that IRN had been engaged in through the STL
(Elgvin 2023a). Mushtaq was therefore challenging fairly fundamental aspects
of how key actors in the IRN had been running the organisation for a good
number of years.

The leader of IRN at the time, Senaid Kobilica, told me more or less the same
story in our interview, but from a different perspective. He had been the leader
since 2007 and stepped down as leader in 2013. According to Kobilica, a conflict
emerged over how much importance one should assign to dialogue activities.

> There began to develop some disagreements on the board. I understood
> that there was talk about the dialogue work, that some people were scep-
> tical. Some people wanted to reduce the number of meetings with MKR
> and STL. So we sat down, and I was trying to understand what it was
> about. Those arguments that we should not focus that much on dialogue,
> or that other organisations were using us for their own gain ... I really

could not accept that. Dialogue had been one of the cornerstones of the IRN. Almost everything we had achieved had been through dialogue.

Interview with SENAID KOBILICA, 21.10.2019

Interviews with activists from both the MKR and IRN indicated that this disagreement on how to conduct dialogue was not fully resolved within the IRN. The board continued to be comprised of some people who wanted to continue the elite- or leader-based way of doing dialogue, and some people who had more sympathy with the dialogue-critical view. In the MKR and STL, there was much frustration because they could not get clear answers from the IRN. Did they want to engage in dialogue and joint activities, or not? The leadership in STL became very frustrated, and described what they perceived as a lack of engagement and professionalism from IRN's side. One actor in STL described it in this way:

> They would often come to meetings completely unprepared. Or late. Or both. They did not respond to emails. They did not work with us on preparing documents and issues. And then in the end they would sometimes complain that we didn't listen to them! Or demand that they should have the final say on personnel! It was incredibly frustrating. You know, if you want to have an influence on something, you need to put down the work, you can't just sit on the sidelines and do nothing for many months, and then demand in the end that everything should be served to you on a plate.
>
> Interview with M, 2017–2019

In part, at least, this lack of engagement may have been a result of the disagreement about dialogue in the IRN. Rather than say a clear yes or a clear no, the organisation withdrew gradually, something which led to much frustration among its external partners.

This criticism of the dialogue work was part of a larger conviction among some actors on the larger Islamic scene: They thought that the IRN needed to focus more on building a sense of community among Muslims and find other sources of income beyond the state. Part of the rationale was the assumption that the IRN would not be able to rely on the funding from the state forever. The funding from the state was not sanctioned by law – it was predicated on good will. On several occasions, politicians and media pundits had called for IRN's funding to be cut off. The external environment the IRN operated within was therefore both unpredictable and not highly institutionalised.

UNSTABLE INSTITUTIONALISATION

Irfan Mushtaq told me that this had been an ongoing discussion almost since the beginning of the funding:

> We didn't think that we could rely on that money. We assumed that one day we would not get it anymore. All the time there were politicians talking about taking the funding away from us. So we thought: How can we stand on our own two feet, not rely on the handouts from the politicians?
>
> Interview with IRFAN MUSHTAQ, 03.05.2019

Kobilica confirmed that there was disagreement on whether the IRN should rely on the funding from the state, but had a different take on the disagreement:

> There was talk about becoming more independent. That we should not rely on money from the authorities, that the halal revenue could be enough, etc. I didn't agree with that. Don't we pay taxes? We, the Muslims, we are part of this society and we pay taxes like everybody else. Why should we not then apply for funding from the government, like everybody else does?
>
> Sometimes there were people who accused us of being too close with the authorities. But let me say this: I have been doing dialogue activities and have had contact with authorities and other actors for more than 20 years. I have never experienced that somebody has put pressure on me. It doesn't work like that. There are many actors in Norway who get their funding from the government. Do they also just do what the government tells them to do?
>
> Interview with SENAID KOBILICA, 21.10.2019

Kobilica and Mushtaq were on different sides of the disagreement, but both of them confirmed what it was about. It does seem that Mushtaq, Afsar and others soon managed to implement some changes in their desired direction. The first change was a revitalization of the Safe Muslim initiative, which had mostly laid dormant since 2008. Sometime during 2012, the IRN redesigned their website, and updated, among other things, the text on Safe Muslim. The text was shortened and simplified, and a section was added at the beginning of the text: "Allah says in the Quran: 'The believers, men and women, are protectors and supporters one of another' (Quran 9:71). Ummah is a joint responsibility, together we are stronger" (IRN 2012).

This section highlights the joint responsibility of Muslims for strengthening the ummah – the community of believers. This very phrase – *Ummah er et felles ansvar*, "Ummah is a joint responsibility" – would go on to become a semi-official slogan for many of the IRN's activities. Starting in 2013, a picture with the slogan became the top picture on IRN's Facebook page, and it has remained so until the present. Ummah means community or group in Arabic and is usually used to designate the religious community of Muslims as such, which transcends ethnic and national barriers. The different endeavours of the IRN during these years can then be understood as aiming towards strengthening the Muslim community in Norway.

In order to distinguish this approach from the dialogue path which was described in the previous chapter, I will label it the *community path*. It must be emphasised that these currents were not completely opposed to each other, at least early on, and did not crystallise as clear choices until later. Proponents of the dialogue path would emphasise that it was an important goal to strengthen the Muslim community, and proponents of the community path were not opposed to dialogue per se. It was instead a question of emphasis. Whereas proponents of the dialogue path thought that the Muslim interest was best served by dialogue and alliances with external actors, proponents of the community path thought that the Muslim interest was best served by strengthening the Muslim community internally. Nevertheless, the overall profile and activity of the organisation became markedly different in the 2010s, and it makes sense to label it as a new path for the organisation.

4.10 Halal Certification and Financial Independence

In addition to the Safe Muslim initiative, the most important endeavour by the proponents of the community path was a large project on certification of halal meat – alongside enrolling a lot of new mosques as members. After he joined the IRN board, Mushtaq soon started to voice critical questions about how IRN was handling the issue of halal meat. As stated in the last chapter, the halal issue had led to a large controversy in 2007 and 2008. Was the meat marked halal *really* halal? Even though the IRN's imam committee had accepted the way of slaughtering of chicken in 2008, doubts apparently remained in some quarters.

When Mushtaq joined the IRN board, the person responsible for halal food on the board was Asghar Ali. IRN and Ali had made an arrangement in 2010 where they outsourced much of the responsibility for the halal certification to one external business – the small and newly founded company *Al-Salam* (Sleipnes 2010). This company was owned and run by Alexander Mousavi. Mousavi had migrated to Norway from Iran in 1992 when he was in his early 20s.

UNSTABLE INSTITUTIONALISATION

In 2003, he had founded an organisation or think tank called *Samarbeidsrådet for integrering*, "The cooperation council for integration" (SARFI) (Flatøe 2003), the objective of which was to advise different actors and bodies on integration. There are almost no traces of what this organisation did in the newspaper archive. But the organisation did open several businesses, among them one of the largest stores for halal meat in Oslo (Bleskestad 2010; Haakaas, Magnussen, and Stokke 2010).

In my interview with Asghar Ali, he revealed that he and Sultan were unsure as to how to deal with the halal situation. How were they to ensure that the meat that was slaughtered as prescribed? At this time there were few major actors on the Norwegian market providing halal meat. Mousavi, through his involvement in the halal meat store, was one of those who was most involved in the business. What the IRN did in 2010 was therefore to make an agreement with Al Salam, a new company founded by Mousavi, given Mousavi's knowledge of the market. Al Salam got the right to be a distributor for IRN-certified halal meat in Norway, and distributed this meat to different supermarkets and restaurants (Sleipnes 2010).

This arrangement seems to have worked out reasonably well, as Al Salam quickly got contracts with several meat producers. However, among some actors in the more conservative Muslim communities, this arrangement was controversial, partly because Al Salam had effectively been granted a large share of the market for halal meat in Norway. Moreover, it had to do with the fact that Mousavi himself had never had a pronounced public profile as an outwardly practising Muslim. As leader for SARFI he had also espoused views calling for stricter integration policies, for example (Brandvold 2009). Could practising Muslims put the halal certification business into the hands of someone whose religious credentials were not clear-cut? These were questions that Mushtaq raised when he joined the IRN board. According to several of those involved, strong arguments and disagreements ensued. It ended with Mushtaq taking over the responsibility for the halal certification, and Asghar stepping down from the board.

Mushtaq immediately set in motion many projects relating to halal. The first thing he did, he said in our interview, was to contact the imams in almost all of the member mosques to conduct a review of the theological legitimacy of the Norwegian way of halal slaughter:

> In 2012, for the first time, we wrote a theological and technical document which was a *halal-standard* for Norway. It wasn't just the IRN saying "this is ok"; it was an elaborate document which we had worked with internally for a long time. I had discussed it with the imams in Norway, I had

involved imams abroad, we had looked at fatwas, we had considered that mechanical slaughter and stunning was a challenge. But we reached a compromise, based on the rules of exception [from the traditional theological requirements] the imams could agree to.

Interview with IRFAN MUSHTAQ, 30.11.2018

I was not able to procure the full and complete document from IRN, but the Internet Archive had saved the first part of it from IRN's website (Mushtaq 2012). The essence of it was not that different from what the IRN had previously agreed to, namely to accept stunning before slaughter, as long as the animal did not die from the stunning procedure itself. The difference seems to be that this document was more extensive in its regulation of the slaughtering process and was more comprehensive than the statement the IRN had made earlier. Theologically, it seems to have had a more restrictive starting point, even though it arrived at the same conclusion as before. Instead of saying that stunning animals before killing them was not problematic, this document said that it was not ideal – but could still be acceptable given the societal circumstances in Norway.

Another difference was that the document seemed to have a stronger acceptance in a larger group of mosques, particularly among the Barelwis. As was previously discussed, the IRN was put in a difficult position in 2007 when a group of mosques and imams took the initiative to boycott chicken meat more or less on their own, without the full involvement of the IRN organisation. At that time, the Pakistani Barelwi/Sufi mosques in particular seemed to be the ones that had revolted against the more lenient approach the IRN had been advocating. But this time, Mushtaq – himself from a Barelwi background – managed to get Barelwis, Deobandis, Somalis and Arab post-Islamists on board with the halal approach he was promoting.

After he had secured the backing of the mosques, Mushtaq and the IRN embarked on an ambitious project to secure complete control over halal certification in Norway. As has been discussed by some scholars of Islam in Europe, controlling the right to pronounce something as halal or not confers great symbolic power. The person who can say that something is halal is effectively asserting a claim to speak for Islam. In France, for example, there are several different bodies, all of which compete for the right to certify meat as halal (Arslan and Adraoui 2013, chap. 10). When they claimed the right to certify halal, the IRN was also laying claim to symbolic power. One of the first steps the IRN took was to stop cooperating with Mousavi and Al Salam and take the process of halal certification into their own hands. After the new halal standard had been approved, the IRN made provisions for certifying businesses or restaurants as halal in exchange for a fee. This fee, it was said, would cover the costs associated with certifying that the enterprise indeed was halal. For example, did the kitchen serve anything non-halal on the same plates, even though only halal meat was used for the halal dishes? In the beginning of the process, the IRN employed a fairly harsh tactic. If a business did not want to be certified because they did not want to pay the certification fee, the IRN from time to time published a piece on their website or Facebook which said that this or that restaurant was *not* halal. When a restaurant or business chose to become halal-certified, on the other hand, the IRN would often publicise this, for example accompanied by a statement that "the Muslim consumer can now safely enjoy the good food that is served by this restaurant" (Mushtaq 2013a, 2013b).

Quite understandably, perhaps, this hard-nosed approach created friction and resistance. Several business owners thought that it should suffice that they only used halal-certified meat on their premises, and had difficulty understanding why they needed to pay a fee to the IRN in order for the IRN to ensure that they did what they were already doing. The argument from the IRN's side, on the other hand, was that the Muslim consumer had no way of knowing this. Yes, the individual Muslim restaurant owner could have a clean conscience – but how could the Muslim consumer actually know who conformed to the halal requirements and who did not? By creating a system of certification, they were enabling the consumers to make informed and safe choices: They would *know* that the business in question was halal.

After the initial period of resistance, the IRN succeeded in its endeavour. More and more businesses, stores and restaurants owned by Muslims came to IRN and asked for certification. After a while, this began to generate a substantial source of revenue for the IRN, allowing them to employ two full-time employees who only worked with halal certification and halal agreements. It also allowed them to move into new and more representative premises in 2016. IRN had succeeded in becoming the de facto certifier of halal in Norway, a feat that gave the IRN no small amount of symbolic power among Muslims.

Additionally, Afsar, Mushtaq and others on the board made a point of recruiting new members. They had an active policy of getting new mosques to join. They frequently visited mosques, members and non-members alike, many of them on the outskirts of the big cities. Thus, the number of members nearly doubled in only a few years. The membership base of the IRN had been stable for many years, ranging from 16 to about 20 mosques. In 2013, according to minutes acquired from the Brønnøysund registry, they had 43 members. That kind of growth was remarkable. All of these developments went in the same direction: Emphasising that the IRN should be an interest organisation for Muslims, advocating the interests of Muslims, in a society in which Muslims frequently felt that they met hostility: *ummah, a joint responsibility*.

4.11 Seeking Community or Seeking Allies

Why did these two competing visions emerge in the organisation? The dialogue path, which crytallised during Shoaib Sultan's tenure as secretary general, emphasised that the IRN should reach its goals through dialogue and alliances with external partners. It also emphasised that the IRN should not paint itself – and the Muslim communities in general – primarily as victims of Islamophobia, but should also attempt to be seen as constructive and pro-active partners in society. The community path, which crystallised during Mehtab Afsar's tenure as secretary general, emphasised that the IRN should focus on building solidarity between Muslims, and provide services to Muslims such as halal certification and legal support for Muslims who experienced discrimination. It also emphasised that IRN should take a more independent stance with regards to the authorities and its dialogue partners.

To a certain degree, these changes happened by chance. The immediate cause for the change of direction – and the resulting conflicts between the adherents of the two visions for the organisation – was a change on the micro level, with the introduction of new persons into the leadership. In an article on internal conflicts in organisations, the sociologists of organisation Anne-Claire Pache and Filipe Santos suggested that such changes may be partly accidental: "[internal disagreement] can be the outcome of hiring practices that, accidentally or purposefully, bring into the organisation members who adhere to various normative and cognitive templates" (Pache and Santos 2010, 468). The fact that Afsar, Mushtaq and other new persons joined the IRN and set their mark on the organisation came about partly by chance. It is likely that the trajectory of the organisation would have been different without the presence of Irfan Mushtaq, for example, who was able to set up their successful system for halal food certification. In a similar way, both of the two secretary generals – first Shoaib Sultan, and then Methab Afsar – set their distinctive marks on the organisation. Whereas Sultan was usually soft-spoken and mild-mannered, Afsar could become combative when conflicts arose.

But these personal patterns were also impacted by patterns and developments at the macro level – in society at large, and in the general external environment outside the organisation and its members. Pache and Santos expressed it in a somewhat cumbersome way: "Internal representation is also influenced by broader societal institutional logics that provide organisational members with cognitive templates that influence their perception of which

UNSTABLE INSTITUTIONALISATION

objectives and practices are appropriate" (Pache and Santos 2010, 460). I take this to mean that individual persons in organisations are influenced by broader norms and patterns of thought in society.

Both the dialogue path and independence path were responses to the same external environment in which the IRN was facing increasingly strong pressure from multiple directions and from different actors – and these pressures made it more difficult to navigate in a flexible and balanced way. The 2000s and first half of the 2010s saw an intensified public debate over Islam in Norway. This also affected the IRN and made it pertinent for the organisation to find a way to respond to external demands. In line with the theory of Kraatz and Block, an organisation may react to competing pressures by balancing acts, as has been detailed in previous chapters. But it can also respond by attempting to decouple or withdraw from sources of pressure, or by reaching independence (Kraatz and Block 2008). Fundamentally, when the IRN met hostility and difficult demands from mainstream society, it could live with these demands by seeking allies, by seeking independence, or both. In the late 2000s, several of these approaches had been employed at the same time. The balancing approach was most prevalent – but the withdrawal and decoupling approaches were also employed at times.

Signs of the independence approach could also be seen, for example with the original introduction of the *Safe Muslim* initiative in 2008. As the happenings from 2008 and onwards show – i.e. the youth demonstrations, the push for a more combative IRN – there was a clear sense among many young Muslims that they were alienated and discriminated against and needed to stand their ground. Indications of this can be found in several interviews, in fact in particular among those who supported the dialogue path. Some of them said, for example, that certain positions might be "popular on Facebook". One of them put it in the following way, with reference to a controversy in 2016 which will be covered later, when the IRN had hired a woman wearing the niqab to work in their office:

> When the conflict came out in the open, they started to attack us on Facebook. Every time they did that, they got lots of "likes"! They were just playing on emotions. They got lots of support. So, when they hired Leyla Hasic [who used the niqab], they received a whole lot of support from the youth, who thought – hey, now the IRN has done something really cool here.
>
> Interview with C, 2017–2019

This quotation does indicate that the community path tapped into something real among segments of the Muslim youth. The later hiring of the niqabi Leyla

Hasic was met with empathy. This was probably not because of support for the niqab as such, which remains a marginal garment in Norway, but rather because it was seen as an assertion of Muslim rights.

Around the time when Hasic was hired, I did a group interview with activists in the largest mosque in Bergen, which has a soft and dialogue-oriented profile. Most of them said that they were critical towards the niqab themselves, and most of them thought that the IRN had become too combative in recent years. They nevertheless had much sympathy with the IRN when it came to how the niqab controversy had been handled in the media. One of interviewees explained it as follows:

> You know, it is not that we support the niqab as such. I don't think there's anybody in this mosque who really likes the niqab. It is rather that we think that if the politicians ban the niqab, what will come next? The hijab? The right to have halal food? So it is a symbol, in a way. To support Hasic and her right to be employed with the niqab is, in a way, a show of support for the rights of Muslims more generally. We need to stand our ground.
>
> Interview, Bergen, 05.05.2017

And as will be recalled from previous chapters, the approaches of withdrawal and independence were seen all the way back to the 1990s in several of the mosques. During the blasphemy controversy in 1995, representatives from one of the Turkish mosques had made a point of letting it be known to the Norwegian public that they supported the blasphemy verdict in Pakistan, even though they had nothing to gain from this in society – and did not even hail from Pakistan themselves. This was clearly an act of defiance – and possibly a way of asserting independence. When VG interviewed mosque leaders in 1995, many imams and mosque leaders let it be known that they did not want to answer any questions (Schmidt and Hansen 1995). In the 2000s, as was seen in the previous chapters, several key actors in the IRN began to withdraw, as they perceived the media atmosphere as too challenging.

The anthropologist Christine Jacobsen also documented in her thorough study of Muslim youth in Norway that several competing discourses existed among young Muslims in the 1990s and early 2000s. Some wished to follow Tariq Ramadan in proudly proclaiming that they were 100 percent Muslims and 100 percent Norwegians. Others were sceptical, and "suspected that Muslims would never be fully accepted as a part of Europe unless they were willing to 'give up their identity' and 'become assimilated'" (Jacobsen 2010,

UNSTABLE INSTITUTIONALISATION

127). The community path was therefore not something new in IRN's history, or in the broader Islamic field in Norway. It was a crystallisation and clarification of tendencies that had been there for a long time, but which were forced to the fore by the more intense debates about Islam in the late 2000s and early 2010s.

The dialogue path, meanwhile, emerged as an alternative way of navigating the same external environment. Actors in the IRN early on understood that they could achieve significant gains in the Norwegian context by focusing on dialogue, and by allying themselves with actors who were trusted in mainstream society. In the 1990s, their contact with the MKR, and later with the broader alliance of minority religions in ALIS and the STL, ensured that they received both significant gains and symbolic recognition. Later on, in 2006, the dialogue path chosen during the cartoon crisis propelled the IRN right into the halls of power. Furthermore, this dialogue path gave them a clear sense of having some friends in an otherwise hostile environment – MKR, STL, some journalists and policymakers – friends who could help the IRN to achieve their goals. Several of the interviews I did with key actors indicate that this way of thinking had become common among key actors in the organisation. Senaid Kobilica, who was a key actor in the IRN throughout the 2000s and well into the 2010s, put it as follows:

> We knew [during the conflict in the 2010s] that what IRN had achieved, we had achieved through dialogue and cooperation with others.
>
> Interview with SENAID KOBILICA, 21.10.2019

A similar statement was made by one who was on the other side of the conflict. In an IRN meeting in 2015, he told me that the discussion happened like this:

> There is one meeting which I remember very clearly. One of the others opened the meeting by saying this with great emphasis: "Our friends are unhappy!". I remember that I was like: "Who are they exactly, our friends?" But they didn't want to specify it. They just said that these friends were unhappy, and that this was not good for the organisation.
>
> Interview with R, 2017–2019

It also appears as if the dialogue path became even clearer to its proponents during the conflict, when it was contrasted with the independence path. Both of these two organisational visions, which crystallised as distinct options for the organisation during the 2010s, were therefore related to the broader macro-environment the IRN found itself within.

CHAPTER 5

Towards the Split (2013–2018)

This chapter details how the conflict and disagreements in the organisation deepened and ultimately led to a split. In 2018, a faction decided to break out of the organisation in order to create the competing umbrella organisation *Muslim Dialogue Network* (MDN). The disagreements that led to the split were partly about personal conflicts. But there were also ideological disagreements over whether the organisation should pursue the dialogue path or the community path.

This chapter brings together the various analytical building blocks from the book, and proposes an answer to why the IRN ultimately split up. The cross-pressures the organisation was under became more intense in the 2010s, and led to the competing strategies of focusing on either dialogue or community building. Coupled with the multipolarity on the Islamic scene in Norway, this made it more difficult to arrive at compromises in the organisation that were acceptable to all – particularly given the low level of institutionalisation both within the IRN and in their external environment.

5.1 Deepening Conflicts

Around 2013 and 2014, it began to seem as if those who favoured the community path had prevailed in the organisation. IRN had thrown its weight behind the halal certification project; the Safe Muslim project was slowly gaining ground, and the membership of the organisation had increased substantially. Most of the pronounced critics of the new course had left the board. A new board was elected in 2013, headed by the veteran Mohamed Bouras. Although there were disagreements on this board as well, relationships were less conflictual than they had been previously.

At the same time, conflicts were never far away, both internally and externally. Simmering below the surface was a continued disagreement within IRN on how it should relate to its external dialogue partners. This became pronounced in early 2013, when IRN, MKR, and the Jewish community embarked on its most ambitious dialogue project so far. Starting in 2011, the three communities – Christians, Muslims and Jews – had engaged in a tripartite dialogue/trialogue project called "Abrahams barn", *Children of Abraham.*

© OLAV ELGVIN, 2025 | DOI:10.1163/9789004701144_006

This is an open access chapter distributed under the terms of the CC BY-NC-ND 4.0 license.

TOWARDS THE SPLIT (2013–2018) 137

In February 2013 representatives from these three communities as well as the Catholic Church in Oslo went on a joint trip to Israel and Palestine. The idea, according to the official report from the trip, was to decrease tension between Christians, Muslims and Jews in Norway (MKR, IRN, and DMT 2013, 1). The Israel-Palestine issue had been a thorny issue for many years, which had led to tension in the dialogue meetings. This tension had partly been between Jews and Muslims, but also between Jews and Christians – as MKR was very critical towards Israeli policies, and supported limited sanctions against Israel.

The idea behind the trip, I was told by two of those who had organised it, was to tackle the most difficult issue between them head on (interviews with D and F, 2017–2019). If one was able to deal with Israel-Palestine issue, they thought, one would be able to deal with other issues as well. The result, however, was the opposite. Discussions became heated between the participants, and the atmosphere was not always pleasant. In the report from the trip, IRN mentions specifically that they found it upsetting that the Muslim participants were held back for several hours in the checkpoint when they left Gaza, whereas the Jewish and Christian participants were allowed to leave straight away (MKR, IRN, and DMT 2013, 9). For both the Muslim and Jewish participants, the trip evoked strong emotions, according to the report. Instead of improving inter-religious relations, the trip ended up doing the opposite. Following the trip, there would never again be any tripartite dialogue between MKR, IRN and DMT, as the newspaper Vårt Land reported in 2015 (Lindekleiv 2015).

An issue which was not reported in the media or in the official report from the trip, however, was that this project also led to subsequent complications within the IRN. Interviews with actors in both IRN and MKR revealed that there had been significant disagreement in IRN about the trip. Parts of the board had thought that the trip was premature. According to one interviewee, the board actually decided in 2012 that IRN would not participate. Some people in IRN were nevertheless so interested in participating that they said yes without getting the final approval of the board, and presented it to the board as a *fait accompli*, according to one interviewee (interview with R, 2017–2019). A representative from MKR also had the perception that the IRN representatives were unusually quiet about their participation in the trip, and did not post anything about it on social media – unlike what they usually did with such trips or projects (interview with S, 2017–2019). The fallout from the trip was therefore that IRN became more sceptical towards participating in dialogue activities. None of the interviewees from IRN mentioned anything about the precise discussions that took place following the trip. The perception in MKR, though, was that the trip to Israel/Palestine effectively killed off all dialogue with IRN.

Conflicts began to rekindle again in 2014. This time the issue was Afsar's employment status as secretary general. Both Sultan's and Afsar's positions had been defined as temporary. They were to last for a term of three years, with the possibility of renewal. Sultan stepped down after his first period ended. After being hired, Afsar started to enquire about the possibility of a permanent position. When his period was about to end, at the end of 2013, he stepped up his enquiries, according to several sources. According to Afsar, he needed a permanent position for several reasons. He needed the economic security and stability a permanent position would provide, and it also played a role for what kind of mortgage he could get in the bank. Afsar also wanted to have a higher salary, as his original salary was indeed fairly low by Norwegian standards.

Many on the board and in the broader organisation were undecided. Some were actively against making the position permanent, particularly people from the ICC, the Rabita mosque and the Bosnian mosque. When it came to the salary, the conflict lines were somewhat different. Irfan Mushtaq – who had been allied with Afsar when it came to halal food for example – was actively against raising the salary. According to several sources, Afsar exerted quite a lot of pressure to get his way and said that if he did not get an offer of a permanent position, he would not seek a new period and would immediately resign. The board then hired a lawyer, who gave the board legal advice about what their obligations were and what options they had. The end result was that the board offered Afsar a new contract with a permanent position, which was approved by the annual IRN meeting in April 2014 with only a few dissenting voices, after a prolonged discussion during which Afsar had to leave the room.

This disagreement, though, seems to have deepened and exacerbated the conflict in the organisation. Several sources claimed that the affair had an impact on Afsar – he felt hurt that there were actors in the organisation who did not want to offer him a position. On the other side of the conflict, this outcome also had an effect. One of the members, who later broke out, framed it in this way:

> After Mehtab got that permanent position, many of us felt that it became even more critical. Now it was not only temporary, how he affected the IRN. It had become permanent. So we thought about what we could do.
> Interview with U, 2017–2019

Whatever the cause, disagreements became increasingly heated. Ordinary interactions could suddenly turn into conflicts. Some of those involved seemed to change their behavior during this period. They became more combative, and became less interested in reacting to others in good faith.

5.2   The Dynamic of Conflict and the Role of Individuals

Why did this development take place? In my original PhD thesis, I attributed most of this development to structural challenges for the IRN organisation on the meso and macro level. Multipolarity and cross-pressures became even more difficult to deal with in the 2010s. As will be detailed in the next section, IRN was put under an increasing amount of pressure in the 2010s concerning how to deal with radicalisation and terror. This coincided with a continuation of the conflict about approach and direction: Should IRN seek allies, or seek internal strength? Such external and internal pressures could make it easy for conflicts to flare up.

When various actors in IRN and other organisations read my thesis after my PhD defence, however, this was the point where I received most pushback. Some of those who read it thought that I placed too little emphasis on the personal aspect. There were those who thought that the conflict in IRN was more or less in its entirety about difficult personalities who were not able to cooperate. Some pointed in particular to the secretary general, Mehtab Afsar and his increasing stridency – at least those who had found themselves in a conflict with him. Others did accept that cross-pressures and multipolarity had played a role. But they still thought that there was an interplay between these larger societal developments and the personal aspect. Others, though, mostly agreed with the framing I had chosen. This disagreement over the ultimate causes of the conflict reflects the disagreement in the organisation about what they were actually disagreeing about.

This criticism nevertheless led me to reassess the data, both the material from the interviews and the posts from social media I had collected from this period. The interviews indeed contained several stories about conflicts, quarrels, manipulations, etc, some of which are fairly dramatic. The different actors who were involved had very different versions of who did what to whom. This much I had written in my thesis. But after reassessing the data, it did become clear to me that many of these interactions were not only about factual disagreements on whether the IRN should do this or that. Many interactions and disagreements also had a clear personal angle. In the thesis I had left out most of these stories, partly because it was difficult to corroborate what actually went down, partly out of a respect for the privacy of those involved, and partly because I thought that the personal issues were less interesting than the larger analytical and structural arguments. But after reassessing the data when working with this book, I concluded that the critics had a point: Leaving out the personal quarrels altogether probably left the reader with a picture that was not complete.

I will therefore include one such story which was recounted to me, which illustrates how interactions could be during this period. The reason I include this story is that it was recounted to me by a person who was not party to the conflicts in the organisation, and therefore did not have a motive in painting people in the organisation in a bad light. I met this person at an informal gathering in 2016, and he asked me what my thesis was about. When I told him that I wrote a thesis on the Islamic Council of Norway, he immediately erupted: "You write on THEM? You know, I actually had a very strange interaction with them." (fieldwork notes, October 2016). This person was working in the Church of Norway in a smaller town, and had attempted to set up a dialogue project with a local Muslim organisation. Prior to this project, according to his recounting, he had no interactions with IRN and had not held any strong opinions on the organisation. Then the following episode happened, in his telling – here reconstructed from my own notes later that day:

> Suddenly one day I received a phone call. I didn't know the number and picked up. The caller introduced himself as calling from the Islamic Council of Norway. After some courtesies, he started asked rather briskly about this dialogue project, and asked why we had not contacted the Islamic Council of Norway when setting up this project. I replied that we didn't think it was necessary, you know, it was a small local project, so why should we contact the Islamic Council of Norway? Then he exploded! Like out of nowhere! He said that it was unacceptable to undermine the authority of the IRN in this way, and asked why we were working against them. I hung up afterwards and wondered what had just happened.
>
> Reconstructed from fieldwork notes, October 2016

The result was the dialogue project continued, but without the involvement of the IRN. The phone call convinced some of the organisers that IRN was not a good dialogue partner, according to my interlocutor.

When I went home that evening, I wrote the story down, as I thought it was rather remarkable. I did not include it in the thesis, as I could not corroborate independently that the episode happened in that way. I have therefore anonymised the persons involved. I was able to corroborate, however, that the person who spoke to me did initiate a local dialogue project around this time, which happened without the involvement of the IRN. Furthermore, he did not have a public record of speaking out against the IRN or other Muslim organisations.

The phone conversation may not have transpired exactly as he told it to me, of course. I still regard it as likely that his recounting contains an element of truth. I do not think that this person had any interest in misrepresenting to me what happened. Whatever the truth of the matter, the episode at the minimum reveals that there were outside actors during this time who perceived actors in the IRN as difficult or behaving in an erratic way – even when they were not involved in a conflict with them. The story also indicates that there were actors in the IRN during this time who acted in a combative manner, even when it could have been possible to solve disagreements without resorting to forceful language. In this case there was no conflict to begin with, and it is not unlikely that the IRN could have become a partner in the project if their initial approach had been softer. The communication style of the person from IRN therefore seems to have played a role in the ensuing outcome.

I have not picked up that the main actors in the conflict were involved in similar conflicts prior to the conflict in the IRN. Some of them were also involved in other organisations. I asked some people in these organisations about them, whether they were perceived as combative or difficult, and the answer was no. It is therefore likely that it was the features of the situation – an escalating conflict due to internal disagreements – led many of the persons involved to act in a more conflictual manner. They were caught in a conflict dynamic, which made them more likely to act in a certain way (Bar-Tal 2013). This behaviour may then have had spillovers to other situations. In the recounting of the phone call above, for example, the representative from IRN claimed that the lack of involvement of IRN amounted to an undermining of their authority. Would he or others in the organisation have perceived it the same way if there was no ongoing conflict? We cannot know for sure. But it is not unlikely that the conflict led him and others to perceive episodes in a more conflictual way, and to behave more combatively – even to outsiders. At the same time, the way certain individuals reacted to this situation clearly mattered. Combative behaviours became more common. This made it difficult to solve disagreements, and the conflict became ever more entrenched.

5.3 Turning Up the Heat: the Debate over Fundamentalism and Radicalization

At the same time, an important piece of the puzzle is also that there were developments during this period which increased the pressure on key actors in the IRN. In the 2010s, the politicization and securitization of aspects having to with Islam reached new levels. The wars in Iraq, Afghanistan and Syria; and the Jihadi networks in these countries and their attacks in Europe had made jihadism and radicalization a key issue for most European states in the 2000s (Nesser 2019).

The 2010s witnessed additional developments that further increased the politicization of Islam in Norway. On 22 July 2011, Norway had its worst ever terrorist attack. Far-right activist Anders Behring Breivik bombed the government quarter in Oslo, and then attacked the summer camp of AUF, the youth division of the Norwegian Labour Party (AP) on the island of Utøya. He killed 69 children and adolescents and severely injured more than 50. Even though this attack reinforced the commitment of some policymakers to the notion of a multicultural society, it also had a paradoxical effect on the public sphere. Some politicians and media commentators drew the conclusion that Breivik – and those like him – had been radicalised because they had not been invited into the public discussion, where their arguments could be met (Tajik 2013). As a result, far-right actors such as Hege Storhaug and Breivik's ideological guru, Peder "Fjordman" Jensen, would go on to publish more op-eds in the press about the threat from Islam than they had ever done before the attack (Figenschou and Beyer 2014, 442–44). Key politicians from the far-right Progress Party also intensified their rhetoric against Islam and Muslims (Bangstad 2016, 57–61). The IRN also faced mounting criticism from Muslim actors for being too conservative and too hesitant to confront Muslim radicals (VG 2013).

In addition, there were recurrent calls from policymakers and journalists for the state to discontinue the IRN's funding. Ever since the IRN began to receive funding, there were political actors who wanted to take it away. This included far-right politicians from the Progress Party, but also politicians in the Socialist Left and the Labour Party. The first time this occurred was after the homosexuality controversy in 2007, right after the IRN started receiving funding for the first time (Utrop 2007). The next time these calls came with force was in 2011, when the activist Sara Azmeh-Rasmussen had her sit-in demonstration outside the premises of the IRN. This time it was an MP from the Labour Party who called for the government to stop the funding the IRN, even though the minister – also from Labour – turned the proposal down (Dagsavisen 2011).

On the Muslim side, the IRN was also facing challenges it had to deal with. In 2012, Norway for the first time saw the establishment of a full-blown Salafi-Jihadist group, called *The Prophet's Ummah*. Mohyeldeen Mohammad – the man who had warned of a terror attack on Norwegian soil in 2010 – was a central person in the group, although he was not formally the leader. Irfan Bhatti, the former criminal who had taken the initiative to the demonstration in 2010 which was covered in the previous chapter, was another member. The group seemed to be fully organised by January 2012, when they arranged a demonstration outside the Norwegian parliament against the Norwegian participation in the NATO's war in Afghanistan. A person in the group – who would later join ISIS in Syria and be killed there – also published a video on Youtube which made explicit threats against the Norwegian prime minister, the Norwegian crown prince and the Norwegian foreign minister (Ihlebæk and Færaas 2012).

TOWARDS THE SPLIT (2013–2018)

The IRN needed to decide how to deal with the challenge from the jihadists. Later in 2012, the jihadist group once again made noise and forced the IRN to act. This was occasioned by the short anti-Islamic movie *The Innocence of Muslims*, an amateurish film uploaded on Youtube on 12 September by anti-Islamic Christian activists in the USA. For some reason, this movie attracted significant attention from the media. This led to international protests against the film, including in Norway. Once again, people associated with what was now publicly known as *The Prophet's Ummah* were calling for a demonstration. But this time, the IRN chose a different tactic: rather than warning against demonstrating, they decided to hold a demonstration of their own, to give Muslims a peaceful venue for venting frustration. The IRN therefore arranged a large peaceful demonstration in central Oslo, which drew 3000 participants. But they cooperated with other actors in society, such as the bishop of Oslo, Ole Christian Kvarme, and were careful not to create an us-vs-them narrative. At the same time, the Prophet's Ummah held their own small demonstration outside the American Embassy in Oslo, in which around 150 people participated. In that demonstration, they hailed "sheikh" Osama Bin Laden, and carried the black Jihadist flag (Hirsti 2012). But even though the IRN attempted to counteract the appeal of the young Jihadists, they were also criticized by other Muslim organisations that claimed the IRN was not doing enough to combat radicalization (Decap 2013).

The 2010s also saw the emergence of a non-violent and peaceful Salafi-inspired movement in Norway, which also challenged the IRN at times. The largest and most influential of these was *Islam Net*, which emerged in 2008 as an Islamic Student Society at the University College of Oslo – an educational institution for vocational education. In later years, Islam Net has changed their profile, have moderated their stances and arguably become part of a reformist post-Salafi tendency (Qadhi 2014; Thurston 2018). In the first years, however, Islam Net attracted fairly large numbers of young Muslims to large-scale conferences, to which they invited charismatic speakers from abroad. Several of the guest speakers were on record for having made controversial statements. This led to heated public debates on several occasions. In early 2012, a public conflict erupted between Islam Net and the IRN, following some statements by IRN leader Senaid Kobilica (Brandvold 2012; Qureshi 2012).

When the authorities, the media, society at large and various Muslim groups began placing stricter demands on the IRN, it became more difficult to navigate the field in a flexible way and to find balanced solutions that could satisfy all the different parties. This kind of tension between different demands had been a part of IRN's predicament since the very beginning, as the preceding chapters have shown. But the tension arguably grew more intense in the 2010s, forcing key actors in the organisation to take a more defined stand on how the organisation should respond to these pressures. It is fair to say that the IRN leaders in the 2010s faced more cross-pressure than previous leaders in IRN. Combined with the more combative way of responding to conflict that some of the leaders displayed, this led to more quarrels and disagreements than before. It also led those who were in charge to double down on the community path as the way forward for the organisation.

5.4   The Challenge of Multipolarity Once Again

Even though the conflict was not primarily about doctrinal or theological differences, the diversity and multipolarity of the IRN membership and on the Islamic field in Norway also contributed to the entrenchment of the conflict. IRN's membership had been stable for a good number of years, and the organisation was dominated by a few influential mosques – particularly the post-Islamists and the Balkan mosques. During the 2010s, membership increased substantially, which meant that the relative standing of the mosques which had been dominant became weaker. The 2010s also saw an increased assertiveness among the Barelwi mosques, which had previously stayed out of the spotlight – and occasionally had internal conflicts between themselves. This tendency first came to the fore with the halal controversy in 2007 but intensified later – and coalesced around the new halal certification project in the 2010s.

According to several sources, there were actors in the organisation who mobilised around the conflict by playing on the identities of Barelwi or Sufi Muslims and the post-Islamists. When I did interviews with people from Barelwi mosques from 2017 to 2019, I was initially surprised that several of them spoke disparagingly of the post-Islamists or Islamists in the Rabita and ICC as "Wahhabis". Previously – in the late 2000s, and in the early 2010s – I had never encountered those kinds of accusations. One former key actor in IRN, for example, who had worked alongside the post-Islamists for a long time, said this:

> They are Wahhabis. Not like us, the Muslims. You know, the Sunni Muslims. They just follow the Saudis, do whatever they say.
>
> Interview with K, 2017–2019

Wahhabism is a term often used for describing a Saudi-oriented type of Islam which emphasizes very strict readings of the Islamic tradition. These days it

TOWARDS THE SPLIT (2013–2018)

is more common to call it *Salafism*. Most researchers of Islam see clear distinctions between Salafism and the Islamist or post-Islamist interpretations of Islam (Shavit 2015). As a practical example, Salafis in Norway have sometimes warned against greeting non-Muslims with sayings such as "merry Christmas", because they think that it involves an implicit recognition of the religious validity of the Christmas holiday. The post-Islamist groups in Norway, on the other hand, only see sayings like that as customary expressions which are about politeness and social norms. This is only one of several fairly fundamental differences between the Salafi and the post-Islamist approaches to Islam in the West. I was therefore surprised, initially, to hear the Barelwi Muslims label the post-Islamists as Wahhabis. But research on the relations between Barelwi and Deobandi Muslims in South Asia indicates that these Barelwi Muslims were tapping into a long-standing discourse in South Asia. Leading Barelwi scholars have made such claims since the late 19th century – often calling their South Asian Deobandi competitors "Wahhabis" (Jackson 2013, 113). The discourse in which Barelwi Muslims themselves are said to be nothing but *Muslims* or *Sunni Muslims* also has long historical roots (Jackson 2013, 5). What I heard in these interviews, then, was probably the re-activation of a discourse that had been used previously in their movement in Pakistan, but which to my knowledge had not been used much in the Norwegian context previously.

Indirectly, some actors from Barelwi mosques confirmed that the conflict between Barelwis and Deobandis/post-Islamists had been activated. One of them framed it like this:

> I grew up in a Barelwi household. But as kids we were only raised to be Muslims, not more than that. It wasn't like we were told that we were Sufis and that the other guys were Deobandis or Wahhabis. When I became an adult I kind of thought we were finished with that stuff, you know? But then I understood that it mattered a whole lot. The Arabs, the Ikhwanis [the Muslim Brotherhood], they had been used to being in control. And then suddenly it was the Sufis who were in charge. They didn't like that.
>
> Interview with R, 2017–2019

On the other side of the conflict, I did not hear equally distinct allegations that it was about Sufis or Barelwis vs the post-Islamists. What I did hear, however, was talk of ethnicity. One IRN activist said straight out that it may have been about "the Pakistanis":

> For a long time, it was the Arabs who dominated IRN – not only the Arabs – there was also the ICC and the Bosniaks. But the Arabs were important. And then the Pakistanis increasingly took over. You know

what we call it now, jokingly? Not "the Islamic Council of Norway" but "the Pakistani council of Norway". The Pakistanis have all the important positions. I haven't studied it in depth, so I will not make any grand claims here. But it is interesting, right? Before the Pakistanis took over, things were going well. Then the Pakistanis took over, and it all went down the drain. It is interesting, I think.

Interview with T, 2017–2019

It does not seem that these disagreements played out as strong *theological* conflicts, though. The clearest disagreement that can be attributed to doctrinal differences was about halal slaughter, as was discussed in the previous chapter. Traditionally, the Pakistani Barelwis have been more focused on the minutiae of halal meat than the Deobandis, the post-Islamists or the Bosniaks. This could be seen already in 2007, when the Barelwi *Ahle Sunnat Imam Council* – led by the Ahle Sunnat mosque in Oslo – led the charge against the slaughter of halal chicken involving stunning, with opposition from mosques like the ICC.

Some of those in the post-Islamist camp went as far as to say publicly that the halal certification was "not important" (Brandvold 2016a). In one interview with an activist in the post-Islamist camp, when I brought up the subject of halal certification, he responded:

Oh my … the halal thing, what a disaster that was. A disaster! We should never have started to get entangled in that. Never! Halal meat is, well, halal, and it doesn't matter what we in the IRN do about it.

Interview with T, 2017–2019

For many Barelwis, it would be unthinkable to say something like that. This disagreement about halal seems to have been joked about internally, even though not everybody thought that it was a thing to joke about. One of the Barelwi interviewees mentioned to me that he had been sitting alongside an imam from one of the post-Islamist mosques at an IRN gathering, which took place in the mosque this imam belonged to. They were eating pizza.

Then the imam turned to me, looked at me mockingly, and said in what was apparently a joke to him: 'Hm … are you 100 percent sure that the cheese on this pizza is halal? Perhaps not, hm?' I was shocked! How could he as an imam not be sure whether he was eating cheese which was halal or not? Didn't he know that cheese can be made with animal leftovers, that may not be halal? How was this a joke for him?

Interview with K, 2018

One may of course interpret this story in different ways. It is likely that the imam actually knew whether the cheese was halal or not, given that it was in his own mosque, and that he instead was mocking what he perceived as over-zealotry in his interlocutor. But the exchange does reveal that they disagreed on this issue and had different perceptions of how one should approach the issue of halal food. This disagreement on the importance of halal certification does seem to have theological roots, at least in part, and played out through the shifting importance of the different mosques in the organisation.

But beyond differences of theology, relations between Barelwis and post-Islamists may therefore have been about basic mechanisms from group psychology. People supported other people in their own in-group, irrespective of whether there was any substantial theological disagreement or not. Even though the conflict probably did not begin as a conflict about sectarian differences, the multipolarity and diversity among IRN's members probably contributed to the prolongation and intensification of the conflict.

5.5   Unstable Internal Institutionalisation and the Failed Intervention

All of these factors may have contributed when some of the actors in the organisation decided to undertake what some of them referred to as "an intervention". Had the IRN been more instutionalized internally, it is not unlikely that this intervention would have succeeded – or never taken place in the first place.

The final phase in the history of the IRN as a more or less unified organisation began at the annual meeting in the spring of 2015. One year previously, in 2014, the annual meeting had chosen an electoral committee. This committee consisted of many people who were sceptical towards the new course of the organisation. Their proposal for the new board included many candidates who hailed from the large mosques that for a long time had been central in the IRN – Rabita, ICC and the Bosnian mosque. Many of the proposed candidates were IRN veterans: Basim Ghozlan, Senaid Kobilica, Arshad Jamil and Ghulam Abbas. In addition, and significantly, the original proposition of the electoral committee was that Irfan Mushtaq should not be re-elected to the board. They proposed another candidate for the position as the person responsible for halal food.

At the annual meeting, Mushtaq made it clear that he wanted to continue. This was not taken lightly by several of those who wanted another direction. Many of those who were candidates for the new board made it clear that they would not stand for election if Mushtaq was part of the board. But in the end, those who were elected to the new board – Kobilica, Ghozlan, Jamil and others – accepted Mushtaq's candidacy, and they were elected together. The majority of the new board, however, wanted to reverse what they saw as the new course in the IRN. This seems to have been a conscious decision from early on by several of those involved. One of the newly elected board members confirmed as much to me in our interview:

> When we got elected to that board ... it was an attempt at an intervention. We saw that everything was going the wrong way. So we wanted to give it a shot. To see if we could put the ship on the right course.
>
> OE: What made you intervene?
>
> Everybody was complaining. Everybody! All of our partners and friends. Everybody! Journalists, people from the authorities, our dialogue partners ... there were complaints about the IRN all the time. IRN did not answer the phone, IRN could not be trusted; it was difficult to cooperate with IRN, and so on. There were only complaints. So we felt that we needed to do something, so that it would not all go to waste.
>
> Interview with U, 2017–2019

I heard similar stories from others among those who wanted to change direction. Almost all of them mentioned that people on the outside were unhappy (interviews with D, C and T, 2017–2019). They seem to have perceived this as a significant liability for the organisation. Their view was that the IRN had achieved victories through cooperation. They perceived the worsened *reputation* of the IRN as a significant liability. Without a good reputation, they assumed, the IRN would not be able to achieve its goals.

What happened after that depends somewhat on perspective. The people I spoke to, on different sides of the conflict, tell more or less the same story – but from different viewpoints. What seems clear is that the majority on the new board attempted to rein in Mehtab Afsar in his role as secretary general and were also trying to isolate Irfan Mushtaq. In the words of those who were sceptical of Afsar, it was a question of having him fulfil his actual duties as a general secretary – writing reports and minutes of meetings, answering the phone when journalists called, etc. In the words of Afsar and Mushtaq and their allies, it was an attempt at micromanagement: stripping Afsar of his proper responsibilities as general secretary. One of the new board members put it this way in our interview:

> When we were elected to the new board, we wanted to give Afsar a chance. We made clear what the expectations were, what we were asking

TOWARDS THE SPLIT (2013–2018)

of him. We wanted him to show that he could deliver on that. But he did not fulfil his obligations.

Interview with C, 2017–2019

When Afsar was interviewed one year later, by the newspaper Vårt Land, he claimed that he had been "stripped of responsibility" early on (Huseby 2016). In an interview with me a couple of years later, he repeated this, and said that he had been micro-managed by the board (interview with Mehtab Afsar, 08.10.2017).

The journalist Åse Brandvold at the newspaper Klassekampen, who followed the conflict closer than any other journalists at the time, received access to internal emails, and could reveal that people on the board began to discuss firing Afsar early on – from May 2015, just one month after taking on their roles (Brandvold 2016b). Two people, independently of each other, told me that this email discussion had not been a formal email discussion between all of the board members. It had rather been a selective discussion between some of the board members, who discussed how to get rid of both Afsar and Mushtaq. It is clear in any event that a majority on the board were unhappy with Afsar and with the general direction of the organisation that Afsar, Mushtaq and others had pursued. At some point in late 2015, Irfan Mushtaq decided that he had enough, and resigned from the board. Another board member – the imam Najeeb Naz from the Barelwi mosque World Islamic Mission – did the same.

The board then gave Afsar a notice that he was fired, and on 4 June convened the council of the IRN – consisting of representatives from all the member mosques – to brief them on the decision. This did not work out as planned, in part due to the unstable institutionalisation in the organisation. The board had assumed that it had the legal right to fire Afsar. The problem was that the IRN did not have any statutes for such cases. Afsar had become a regular employee in 2014, but neither his contract nor the statutes specified the person actually authorized to fire him. Was it the board, or the larger council? This was juridically unclear. The board took a chance and fired him. At the council meeting, though, most of the delegates voted to reinstate Afsar. The result was clear: 16 delegates voted to uphold the firing of Afsar, whereas 40 voted to reinstate him. When this happened, the sitting board dramatically announced that it would step down.

In their place, an interim board was appointed. This interim board consisted of veterans of the IRN who stepped up to be caretakers while the organisation figured things out. Kebba Secka – the leader who had to step down after the FGM controversy in 2000 – was appointed as the leader. Zahid Mukhtar, the first secretary of the board, who left the organisation after a media controversy in the 2000s, also sat on the board. The last person was Mohammed Ibrahim, from the Somali Tawfiiq mosque. The job of the interim board was to assess the situation and prepare the ground for an election of a new board. The reason they were chosen for this task, according to a couple of interviewees, was that they were veterans who knew the IRN but who did not have any stakes in the conflict. They had not been involved in the IRN for a long time and were therefore expected to be more impartial than those who had recently been involved in the organisation.

But in the larger public sphere, it was not taken lightly that two controversial figures who had previously fallen from grace – Kebba Secka and Zahid Mukhtar – would now be leading the organisation. The fact that the board stepped down also led to widespread public and political unrest among journalists and politicians. The minister of culture and religion, Linda Helleland, therefore wanted to send a clear signal to the IRN that she expected them to get their house in order. She decided to withhold their funding until she received clarification about what was happening. This was the first time that the ministry told the IRN in such strong and unequivocal terms that they were not happy with what was happening; not only through words, but also through actions.

Then in October, a new board was elected. For the first time, there were no representatives on the board from Rabita, the ICC or the Bosnian mosque, all of which chose not to have any candidates stand for election. Quite soon, in October and November 2016, some of them began talking publicly about breaking out and creating a new organisation (Brandvold 2016a). It thus became clear that the *interventionists* had failed in their intervention – and were considering other options. Nevertheless, the new board managed to get the funding from the government back, and thus the operation of IRN continued.

In October 2016, the new board was elected, with Zaeem Shaukat as the leader of the board, who hailed from the same mosque as Afsar. Even though some of the former board members from the losing side had begun to talk publicly about breaking out, they hesitated to do so. During the winter of 2017, a fact-finding task force was commissioned, comprising a team of lawyers from the law firm *Aurelis* in Oslo. Their report largely cleared Afsar, and said that the firing had in fact been contrary to Norwegian law (Brandvold 2017b). Even though those who had attempted to fire Afsar accepted the legal ruling of the report, they thought that the report was unbalanced and mostly presented one side of the story.

This nevertheless gave Afsar a moral victory. It seemed as if Afsar and those who supported him had won, and that they had consolidated power over the organisation. In retrospect, it is possible that this could have been the final

TOWARDS THE SPLIT (2013–2018)

result, and that the organisations and actors who lost the battle over the direction of the organisation would have accepted the loss. What changed all of this, however, was an affair that came under the scrutiny of the public eye at the end of March 2017.

At some point during 2016, the IRN had applied to the ministry for additional funding. The application stated that they had too much work and too few resources; they needed more funds to do their work – including dialogue and bridge-building. They therefore applied for funds that would cover a new part-time position as secretary and office-manager. According to one board member at the time, this had happened on the initiative of the ministry:

> We had a meeting with two persons from the ministry. They said that they were unhappy with the direction of the organisation, particularly our focus on halal certification. They thought that, as a voluntary organisation, we should not make money on halal certification that way. We told them that we made a clear distinction between the two: The money from the halal certification went to the salaries of those two employees who worked with halal, whereas the funding from the ministry went to fund Mehtab's job, and other assignments. We also said that the funding from the ministry wasn't enough to cover all the activity the organisation did. We said that we had applied for more funding several times and had been turned down. So why were they complaining that we got other sources of revenue?
>
> Interview with F, 2017–2019

According to this board member, the representatives from the ministry then proposed that the IRN should apply for additional funding. I interviewed a couple of bureaucrats from the ministry, and they also confirmed that they had told the IRN that the funding could not be used for internal purposes such as the halal business – and that they attempted to meet IRN with flexibility by offering them additional funding (interviews with H and X2, 2017–2019). One interpretation is that the ministry saw this as a way of giving the IRN a carrot: To get the IRN to adjust their profile to align more with what the ministry wanted, by providing them with further incentives.

The ministry said yes to the request for additional funding, which IRN then used to create a new position as a part-time office secretary. There were 16 applicants for the position. The person offered the job was not just anyone. It was Leyla Hasic, one of the most publicly vocal niqabis in Norway. She was of Bosnian origin and had grown up in Norway. I did an interview with her in 2012, long before she showed any interest in the IRN. A couple of years before our interview, she had been «born again» as a Muslim, after having lived an essentially secular life during the previous decade. At the turning point in her life, she was a single mother working in a bar and had come to the conclusion that she was living a sinful life. She soon became more conservative and at some point, decided to wear the niqab, as one of very few women in Norway. She started to write comments online and in newspapers, in which, among other things, she accused the Muslim leadership – including previous IRN secretary Shoaib Sultan – of not supporting her and thus of abandoning the cause of the Muslim community. She also had loose associations online with a group of Muslim radicals, among whom several would go to Syria to join IS at a later stage.

After this, she moved out of the spotlight for some years and then suddenly re-emerged in 2017. She had applied for the position and wanted to move from the smaller town of Fredrikstad to Oslo together with her son. According to sources in the IRN, she had left behind the radical ideas she had been toying with some years earlier. But she was still wearing the niqab. She was the one who was offered the job at an IRN meeting in February.

It must have seemed obvious that this would lead to angry reactions in the press and mainstream society. After all, the niqab was and is very controversial in Norwegian society, and the government had toyed with the idea of banning it in several public institutions. Afsar's motivation for hiring her was simple, he explained to me: She was the best qualified candidate.

> She was best qualified. It is as simple as that. Should we *not* employ her because she wears the niqab? Wouldn't that be very discriminatory? And is this not a liberal society?
>
> Interview with MEHTAB AFSAR, 08.10.2017

According to two independent sources, Hasic had actually not been the first choice of the hiring committee. Out of the 16 applicants, there were three who had relevant formal qualifications. Hasic, for example, was in the process of finishing studies to become an auditor. They had initially preferred another applicant, who was actually Christian and who had more experience than Hasic doing secretary work. They had called this candidate in to a second interview, but the day before the second interview she called and said that she had accepted another job. This left them with Hasic as the most qualified candidate, according to a couple of the interviewees. This account may validate IRN's claim that Hasic may indeed have been the best qualified candidate IRN had.

TOWARDS THE SPLIT (2013–2018)

It is impossible to know whether the motivations of the IRN board were as pure and simple as reported. One may also see Hasic's hiring as a sign of defiance – the hiring of a woman who wore precisely the kind of religious clothing that the government had talked about banning. Yet another possibility is that Afsar may have wanted to show that the IRN would not bow to whatever dictates the government put out. In our interview, Afsar did confirm that he understood that there would be reactions:

> Of course I understood that there would be reactions. I am not stupid. Still, she was the best qualified. I really mean that we needed to hire her then. Take a hypothetical case where the best applicant was a woman who insisted on wearing a mini skirt and high heels and was the most qualified. I would have insisted that we hire that person as well!
> Interview with MEHTAB AFSAR, 08.10.2017

There are no indications that Afsar or others on the board themselves supported the use of the niqab for Muslim women. Quite to the contrary, Afsar appears to have advised Hasic in private to stop wearing the niqab, even though he never said so publicly. Whatever Afsar's motivations were, the consequences were dramatic.

The affair became known in the media at the end of March. The reactions from politicians and media pundits were fierce (NTB 2017b). Many politicians – several of them Muslims – said that the IRN had outlasted its role, and that it was time to remove their funding. This sentiment was echoed widely in the traditional media and on social media, and the voices who defended the IRN were close to non-existent in the public sphere (Henriksen 2017). The Church of Norway – which usually refrained from public criticism of the IRN – was among the voices that criticized the hiring of Hasic (Brandvold 2017c). The minister of culture, Linda Helleland, called the IRN to a meeting to ask about what was happening. When the IRN showed up, they had brought a lawyer along. One of the bureaucrats I interviewed remarked rather dryly in our interview:

> As you may imagine, it is not exactly a boost for the social atmosphere when you bring a lawyer with you to a consultancy meeting with the minster.
> Interview with H, 2017–2019

The minister said afterwards that this meeting did not restore her trust in IRN. Other developments also made the situation difficult for the organisation.

Leaders in several of the largest mosques – the Bosnian mosque and Rabita – announced that they were thinking of leaving IRN. They also spoke of setting up a new umbrella organisation (NTB 2017a).

After the summer, STL did an unusual thing. Their leader went public in the media and said that they no longer had confidence in the IRN as a partner (Huseby 2017). This was new ground for STL, which almost never chose to criticise its own members publicly. The backdrop was prolonged frustration in STL circles with Afsar and the IRN. Apparently, there had been several personal disputes between persons in STL and the IRN, some of which became relatively heated. In October, STL and IRN jointly announced that the IRN would take a six-month "leave of absence" from the organisation (STL and IRN 2017). According to several sources in the STL and MKR, the IRN would have been at risk of being expelled from the organisation otherwise – and this leave of absence was a way for the organisation to save face. When the leave of absence ended in 2018, the IRN announced that it had withdrawn entirely from the organisation.

Later in October, the IRN took another blow. Nortura – the main purveyor of halal meat in the IRN's halal system – stated that they no longer knew if IRN was a partner with whom they could cooperate and broke off their business relations with the IRN (Nortura 2017). They would still produce halal meat in the same way but would not have an agreement with IRN which allowed the IRN to certify the products. This meant that one of the main sources of income for the IRN – the halal certification – was about to crumble. Finally, several of the largest mosques in IRN announced that they no longer had confidence in the IRN and that they were discontinuing relations. These included the Bosnian mosque, the Rabita mosque, the Moroccan Centre Rahma mosque, the Ahl-e-Sunnat mosque, the Albanian mosque, and the Islamic Cultural Centre. All in all, these mosques had around 25,000 members, and their exit from the IRN was a significant blow to the organisation. After a lot of ifs and buts, the Barelwi Ahl-e-Sunnat mosque – still the largest mosque in Norway – decided to re-join the IRN.

Then, in November 2017, IRN received the coup de grâce. The ministry announced that they would not transfer the second half of IRN's funding for 2017 (Kulturdepartementet 2017). According to bureaucrats in the ministry, arriving at this decision involved a huge amount of manpower. Legally, it would have been non-problematic to only refuse to renew IRN's funding for the next year, 2018. Stopping their funding during the year, however, was a legal minefield which could leave the ministry vulnerable to lawsuits. They therefore prepared their case very thoroughly, through a detailed document consisting of 21 pages. This apparently led to some raised eyebrows in the bureaucracy.

TOWARDS THE SPLIT (2013–2018)

The decision was seen as being driven mainly by political considerations. One of the bureaucrats in the ministry had this to say:

> You know how much money it was? 650,000 NOK. It is peanuts. Every year, we disburse millions and millions to all kinds of organisations and causes. But we spent huge amounts of time dealing with this. I would assume 20 man-years in total. Not only here, but in lots of departments and ministries. It was a huge undertaking. Everything needs to be totally vetted you know. We send it to someone over at that section; they send it back; we send it back to them again, and so forth. We needed to be completely sure that we had covered every angle so we would not be in danger of a getting a court ruling against us. An enormous amount of resources was spent – just to be able to stop the funding a few months early.
>
> OE: Why was it important to stop it in the middle of the year, instead of just stopping it next year?
>
> It was political. Around that time, the negative atmosphere against the IRN was fairly massive, in the media and among politicians. It was probably quite difficult for the government to be seen as continuing to give money to the IRN.
>
> Interview with H, 2017–2019

When this happened, it was 'game over' for the IRN organisation in the form it had had for the past years, with a paid secretary-general, a part-time office administrator, a burgeoning halal franchise with two full-time employees, all located at a centrally located office. Key actors in the IRN decided to continue the organisation, but they had to do it without any paid employees, without an office of their own, and without a halal franchise.

5.6 Unstable External Institutionalisation and the New Organisation

The mosques who broke with the IRN announced around the same time – at the end of October – that they would form a new organisation, called *Muslimsk dialognettverk* – "Muslim dialogue network", or *MDN* as it would be called colloquially (Kvamme 2017). This was an organisation that consisted of the five mosques which had broken away from the IRN – Rabita, ICC, the Moroccan Mosque Centre Rahma, the Bosnian mosque, and the Albanian mosque. This constellation of mosques gave MDN a clear theological and ethnic profile: It consisted of the post-Islamists in Rabita and ICC, a profile which also found sympathy in the Moroccan Rahma-mosque, and of the two mosques in Norway that hailed from the Balkans. The numerically largest groups of Muslims in Norway – Somalis and Barelwi Pakistanis, as well as the Shia – were absent.

In the first interview that representatives of the new organisation gave to the press, they spoke about the need to "regain the trust" of actors in society at large. When asked if they would work with halal certification, Arshad Jamil from ICC said this:

> For our part, the dialogue work is most important, and then we'll see what the future brings. Right now, there is a vacuum we are trying to fill. We need to regain the trust of society and actors in society, and we have a big job to do.
>
> KVAMME 2017

There were many signs that this new organisation was immediately met with goodwill from important actors in society. The leader of STL, Ingrid Rosendorf Joys, and the general secretary of the MKR, Berit Hagøy Agen, both welcomed the organisation (Kvamme 2017). Right before Christmas, it was also announced that the new organisation would receive some of the funding that had been taken away from the IRN (Brandvold 2017a).

During the following year, the MDN held a relatively low profile. In March 2018, MDN was also taken up in STL as a member. In October, it was announced that MDN would formally start receiving state funding on an ongoing basis, as had the IRN previously (NTB 2018). This meant that MDN had all but replaced the IRN in all the ways that mattered to society at large: It had taken its place in STL; it was receiving the funding from the state that IRN had previously received, and it was consulted by journalists and policy makers on various issues.

This was by all accounts a conscious strategy from the organisation, as Arshad Jamil had said in the first media interview. They saw it as their job to regain the trust of mainstream society. This was also reflected in their first large undertaking, which was a "Dialogue conference" which took place on 28 January 2019 (MDN 2019). This conference was by invitation only, and was attended by a large number of influential policymakers, dialogue partners from the church and STL, journalists, etc. The first session was called "Dialogue – a necessity in 2019?" (MDN 2019). Both in content and format, this conference signalled what the MDN saw as their most important job – to create ties with influential actors in mainstream society and become a trusted partner. This was a break with the direction that the IRN had pursued since 2011.

An important institutional feature which made the option of breaking out more attractive was the unstable institutionalisation in the external environment of the IRN. The most common way of conceptualising the incorporation of interest groups like the IRN in Norway and Scandinavia is by referring to it as a neo-corporatist arrangement – where representative interest groups get a formal seat at the table, in exchange for moderation and displays of societal responsibility. This term was the one Laurence employed in his study of Muslim councils in Europe (Laurence 2012). Neo-corporatism has been distinguished from pluralist arrangements, where interest groups do not get formal seats at the table but have to compete with each other over influence. Pluralist arrangements are often more unstable than corporatist arrangements: There is no guarantee that one will be heard, get funding or have a seat at the table.

In some ways, the public funding of IRN was clearly neo-corporatist: The authorities chose IRN as a partner and gave it funding. At the same time, several scholars have noted that Norway has grown less corporatist in the last couple of decades, and some have proposed that neo-pluralism is a more fitting descriptor than neo-corporatism (Rommetvedt 2005). A central venue for interest group influence of Norwegian policy has traditionally been temporary advisory commissions, for example, which examine major policy issues and provide advice about solutions. In the words of Johan Christensen and Cathrine Holst, "advisory commissions have played a particularly vital role in the formulation of public policy [in the Nordic countries], to the point that they have been described as a core element of the consensual Nordic model of government" (Christensen and Holst 2017, 1). But when it comes to the actual composition of such advisory commissions, there has been a "marked rise in the participation of academics over time and a stable or declining representation of interest groups" (Christensen and Hesstvedt 2019, 91) This may be an indication that interest groups have less corporatist influence over Norwegian policymaking now than they had in the past. Rommetvedt et al. have proposed that interest groups in the Nordic countries have begun to engage in lobbying rather than representation. Interest groups do not necessarily have a formal seat at the table, but they attempt to influence politics informally through lobbying and influencing members of parliament (Christiansen and Rommetvedt 1999; Rommetvedt et al. 2013) A recent analysis by Daniel Arnesen has indicated that this development may not actually have weakened the influence of interest organisations per se, but has favoured the interest organisations that are most organised and resourceful (D. Arnesen 2019, 49).

Restricting ourselves to the kind of sector in which the IRN operated – religion and multicultural society – it may be argued that what can be seen in Norway is a hybrid between corporatism and pluralism. We may label it as a pluralist corporatism: it is a type of corporatism with pronounced pluralist traits. Organisations are funded by the state and meet clear expectations associated with this funding. They also get a certain standing due to this funding, and are therefore invited to participate in public events; they may be asked to make statements to the media, etc. For faith communities and congregations, this funding is mandating by law and not subject to political whims. But for other kinds of religious organisations – umbrella organisations like the MKR or STL, or religious organisations which are not tied to a congregation – funding or representation is far from guaranteed. These organisations are not given any formal representation in the policy-process, and have to compete for influence and power. Furthermore, their standing is not necessarily dependent on democratic representation – that they represent certain constituencies – but rather on their broader reputation in society. The result is that the state funds and incorporates a number of groups that compete with one other for standing and influence. This is different from how corporatism in Norway functions on the labour market, for example. Labour and employer unions play roles in society that are tightly regulated by both laws and convention, and representativeness is paramount. On the multicultural and religious field, however, influence and representation is more fluid.

To the best of my knowledge, this development has not been described in detail elsewhere, but it is in line with research from other countries (Laurent et al. 2020). How this has played out can be seen in the development of the Norwegian multicultural NGO field during the 1990s, 2000s and the 2010s. During this period, when questions having to do with Islam and integration became increasingly politicized, the government started to fund particular organisations working on integration issues. In the early phase, this funding went to associations of a more or less multiculturalist orientation: The Norwegian Centre against Racism, and The Organisation against Public Discrimination. In the early 2000s, as a part of a deal with the far-right Progress Party, the government also began to fund the far-right anti-Islamic NGO Human Rights Service. In the 2010s, the focus began to shift once again. Now, the authorities began to fund organisations consisting of people of a Muslim or migrant background, who wanted to reform their own communities. Examples include the think tank Minotenk, the anti-radicalisation organisation Just Unity, the organisation for secular Muslims LIM, and finally an organisation that worked against the honour culture and social control, Born Free. All of these organisations became formal or informal advisors to the authorities, politicians or public bodies at various periods. But given that they were funded via goodwill – and their funding could be taken away – they also had to compete for the favour of the politicians or the bureaucrats. Some representative faith-based umbrella

TOWARDS THE SPLIT (2013–2018)

organisations also received funding during these years – STL, IRN, and the Christian Council of Norway.

For many of these organisations, reputation can be as important as representation, when it comes to gaining standing and legitimacy. In the earlier period of IRN's history, formal representation seems to have been a more important aspect in the external environment of the organisation, even though the organisation was not officially recognized by the government on a central level. The Church sought a representative partner it could deal with, as it sent out a letter to all of the mosques in Norway. Later on, some of the assignments of the organisation were formalised. In the 1990s, it got the right to comment on the content pertaining to Islam in the books that were to be used in the Norwegian public schools, just like the Jewish community got the right to comment on the content pertaining to Judaism. These were formal types of representative roles that were tied to the very fact that IRN was a representative. After some years, this arrangement was discarded, and the IRN did not retain any formal public assignments that were explicitly about its representative functions. To gain influence, the IRN had to work through informal channels – lobby, build alliances with others and be present in the media. This does not mean that representation completely lost its importance later on. The standing STL has enjoyed, for example, has to a large degree been based on the fact that it has functioned as a representative for almost all religious communities in Norway. But for key actors in IRN, ensuring a good reputation was nevertheless seen as crucial.

When a faction in IRN decided to leave the organisation, they did so with the knowledge that they would have the full support of powerful players in Norwegian society. The reason was that they knew that their new organisation would be met with more goodwill and have a better reputation, and that this could matter more than representativeness. If the role of the IRN had been formalised and institutionalised more, and tied to its role as a representative organisation, it is doubtful that the organisation would have split in two in the same way.

CHAPTER 6

Breaking Up and Starting Over (2018–2024)

This short chapter details the most recent part of the history of the IRN, and its new competitor, the MDN. After the split, it was uncertain whether IRN would survive as an organisation. After a rough start, however, IRN managed to reestablish themselves as the major umbrella organisation for Muslims and mosques in Norway. They clarified their profile, and sought to be both an interest group for Muslims and a partner in dialogue. The MDN and IRN increasingly accepted each other's presence, and engaged in a relationship of both competition and cooperation.

6.1   Clarifying the Profile

Following the loss of funding – both from the government and from the halal certification – IRN went through a period of introspection. Throughout 2018, it was difficult for me, for the first time, to get in touch with key actors in the IRN. When I tried to contact board members about interviews, I received no response. It was later revealed that Mehtab Afsar stepped down during this year, and IRN stopped having employees. For some time, it appeared uncertain whether the IRN would in fact survive as an organisation. But during 2019, it became clear that the IRN not only survived, but envisioned a clear role for itself as the largest umbrella organisation for Norwegian Muslims and mosques, and a partner for the authorities and other organisations. A new board was elected in 2019, which decided to re-enter the public sphere and wished to continue playing a role. At some point during 2019, they also set up a new office, which was located on the premises of the Barelwi *World Islamic Mission* mosque in the *Grønland* area of downtown Oslo. The organisation also re-started their contact with MKR and the Church, and has even been contemplating re-enter the STL – even though it has not happened so far (Kruse 2019).

The new leadership of the IRN did attempt to become less combative in its rhetoric. One example was that the text on its website on the *Safe Muslim* project was revised. From 2008 and onwards, the text had only emphasized that Muslims were discriminated against, and that Muslims needed to stand together. In 2019, it was revised, and now said:

© OLAV ELGVIN, 2025 | DOI:10.1163/9789004701144_007

This is an open access chapter distributed under the terms of the CC BY-NC-ND 4.0 license.

> The Safe Muslim service [...] contributes actively so that Muslims in Norway shall feel safe everywhere, both privately and in the public space. Norway is a pioneering country in many areas, and [gender] equality, equal treatment and freedom of religion are some of those areas. But we have an important job to do on these particular areas for Norwegian Muslims.
>
> You will get this as a member of Safe Muslim:
>
> [..........]
>
> As a member of this service, you take part in strengthening IRN's role as a dialogue partner and bridgebuilder, and you give a contribution to activities for Muslims in Norway in the form of resources and economic support.
>
> IRN 2019C

In this new version, the sole focus was not only on intra-Muslim solidarity, but also on dialogue and bridge-building – and it is emphasised that all is not bleak in Norwegian society. When adopting this kind of rhetoric, IRN moved closer to the rhetoric MDN was using.

At the same time, IRN and MDN did continue to distinguish themselves from each other. IRN changed its self-description on the website in 2022. They now began calling themselves an "umbrella and interest organisation" (Islamsk Råd Norge 2022). They also began to formally accept Muslim organisations which were not mosques as full members. In this way, they continued to distinguish themselves from the smaller organisation MDN, which continued to only focus on dialogue. This was also laid down in the statutes, which were revised in 2021. The new statutes were mostly similar to the older statutes, but added that the organisation should "safeguard the interests, needs, and rights of Muslims in Norwegian society" (Islamsk Råd Norge 2021). MDN, on the other hand, adopted statutes which did not include anything about being an interest organisation, but were primarily focused on dialogue and bridge-building (Muslimsk Dialognettverk 2022). In a more recent strategy document, however, the organisation also maintained that they were a "mouthpiece" for Muslims in Norway, and that they worked for "Muslim perspectives being respected" by policy-makers (Muslimsk Dialognettverk 2024). This means that MDN also moved closer to the profile of IRN, and attempted to represent Muslim interests in addition engaging in dialogue.

One consequence of the split and IRN's initial fall from grace was that the halal certification project crumbled. For actors who did not want the IRN to have a significant source of income independent of the state, that could be seen as a positive development. But the actual consequence seems to be that key actors in IRN and some Muslim communities once again became more sceptical towards the slaughter method that is used in Norway; namely stunning prior to slaughter. When the halal certification agreement crumbled, the IRN quietly began another undertaking. The organisation set up a daughter company which began importing non-stunned halal meat from abroad, and sold it under the brand *Nawal* (Proff 2020). Presumably, this was done because the organisation wanted a new source of income. On all its products, Nawal wrote that it was "slaughtered by hand without stunning" (Matpunkt 2020). On some of its postings on social media, it used the slogan "No doubt, only enjoyment" (Nawal 2020b).

From a legal point of view, this was not controversial. Norway allows a certain quota of imported kosher and halal meat each year, and IRN has the same right as other actors to import and sell meat under this quota. But by engaging in this undertaking, and associating halal meat slaughtered in Norway with the word "doubt", IRN arguably began to undercut the theological agreement on halal slaughter it had so painstakingly worked out in 2012, and indirectly sowed doubt in the minds of Norwegian Muslims as to whether they could be sure that it was Islamically defensible to buy meat from Norwegian halal producers. Later on, however, the Nawal business undertaking seemed to stop. On its Facebook page, for example, the last posting was from June 2020 (Nawal 2020a).

A couple of years later, the IRN renewed its project of halal certification using meat slaughtered in Norway. It emerged in 2021 that the organisation had resumed its dealings with several Norwegian slaughter-houses and were again certifying stunned meat as halal (Capar 2021). But the halal certification program continued to be a source of conflict and tension. In 2024, tensions erupted once again with full force. Nortura, the largest producer of chicken in Norway, had for many years slaughtered chicken according to the halal agreement with IRN. In the fall of 2024, however, they moved their slaughtering operation to a new slaughterhouse. For various reasons, IRN did not accept that Nortura could just change to a new slaughterhouse without consulting closely with IRN (Tassamma 2024; Vogl 2024). Nortura, however, apparently did not want to involve IRN in the process. They did not see a need for external certification, and were adamant that the slaughtering process in the new slaughterhouse would be controlled even more tightly according to halal standards than previously. As a result, IRN announced rather dramatically in the summer of 2024 that there was "No more halal chicken in Norway" (Islamsk Råd Norge 2024). In that blog post, they also emphasised that their goal as an organisation was

BREAKING UP AND STARTING OVER (2018–2024)

to "defend the interests of Norwegian Muslims". Later on, they announced that they had entered into a certification agreement with a different producer of chicken. This hard-nosed way of dealing with external disagreements and conflicts bore some resemblance to how IRN had comported themselves in the years prior to the split.

But in the years following the split, IRN also renewed their status as a dialogue partner for Norwegian authorities. During the pandemic, the authorities cooperated with both MDN and IRN about reaching Muslim populations with information about the pandemic and the vaccines (Eggen 2021). The organisation also began to send input to governmental commissions, which was a way of participating in the Norwegian corporatist system of government (Islamsk Råd Norge 2023).

It thus seemed as if IRN had landed on a defined profile which distinguished them from MDN. It did not continue to be as combative and strident as it had been in the years prior to the split, and was called back into the fold as a cooperation partner for Norwegian authorities. At the same time, it had firmly defined itself as an interest organisation for Muslims, and continued to employ confrontational strategies if they thought it was needed.

6.2   Competition and Cooperation between Two Umbrella Organisations

In the years after the split, MDN and IRN operated as competitors – but increasingly in a relationship of *coopetition*, where they competed but also cooperated at the same time (Azzam and Berkowitz 2018). Following the split, there were in the beginning some rough tumbles and public rows between representatives of the organisations (Gilje 2019; IRN 2019a). But after some time, the organisations also showed an ability to cooperate. Immediately after the split, the long-established theological agreement on Eid celebration and the lunar calendar initially seemed to be in danger. In the last days before Eid ul-Fitr after Ramadan in June 2019, several mosques announced that they would not follow the IRN calendar, but rather follow the calendar in Saudi Arabia or their home country. I witnessed firsthand how this created chaos and frustration among Muslims. In an announcement on their Facebook page, the IRN defended the decision to follow the local astronomical calendar. But as the discussion revealed, many of the largest mosques in Norway decided to not follow the IRN's advice (IRN 2019b). Significantly, this included the Rabita mosque, which had previously been among the mosques which had been most vocal in creating an astronomy-based local calendar that would not be dependent on calendars in other Muslim countries. But this year, they decided not to follow the calendar they themselves had defended previously. They made this announcement only two days before Eid was supposed to take place, and announced that it would take place the following day (Det Islamske Forbundet – Rabita 2019). Many Muslims expressed deep frustration on social media. They simply were not sure when to celebrate Eid and were also frustrated that their Muslim friends celebrated Eid at different days.

Following this episode, key actors in the IRN and MDN decided to pursue a shared holiday calendar once again, according to a couple of interviewees. They set up a shared calendar committee that once again worked out a calendar agreement. This time it was accepted by almost all the mosques in Norway. The result was that Eid ul-Fitr in 2020 was celebrated on the same day (May 24th) by almost all Muslims in Norway. Significantly, the national public broadcaster NRK dedicated a separate live broadcast to the Eid-celebrations on this day, modelled on similar broadcasts that have traditionally taken place during Christmas. Most Muslims who shared their thoughts on social media were very happy about this broadcast and felt that it was a significant recognition of their faith and culture. It is difficult to imagine that the broadcast could have been done in the same way if the mosques had not been able to agree among themselves on a shared calendar for celebrating Eid.

In the coming years, there were also other cooperative projects. The most significant initiative was adopting a joint prayer schedule (Hauge, Acharki, and Bakken 2022). Previously, many mosques in Norway had followed separate prayer schedules, often based on prayer schedules originating from mosques or Islamic organisations in other countries. Following a long process, which involved theological discussions and consultations over a period of a year, IRN and MDN were able to adopt a prayer schedule which got the backing of almost all the mosques in Norway. Almost all the mosques in Norway decided to adopt this new prayer schedule. The most significant hold-out was some mosques connected to the Tablighi movement, which decided to adopt their own prayer schedule, and published a video explaining why on Youtube (Den nye IRN tabellen 2022).

The cooperation between the two umbrella organisations was not limited to internal matters among Muslims, such as the prayer schedule or the holiday calendar. In 2024, the leaders of IRN and MDN published a joint op-ed about the Gaza war in Aftenposten, Norway's newspaper of record, where they warned against dehumanization of Palestinians and genocide (Kobilica and Zubair 2024). The op-ed received much push-back from pro-Israeli actors. The publication of this op-ed was significant as a joint undertaking, as the Gaza war was heavily controversial in the Norwegian public sphere. By publishing an op-ed together, MDN and IRN sent a signal that Muslims in Norway were speaking with one voice on the issue.

The split between the two organisations thus resulted in a situation with two umbrella organisations which assumed different roles and responsibilities. In spite of their differences and the conflict that lasted for almost a decade, they did manage to put their differences to the side and cooperate on issues of common interest.

CHAPTER 7

Lessons Learned? Islamic Representation in Norway and Beyond

Why did IRN end up splitting in two? This has been the animating question of this book, and it is time to offer some answers. This chapter discusses the major findings in the book. It also provides a brief comparison with Muslim Councils in other European countries, and argues that the story of IRN and Norway does offer analytical lessons for other cases. The chapter also provides a short assessment of the larger societal consequences in Norway of the kind of representation that was achieved with IRN and later MDN.

7.1 The Consequences of Islamic Representation

This book has been mostly concerned with understanding conflicts in Muslim representative councils, through the case of Norway. But the Norwegian case is also a testament to the benefits that Muslim representation may bring. Overall, the trajectory of the IRN is in line with Jonathan Laurence's theory about the effects of corporatist incorporation of Muslim representative councils (Laurence 2012). The IRN often displayed moderation in its demands, and attempted to find what I have here called balancing solutions. Throughout most of the IRN's history, the leaders tried to advance the goals of IRN, and the goals of their member organisations, but attempted to do so in ways that would not alienate mainstream society, their partners or the authorities.

This could be seen from the very first phase, when Salman Rushdie visited Norway right before the formal formation of the organisation: Those mosques that continued to act defiantly and engaged in public protest were primarily the mosques that were not taking part in the IRN project. During the blasphemy controversy in 1995, the actor which publicised most strongly that it supported the capital punishment for the Pakistani boy was likewise a representative from an Islamist-leaning Turkish mosque that had never been part of the IRN project.

In addition, a key result of the early contact between MKR and IRN was probably that the IRN decided to throw its weight behind the public-school system, and abandoned plans to pursue Muslim private schools. It is difficult to know counter-factually what would have happened if the IRN had

---

© OLAV ELGVIN, 2025 | DOI:10.1163/9789004701144_008

This is an open access chapter distributed under the terms of the CC BY-NC-ND 4.0 license.

pursued Muslim private schools. Perhaps all such requests would have been turned down. If Muslim schools had been opened, we do not know how it would have affected social cohesion and academic results. A recent monography on Islamic private schools in France, for example, argued that several Muslim schools have achieved excellent results for their pupils, far surpassing the national average for Muslim pupils in the French public school system. The same pattern has been seen in the UK and in Sweden (Bourget 2019, chapter 3; Domes et minarets 2019; Friskolornas riksförbund 2017). Nevertheless, there is no doubt that it has been a political wish in Norway that the public-school system should be the main vehicle for education of youth. Scepticism has been voiced towards the idea of private Muslim schools, partly arising from the idea that such schools could result in less integration and lack of social cohesion. IRN thus aligned itself with an important Norwegian policy goal.

In the late 90s and early 2000s, the IRN helped to popularise and spread ideas about the possibility of being at the same time a good Muslim and a good Norwegian citizen. There were several times when Norwegian politicians publicly let it be known that they were not happy with the IRN – particularly during the controversies over FGM in 2000 and Theo van Gogh's murder in 2004. But beyond these controversies, there is little doubt that the IRN attempted to find balancing solutions aimed at finding compromise that both Muslims and the Norwegian society at large could live with. For the authorities it was arguably during the cartoon crisis in 2006 that the IRN played its most decisive role. Today, the role of the Norwegian government and the IRN during the affair has become a contested issue (for an analysis of the Norwegian discourse surrounding the events, see (Hovland 2012)). But there can be little doubt that the IRN invested a lot of effort during the affair and that this benefitted the Norwegian authorities and Norwegian society at large. The organisation sent delegations to the Middle East and Pakistan to ease tensions and act as goodwill ambassadors for Norway. If the IRN had chosen not to play this role, events would probably have unfolded differently. The IRN played similar roles later on, during similar controversies in 2010 and 2012.

Even during the final years before the split, when the IRN was generally perceived as playing a more combative role, there are indications that the organisation did try to find balancing solutions in several areas. During the protests against the *Innocence of Muslims* film in 2012, for example, IRN actively sought to diffuse the spirits by organising a large and peaceful demonstration in close collaboration with external partners in society at large. The large halal certification project also displayed a clear balancing profile. Islamic actors and mosques who had long been sceptical towards stunning animals before slaughter chose to accept theologically the Norwegian regulation of halal meat. This tendency was displayed in reverse when the IRN's halal certification agreements broke down. For a period, the organisation then reverted to the more restrictive stance that key actors in the Barelwi movement had championed prior to the halal certification project.

At the same time, the trajectory of the IRN does not adhere to all the facets of Laurence's theory. The organisation displayed a clear pattern of balancing and compromise-seeking from the earliest period, even though there was no formal recognition from the state, and no legal pressure to adapt – which Laurence indicates is important for moderation to occur. In the latter period, when they received public funding with strings attached and generally were on the receiving-end of more public pressure than previously, key actors took the organisation in a more critical and independent direction. This pattern can be interpreted in several ways. But in the Norwegian case, at least, it seems as if the mere fact of recognition and public incorporation had a moderating effect. It also seems as if the soft interventions of trusted intermediary organisations like MKR, ALIS and STL led to moderation – just as much as the stricter demands from the authorities and the media. The most recent period, where one witnessed a revised course and a split, also demonstrates that public pressure on an organisation like the IRN can result in backlash effects.

The IRN also achieved several goals during the last decades. Organisationally, it managed to achieve recognition as the official voice of mosques and Muslim communities in Norway. This, as was discussed earlier, was one of the aims it set forth in the original statutes. To a certain degree, the organisation was able to use this position to work for goals which were important for its members. Internally in the Muslim communities, the coordination of the lunar calendar in 2000 was a milestone, when IRN was among the very first national Islamic umbrella organisation to adopt a calculation method based on astronomy, which could unify Muslims. The IRN also achieved some concessions from the Norwegian authorities in terms of concrete policy measures. It was involved in projects to open up more Muslim burial grounds, which was deeply important to Muslims, even though the topic has not been covered in this thesis. The main struggle it engaged it during the 1990s and early 2000s together with its allies – on the teaching of religion in school – was crowned with victory when the European Court of Human Rights in Strasbourg ruled against the state of Norway in 2007.

Some of the most important outcomes the IRN achieved during these years were achieved indirectly, through its role in helping create organisations like ALIS and STL, and what the researcher Cora Alexa Døving referred to as a cross-cutting network of religious elites (Døving 2016). For IRN, STL led to several important outcomes. Firstly, the representation of IRN in STL constituted an early formal recognition of the IRN as the official voice of Muslims. To a certain degree, this had already happened earlier through the dialogue the IRN had with the MKR. ALIS had also been a large step towards recognition, as the IRN would cooperate with new partners, write an official response on the new school subject, and even sue the state with informal counsel from the Norwegian Humanist Association. But through STL, the IRN was officially recognized by the state early on, albeit indirectly. STL solidified and expanded the network that had come to the fore with ALIS, a network of religious leaders, where representatives of different life stance communities would become acquainted with and trust one another. The IRN itself did not have a lot of resources available, given that it was run on a voluntary basis for much of its history. But the IRN had found some important allies in STL and MKR, which may have helped the IRN and the Muslim communities it sought to represent to reach some larger goals.

How about larger effects on society? It is noteworthy that Norway unlike several other European countries did not institute many illiberal policies directed at Islam or Muslims during these years, even though the public debate was at times heated. Policy towards religious communities and congregations – including mosques – remained more or less as it had been. There were occasionally politicians who discussed banning the hijab in school, removing funding from religious congregations if it did not adhere to certain values, etc. Such policies have been instituted in several European countries. But crucially, none of these proposals ever became actual policy in Norway. Compared to most other European countries, Norway has continued to have a fairly liberal policy regarding religious minorities and congregations. Norway's neighbouring country Sweden, for example, instituted a rule in the 1990s that religious congregations needed to have 3000 members to get financial support, and were also required to uphold the "fundamental values of society" (Ekström 2011, 4–7). In Norway, nothing like this ever transpired – even though the Norwegian law on religious congregations was changed in a somewhat more restrictive direction in 2021. It is highly likely that STL played a role in ensuring that Norway maintained a liberal regulation of religious congregations, given the institutional weight and breadth of the organisation. The IRN therefore had an impact, but indirectly – through alliances with others.

It is also likely that the incorporation of the IRN in STL and other networks had effects which can be difficult to measure. When I interviewed Bente Sandvig and Lars Gunnar Lingås from the Norwegian Humanist Association (HEF), both told me that HEF had seen internal conflicts between "hardliners" and softer dialogue-oriented people, from the 90s and onwards. Whereas the hardliners wanted HEF to attack religion and what they regarded as superstition, the dialogue faction preferred to work together with other minorities on ensuring equal rights and treatment for all, irrespective of religious belief. Sandvig, who would become one of the first leaders of STL, told me that the dialogue faction had won, and that STL played a role in this process. When HEF got results through the dialogue approach in the STL, it lent weight to the arguments of the dialogue faction. Without STL and IRN's involvement in STL, it is possible that the Norwegian public sphere would have seen even more anti-religious critique or Islamophobia directed against Islam and IRN, of the type that can be seen in France or Denmark, for example (Brun and Hersh 2008; Purbrick-Thompson 2019).

In the last years before the split, the most important goal the IRN achieved was the implementation of the halal certification project. For those who supported this project, it was a milestone achievement. The project provided the IRN with valuable symbolic standing, as the arbiter of what was and what was not halal. It also drew together the IRN, Muslim businesses and Muslim customers in a tighter ecosystem. Arguably, it thereby contributed to the creation of a symbolic *ummah*, a group of Norwegian Muslims who showed solidarity with each other. This project also provided the IRN with a significant source of additional income, which was used to rent new and representative office premises. Nevertheless, this project was contested internally. And as has been detailed, this was not to last.

7.2   Causes for the Split

At the same time, there were challenges in the project of Muslim representation through IRN which caused a split, and made it work worse than it could have. The following sections contain an analytical summary of why the organisation split in two, and thus ceased being a functional representative for a number of years.

7.2.1   *Multipolarity*
The existing research on conflicts in Muslim organisations – or the lack of collective action in Muslim organisations – has often pointed to diversity, or as I have labelled it here – multipolarity (Godard 2015; Pfaff and Gill 2006; Shavit 2016; Warner and Wenner 2006). As has been shown in this book, this observation does contain some truth. But the challenge was not diversity in itself, but rather the existence of different centres of power within the Islamic field. In the most recent years the post-Islamists – Arabs, converts and Pakistanis – constituted one centre of power, and Barelwi Pakistanis constituted another.

There were other mosques and organisations which also welded influence, like the mosques which catered to the Turks, the Balkan Muslims or the Somalis.

This multipolarity was a challenge when setting up the organisation. It is important to emphasise, however, that this challenge was not insurmountable once the organisation was up and running. Once in place, the organisation was able to deal with the challenge of multipolarity, partly because one of the factions initially became dominant. The process of dealing with multipolarity also became easier when the organisation had some flexibility concerning how to work out solutions that were acceptable to the different factions of the organisation. Multipolarity did become a challenge once again, however, when the organisation started experiencing conflicts and difficulties. When new mosques and actors challenged the hegemony of the old dominant coalition, conflicts ensued. In the years that led up to the conflict, the heart of the disagreement was not about theological or ethnic divisions. But theological disagreements and divisions began to overlap with broader disagreements of strategy and approach to the authorities and society at large.

7.2.2   *Different Ways of Responding to Cross-Pressures*

There was a clear element of ideological conflict in the organisation, relating to organisational strategy and approach. This conflict cannot be reduced to a simple question of being "moderate" or "conservative". On different sides of the conflict there were people who were theological traditionalists, and people who were inclined towards reform. The ideological difference had more to do with how IRN and the Muslim community should adapt to the situation it found itself in, with cross-pressures and different expectations and demands from authorities, media, external partners, member organisations and the Islamic field in general. The proponents of the dialogue path – which included some theological traditionalists – preferred a dialogue-oriented and balancing approach, with an emphasis on building alliances with external partners. Like Margot Dazey has argued in her work on the UOIF in France, they sought *respectability* (Dazey 2021b, 2021a). The proponents of the community path, meanwhile, thought that the IRN and the Muslim communities could not rely too much on external alliances, and instead needed to build up the community internally and pursue more independence. These ideological currents were not isolated to IRN but could be found in the larger Islamic field as well.

Ever since the late 2000s, both of these lines of thought had been internally represented in IRN, and proponents of the different approaches were able to co-exist. This co-existence became more challenging once the cross-pressures on the organisation grew ever stronger. This began in the late 2000s, during the years of the "war on terror" and the controversies related to cartoons and freedom of speech. Internally, actors on the Muslim field wanted the organisation to take a tougher stand against Islamophobia and discrimination towards Muslims. But when the organisation did so in the 2010s, it was also criticised by other actors who thought that the organisation became too strident.

These intensified cross-pressures made it more difficult to arrive at balancing solutions that were acceptable to a large number of actors inside and outside the organisation. Instead, the organisation sought withdrawal and independence. This, however, led to both internal and external tension.

7.2.3 Unstable Institutionalisation

The internal conflicts in the organisation were also related to the lack of sufficient institutionalisation internally and externally. Seen in retrospect, the funding from the authorities which led to increased institutionalisation was a double-edged sword. It provided the organisation with sorely needed funds. At the same time, this increased the number of demands placed on the organisation. The financial support came with clear strings attached, as it was only directed towards external engagement, not to building up the organisation internally. Crucially, this financial support was not enshrined by law. From time to time, politicians from various parties threatened to remove this funding. This created insecurity in the organisation, where some actors thought that they could rely on the public funding, whereas others thought that they could not.

Internally, the organisation largely continued to operate in the way it had operated when it was run as a voluntary organisation. The rules for how to deal with employees was not sufficiently developed: Who had the right to fire an employee? Who could step in if there were conflicts between an employee and the board? How could one deal with conflicts between members of the board? In organisations and firms which are deeply institutionalised and stable, there are usually rules and regulations in place for different kinds of difficult situations which may arise. In the IRN, this was not the case.

7.2.4 Contingency

Lastly, we cannot escape the conclusion that the outcome in the IRN was to a certain degree contingent – meaning that it could have gone in another direction as well. There were no sociological iron laws which led to this particular outcome. In a small organisation like the IRN, differences in personality matter. If other persons had been involved, it may be that they could have worked through the differences. Ultimately, if the board had not decided to hire a woman with niqab in 2017 – since the non-niqabi Christian applicant withdrew in the last minute – it is uncertain whether some of the mosques would have broken out and formed a new organisation.

LESSONS LEARNED? ISLAMIC REPRESENTATION IN NORWAY AND BEYOND   173

We may thus propose an answer to the overall analytical question in the book, on why IRN split into two. The cross-pressures the organisation was under became more intense in the 2010s, and led to competing strategies of focusing on either dialogue or community building. Coupled with the multipolarity on the Islamic scene in Norway, this made it more difficult to arrive at compromises in the organisation that were acceptable to all. At the same time, the specific persons who were involved clearly played a role for the outcome. Given the low level of institutionalisation both inside and outside the IRN, it was difficult to solve the conflicts once they had erupted.

Were these factors unique to Norway? That will be discussed in the next and final section, where I compare the outcome in Norway with outcomes in other countries.

7.3 Comparative Outlook: Muslim Councils in Other Countries and the Case of Norway

Does the Norwegian story offer insights which may be of value for the study of Muslim countries as well? And can we understand the Norwegian case even better by looking at the trajectory of Muslim councils in other countries? Muslim councils of various types differ a lot from each other across Europe, as was described briefly in the second chapter. Some have been created by the state, some have been created by Muslim organisations themselves, and others have been created as a result of a double search for representation. Some of these councils are recognised as official partners of the state or the authorities, others are independent. Some are democratic, others are not. Nevertheless, I do believe that several of the social conditions that were important for the IRN also mattered in other countries – both when it comes to the creation of the councils, and how they functioned afterwards.

The shadow cases I will cover come from France, Germany, the UK and Austria. The reason for choosing these countries as comparative cases is that they offer much variation in the make-up of the Muslim councils in these countries – they are "most different systems", in a way (Anckar 2008). If there are similar patterns at work across these cases, it is an argument for the larger generalisability of the patterns I identified in Norway.

7.3.1 *France*

The Muslim Councils in France are among the most well-studied Muslim Councils in Europe (Bayrakli, Hafez, and Faytre 2018; Bruce 2018; Ciciora 2018; Godard 2015; Laurence 2012; Laurence and Vaisse 2007). In France, the nationally designated Muslim council was for many years the Conseil Français du

Culte Musulman (CFCM), created in 2003. It has been the subject of several studies (Bayrakli, Hafez, and Faytre 2018; Bruce 2018; Ciciora 2018; Godard 2015; Laurence 2005, 2012; Laurence and Vaisse 2007). The story of the CFCM, however, has been conflict-ridden from the very beginning. CFCM was created as a kind of federation between the various factions in French Islam – Algerian, Moroccan, Turkish, and post-Islamist. Only five years after the creation of the organisation, the Algerian faction in the CFCM decided to boycott the elections for the board of the CFCM in 2008. Three years later, in 2011, they re-joined the elections. In 2013 it was the UOIF – the largest Islamic federation in France – that decided to boycott the elections. In 2015, the future of the CFCM was thrown into doubt when the government wanted to create an additional consultative body for Islam in France, in which many Islamic currents and organisations could be represented, for annual dialogue meetings with the French authorities (Guénois 2015). Later, in late 2018, a large group of Muslim intellectuals, imams and activists decided to launch a new organisation, the *AMIF – l'Association musulmane pour l'Islam de France* (Ben Rouma 2018; Hoffner 2019). Formally launched in April 2019, the organisation wanted to take on the role of being the main institution for Muslims and France – and a direct reason was that the state seemed to disengage from CFCM (Piser 2019). As if the challenge from AMIF was not enough, CFCM was also challenged from the grassroots, by an initiative from the anti-Islamophobia activist Marwan Muhammad, who joined up with several influential activists on the French Islamic scene. They launched the organisation L.E.S. Musulmans in 2018, and later on an association for imams in 2019, which aimed at being a democratic organisation for French Muslims – and not state-dependent like the AMIF or the CFCM (Le Priol 2019).

In 2020 and 2021 a new conflict erupted in the CFCM. The French state demanded that the CFCM and its member organisations should sign a charter where they adhered to certain points and principles. Some of the organisations refused, and deep conflict ensued (Sifaoui 2020). In 2022 the leader of the CFCM voluntarily took the initiative to disband the organisation, after prolonged conflicts during 2021 and mixed signals form the French authorities (AFP 2022). In early 2022 the French state gave what seemed like a death blow to the CFCM, as they announced the creation of a new kind of representative and consultative institution for Islam and Muslims in France (Morrow 2022). The organisation still exists, however, even though it is unclear how representative the organisation is.

In the French case, all of the analytical conditions I identified in Norway also seem to be a play. Multipolarity mattered: Many of the conflicts seem to have been between different factions, which had different national and theological orientations and belongings. Such disagreements clearly mattered in the conflicts in the early years, which has been attributed to struggles over influence and power in the organisation (Godard 2015). But crucially, also in France there seems to have been challenges with external institutionalisation. Externally, the state sent mixed signals – did it trust the CFCM as a cooperating partner or not? These mixed signals probably affected the creation of the AMIF – as an alternative to the CFCM – in 2018. The issue of cross-pressures and how to respond to them also mattered. The conflict in the 2020s was largely about how to respond to cross-pressures from their own communities and the state. Should the CFCM go along with the requirement to sign the charter the state wanted them to sign, or not? Different strategies appeared, just like in Norway. Some wanted to go along, some did not. And from the grassroots the L.E.S. Musulmans initiative arose, which was an attempt to represent Muslims in a more democratic, assertive and bottom-up way.

7.3.2 *Austria*

We then turn to Austria. In this country, the official council has been set up in a way which is different from both Norway and France, which is interesting for analytic reasons. The Muslim council in Austria is probably the most institutionalised such council in Western Europe, with several important representative functions which are enshrined in the law. But even this organization has experienced deep conflicts in recent years. Austria has a longer history of accommodation of Islam than other Western European countries, due to the continuities between the modern Austrian state and the multi-ethnic Austro-Hungarian empire before WWII (Sezgin 2018, 4–7). In the late 19th century, the Austro-Hungarian empire ruled over a large number of Muslim subjects in Bosnia-Herzegovina. In 1912, the empire instituted the "Islam law", which formally recognized Islam and Muslims as equals before the law, and extended to Muslims the rights that had been given to Christian denominations. When the Austro-Hungarian empire broke down after the WWI, the number of Muslims under Austrian jurisdiction became diminutive, and the legal statutes concerning Islam became dormant. This began to change in the 60s, when Austria started receiving Muslim labor migrants. In the 1970s, Muslim organisations and activists started to seek recognition, and wished to reignite the Islam law from 1912 (Mattes and Rosenberger 2015, 134). They succeeded in doing this in 1979. One part of the new Islam policy was empowering a national IRC, the *Islamische Glaubensgemeinschaft in Österreich* – the IGGÖ.

The IGGÖ was set up as a democratic federation of Islamic organisations, with rather complex election rules. Those who vote in the internal elections are individuals, not organisations, but they vote *through* their member organisations, according to a system which also attempts to create a balance between different ethnic groups and denominations. The IGGÖ received important public assignments. One of the most important ones being tasked with creating curriculums and providing diplomas for teachers who wish to teach Islam in the public school (Mattes and Rosenberger 2015, 134).

Existing research indicates that the IGGÖ was relatively stable for a good number of years. There were some conflicts and disagreements, but they played out within the organisation in a peaceful manner (Heine, Lohlker et al. 2012, 55–64). This changed during the 2010s. In late 2018, the young chairman of the IGGÖ, 30-year-old Ibrahim Olgun, was forced to step down after an intensive public dispute. The *Schura council*, which elects the board of the organisation, decided that all the leadership positions in the organisation needed to be filled anew, and called for an extraordinary extra election (Kocina 2018). Elections were held on December 8th. Ümit Vural was elected as the new president (Simsek 2018). This was about more than individual persons: Olgun belonged to ATIB, which is connected to the Turkish state-led Diyanet. Vural belonged to the *Islamische Föderation*, which is connected to the post-Islamist Turkish organisation Milli Görus.

The Austrian press reported that this conflict was related to two developments in the IGGÖ. One development had to do with the response of the organisation to the new Islam law that was instituted in 2015. Throughout the 2000s, the far-right FPÖ party became increasingly influential in Austria, and managed to get the Christan-Conservative ÖVP to take hardline stances with regards to migration, Islam and Muslims (Sezgin 2018, 13–14). This culminated with the new *Islam law* from 2015. Ostensibly an effort to create a more national form of Islam, it forbade mosques and Islamic organisations from receiving any funding from abroad – while not placing similar demands on Jewish or Christian denominations. Until 2018, the new law was not applied (Sezgin 2018, 15). But in the summer of 2018 the Austrian government closed down seven mosques because of accusations about foreign funding, even though they were eventually reopened. The IGGÖ president Ibrahim Olgun was accused by internal critics of cooperating with the government about this, and that he had used it as a pretext to close down mosques which were critical of him. Olgun responded that he only did what he was legally obliged to do. When looking at the case, it does indeed look somewhat curious that a disproportionate number of the mosques which were closed down were Arabic-speaking, and were run by people who had been critical of Olgun (Kurier 2018). Whatever the motivation of Olgun might have been, this created a backlash against him in the organisation, and led the *Shura Council* to demand new elections and a new leadership.

Another issue at play seems to have been rivalry between different Islamic federations (Kurier 2018). According to reports in the Austrian press, the IGGÖ had witnessed several internal conflicts. Arab-dominated organisations were reportedly in conflict with Turkish-dominated organisations. There were also reports about a conflict between ATIB, the state-led Turkish Islamic federation, and the *Islamische Föderation*, dominated by the post-Islamist Milli Görus. Some commentators noted that the Turkish organisations had been relatively absent from the IGGÖ until 2009/2010, but had played a larger in the organisation since then, which seemingly led to tensions (Kocina 2018). This conflict seems also to have been related to a new internal politicization and democratization of the IGGÖ. Partly as a result of political criticism about being conservative and not sufficiently representative of Muslims in Austria, the IGGÖ had adopted a new constitution in 2010, which included new election rules. The old election system had not been strictly majoritarian, but had tried to balance the interests of the different groups among Austria's Muslims. The new election system was more majoritarian, where the individual vote was more important. This seems to have led to a sharpened competition among Austria's Muslim groups over power in the IGGÖ.

The case of Austria and the IGGÖ thus shows that even a country with as long a history of institutionalising Islam as Austria can witness the type of deep conflicts that we have seen in other European countries. The IGGÖ did not break apart, and internal activity did not stop. But a conflict which results in the removal of the entire leadership of an organisation must nevertheless be said to be fairly encompassing.

Several of the factors which mattered in Norway seem to have mattered in IGGÖ as well. The initial reason for the conflict in the organisation was a disagreement over strategy, concerning how the organisation should respond to the cross-pressures and different demands it was facing. Should it comply with the governments demand to shut down mosques or not?

Furthermore, multipolarity clearly played a role. The Islamic field in Austria was composed of both Arab mosques and Turkish competitors, and this had an impact on relations in IGGÖ. The conflict which led Olgun to step down as leader, was also related to an internal conflict between different Turkish Islamic organisations.

But institutionalisation, both internally and externally, clearly also mattered. Up until 2010, it appears as if the different streams of Austrian Islam had found a way of dealing with their disagreements through the IGGÖ. But when they were made to change their decision-making system due to external pressure, this upended the balance of power in the organisation and laid the seed for new conflicts.

But still, the organisation did not break apart. One reason for this may be the corporatist arrangement the IGGÖ was tied to, with a much stronger external institutionalisation than in Norway or France. IGGÖ's role and public assignments were determined by law. If anybody wanted to break out, they would not be able to take on a similar role, even if they secured a better reputation. This differs from the situation in France and Norway, where the Muslim Councils did not have any legally defined roles, and different factions in the organisation could in principle be able to secure the government's favor if they broke out.

7.3.3 *Germany*

Another well-studied case of Muslim councils is Germany (Aguilar 2018; Amir-Moazami 2011; Bruce 2018; Laurence 2012; Loobuyck, Debeer, and Meier 2013; Rosenow-Williams 2012, 2014). Germany currently has two organisations which can be labelled as Muslim councils. The state-sanctioned council is The German Islam Conference – *Deutsche Islam Konferenz* (DIK). It was created by the German interior minister Wolfgang Schäuble in 2006, as the official representative of Muslims in Germany. Unlike the French CFCM which was founded a few years earlier, it never pretended to be a democratic council or umbrella organisation, where the seats on the board were up for election. It still aspired to be representative of Muslims in Germany. Fifteen of the seats were given to Muslim representatives, and 15 seats to representatives of the state. Only 5 of the Muslim seats were given to the largest member-based Islamic federations and umbrella organisations. As in France, several of the large federations have a national or ethnic character. The *DITIB* has close ties to the religious ministry of Turkey, like the French branch of the organisation. The *Islamrat* (IRD) is also mainly Turkish and is dominated by the Islamist/post-Islamist Milli Görus. The *Verband der Islamischen Kulturzentren* (VIKZ) is Turkish as well and associated with the Turkish Sufi-oriented Süleymanci-movement. The *Alevitische Gemeinde Deutschlands* (AABF) also has a Turkish character and organises persons of Turkish descent who belong to the Alevi community, a heterodox Muslim group which is not recognized as Muslims by all orthodox Muslim groups. The *Zentralrat der Muslime in Deutschland* (ZMD) is the only large federation that is truly multi-ethnic and multi-national and is dominated by post-Islamist Arabs and German converts. The other ten Muslim seats were given to "independent" Muslim individuals – activists, researchers and intellectuals – who were assumed to represent the non-organised Muslims in Germany (Bruce 2018, 137).

The pressure from the government in the DIK was instrumental in creating another umbrella organisation for the member-based Islamic federations in 2007: *The Koordinationsrat der Muslime in Deutschland* (KRM). The Islamic federations wanted to resist what they perceived as a policy of divide and rule – that the German authorities seemingly were happy to play the Islamic federations against each other when it suited them (Rosenow-Williams 2012, 360). The KRM was an umbrella organisation for the four largest federations – DITIB, ZMD, IRD and VIKZ – but it did not include the Alevis. The reason for the exclusion of the Alevis appears to be related to theology and the historical relationship between Alevis and Sunnis in Turkey, and scepticism about the Islamic credentials of the Alevis (Gorzewski 2010, ch. 6; Rosenow-Williams 2012, 345).

Both of these organisations have experienced several conflicts, and several of the factors that could be identified in the Norwegian case have played a role. For the DIK, lack of external institutionalisation and stability mattered. At the end of the first phase of the DIK – the consultations between the state representatives and the Muslim representatives – a final declaration was issued. The declaration bore the heavy mark of the state. It did not take a clear stand against Islamophobia, and it did not recommend that Islamic communities should be legally recognized by the state on a similar footing as Christian and Jewish congregations. As a result, the Milli Görus-dominated *Islamrat* refused to sign the declaration. Partially as a result of this, they were not invited by the state to participate in the next phase of the DIK. In solidarity, the multi-ethnic *Zentralrat* (ZMD) also refused to participate further in the DIK. The strident policy of the German authorities thus destabilised the very organisational structure it had created. According to a central interviewee of Bruce (2018, 140) there was even a danger that DITIB, the largest Islamic federation, was going to withdraw from the DIK process after the completion of the first phase. This would effectively have finished the entire DIK project. What the German authorities did when they sensed this danger was to engage the Turkish state directly. Even if it does not want to acknowledge it openly, DITIB is controlled by Diyanet, the official Turkish "state church". When the Turkish state put pressure on DITIB in Germany to stay in the DIK, it did decide to stay put. External meddling thus destabilised the organisation – but also stabilised it again. Following this episode, the state invited in other federations, and from 2014 onwards the DIK seems to have been able to function in a somewhat stable manner. Increasingly, however, it does not have any pretence of being a representative organisation, but is presented more as an arena for discussion on Islam in Germany.

KRM also experienced conflicts. But given that KRM was fully independent from both German and Turkish authorities, the challenges seem different – internal multipolarity seems to have been the most pronounced problems. The original goal of the KRM was to create a democratic and representative organisation, with regional branches, in which all the mosques in Germany could be represented (Rosenow-Williams 2012, 367). But DITIB – the largest Islamic federation – soon decided against this, probably because they feared losing influence. This led to internal disenchantment with the KRM, and insecurity about the role the KRM could play in the future. In the years to come, the role of the KRM therefore became more limited than envisioned, and the organisation does not seem to have played any important role for several years. New conflicts erupted in 2016, when it came to light that imams in DITIB had worked as spies for the Turkish government against the Gülen movement, a Turkish Islamic movement which had fallen out of favour with the Erdogan government (Bruce 2018, 141). This led to souring of the relations between the main Islamic federations, as well as between the Islamic federations and the state. According to media reports from the 2010s, activity in the KRM also suffered during this period (Arens 2016).

It nevertheless appears that the KRM managed to get through these difficulties. In 2019, it was announced that the KRM would take up several new members, organisations representing both Albanian and Moroccan mosques in Germany, which would make them the representative of around a fourth of Germany's Muslims (KNA 2019). It was also announced that it would open up local branches in different parts of Germany (IslamiQ 2019). This had been on the agenda in the early phase of the organisation, but was then turned down, as the DITIB feared that they would lose power as a result. But in 2019, it did seem to come to fruition, and the KRM thus seemed to be able to finally become a functioning organisation. In the 2020s, the organisation increasingly took on representative roles. Representatives from the organisation engaged in inter-religious dialogue with representatives from both the catholic Bishop conference in Germany, and the Evangelical church in Germany (Deutschen Bischofskonferenz 2022; EKD 2022).

In 2023, however, one of the founding members – VIKZ, representing the Süleymanci movement – announced that it was leaving the organisation (KNA 2023). There were no newspapers reports which hinted towards underlying conflicts. The issue seems to have been that VIKZ wanted to be completely independent, and not be bound by statements that the KRM was making. In a sense, then, the leaving of VIKZ may be connected to the fact that KRM was facing external pressure and cross-pressures, and sometimes had to take stances on controversial issues. But the fact that this organisation left did not lead to a larger conflict in the organization.

In the German case as well, then, we see the importance of both multipolarity, institutionalisation, and cross-pressures. The fact that KRM was riddled with conflict early on, but later managed to become a functioning organisation, may indicate that its independence from the state provided it with a level of institutional and organisational stability: It could decide for itself how to act and how to respond to external pressure, without having to rely partly on the state and partly on its members. That may have been a reason why the leaving of VIKZ seemingly happened peacefully and orderly, without threatening stability in the organisation as such. In order to know whether this was indeed the case, empirical research on the organisation would have to be conducted.

7.3.4   *The UK*

Taking a look at the British case – the third European state with a Muslim population numbering in the millions, alongside France and Germany – also shows us two different Muslim councils, with very different trajectories. One – the MCB – is marked by low acceptance from the authorities, but also a high level of stability and internal institutionalisation. The other – the MINAB – was marked by high acceptance from the authorities, but also a low level of stability and internal institutionalisation.

The Muslim Council of Britain was created in 1997. Even though the MCB does not have an official status as a mouthpiece for Muslims or mosques in Great Britain, it nevertheless enjoys an unofficial status as the most important Islamic umbrella organisation. The MCB grew out of an organisation that came into being during the Rushdie affair – the *UK Action Committee on Islamic Affairs* (UKACIA) (McLoughlin 2005, 88–89). In 1994, they received political signals that indicated to them that they would have a better chance of being heard if they were able to unite. Michael Howard, the conservative home secretary, called on them to get together and speak with one voice (McLoughlin 2005, 89). UKACIA activists were quick to respond. After extensive consultation with over 1000 Muslim organisations, the MCB was formally founded in 1997. It was formed as a democratic organisation, but with a rather complex organisational structure (MCB 2011). The creation of the MCB thus has similarities with the Norwegian case. The MCB emerged as a result of a double search for representation, where both internal and external actors saw a need for stronger Muslim representation.

Even though the MCB was in principle open to all Muslim organisations and mosques in Great Britain, certain strands of Islamic activism became more influential than others. Post-Islamist or reformist-Islamist activists became particularly influential. Some other strands of Islamic activism have been underrepresented in the MCB, in particular Shia and Barelwis. A few Shia organisations are affiliates, but they were for a long time not influential in the activities of the MCB (Bowen 2014, 160). Kashmiri Sufis, who may constitute the largest group among Muslims in Great Britain, also have very few affiliates in the MCB (Seddon 2014, 226). Compared with other national Muslim councils in Europe, the membership of the MCB has been relatively homogenous.

Relations between the MCB and the authorities remained good until 2005 and the London bombing on 7/7 that same year (Braginskaia 2015, 109). This led to a general securitisation of Islam, and disagreement on how one should deal with jihadism and radicalisation. The government wanted stricter and harsher policies than did the MCB. Soon, the MCB were no longer a trusted partner for the government – and throughout the 2010s there would be no officially designated representative Muslim council.

Over the years, MCB has proved to be institutionally stable. None of the studies that have been done on either the MCB directly or the Islamic landscape in the UK more generally has revealed any large defections or splits in the MCB (McLoughlin 2005, Bowen 2014, Braginskaia 2015, Hamid 2016). This does not mean that there have been no conflicts at all. There are reports of conflicts and tensions, but none of these seem to have put the organisational unity or functioning of the MCB in danger.

The trajectory of the MCB stands in stark contrast to the trajectory of the other British Muslim council, MINAB, which currently appears dormant. When MCB fell out of favour with the British government, the authorities created a new representative council in 2006 which was closer in structure to the French CFNM and the German DIK – the *Mosques and Imams National Advisory Board* (MINAB). The goal of this board was to "promote best practice" in British mosques (MINAB N.D.). It was set up with four member organisations, each of which appointed members to the board directly. These organisations were the MCB, the Arab-dominated post-Islamist the *Muslim Association of Britain*, the Sufi-dominated *British Muslim Forum*, and the Shia *Al-Khoei foundation*. The funding of the MINAB came from the government. It did not formally launch its activities until 2009, however (Hussain and McLoughlin 2013, 689). Curiously, the MINAB displays some of the same patterns as the CFCM and the DIK. I have found two scholarly investigations of the organisation, a master's thesis at Leiden University by Zahra Shah which includes interviews with some of the main actors involved (Shah 2016), and an article by Nadiya Ali which takes a critical look at the political process surrounding the organisation (Ali 2014). According to Shah's interviewees, activity in the organisation largely broke down as a result of disagreement between the member organisations (Shah 2016, 15). At some point, the MINAB decided to relaunch. It is unclear when this relaunch occurred and who was in charge of it, but a "letter from the chairman" from the summer of 2018 indicates that they got a new board on 30 June of that year and also indicates that the MINAB organisation was envisioning a new start (MINAB 2018). Later activities seem sparse however, and there are few indications that the organisation has become robust. The webpage seems defunct, and the last post on its Facebook page is from 2022.

In the two cases in the UK, both multipolarity, institutionalisation and stability seem to have played role. In MINAB's case it was created by decree, and was to include all the different factions of British Islam. At the same time, Laurence's study shows that MINAB was facing an unstable external environment, even though he does not go into details. MINAB was set up the Labour government in 2006, but the successive conservative government "abruptly changed tack", and did not uphold its commitment to MINAB (Laurence 2012, 194). The main authority which had set up MINAB therefore disappeared from the organisation – and it had no ultimate arbiter in place which could force the different factions to work out their differences.

In the case of the MCB, its stability may have been aided by two factors: Its relative lack of internal multipolarity, and the fact that it was not dependent on the government. Given its independence it did not have to deal with competing expectations from the government and its membership, it was not destabilised by shifting political signals, and no factions had any impetus to opt out and thus secure funding and symbolic recognition – as there was no such funding or symbolic recognition available. But like with the German case, detailed studies would be needed to know whether such mechanisms were indeed at play.

7.4 Concluding Remarks: Better Models for Representing Islam and Muslims?

Does the trajectory of the IRN, and the experience from other European Muslim councils, offer any hints as to how Muslim or Islamic representation in Europe might fare even better? The trajectory of the IRN does indicate that corporatist incorporation of Muslim councils can have value, both to Muslims themselves and to society at large. How can that be achieved without conflicts and splits?

Out of the social conditions and factors that have been surveyed in this book, there are some facts of life for Muslims and society at large which are not likely to change anytime soon. The Islamic landscape in Norway and other countries in Europe will not stop being multipolar. Mosques and Muslim organisations in Europe are connected to a variety of transnational movements, states and organisations, and take different positions on important theological and social questions. The Islamic landscape will therefore stay multipolar for the foreseeable future. We must nevertheless remember that multipolarity in itself does not seem like an insurmountable challenge for a Muslim council to function well. The IRN was able to make their organisation work for many years, even though it organised a multipolar landscape with different power centres and a variety of theological orientations. The same can also be seen other places. The German KRM seem to have overcome the challenge of multipolarity and competition between member organisations, and is now able to function as a representative for a large part of the German Muslims. The same is the case in the UK: MCB holds together and seems to function well, and does an important job in coordinating and representing Muslims in Britain – even though it is not acknowledged as an official partner by the authorities.

If the condition of multipolarity is not going to change, how about cross-pressures and the related issue of competing strategies? The shadow comparison with other Muslim councils does point to some interesting patterns. The IRN was more stable in the years before it started receiving public funding and was drawn into the corporatist apparatus of the state. In Germany and the UK, it seems that those Muslim councils that operated at a distance from the state – MCB and KRM – ultimately proved more stable. One explanation for this pattern may be that these organisations have been under less intense cross-pressures than the Muslim councils who have been closer to the state. Their primary stakeholders have been their members, and they are less beholden to what representatives from the government or the authorities want them to do. This may have made it easier to find compromises that the different members could live with. Following the defence of my PhD, this was the take-away of some of those in the IRN who read the thesis. Their interpretation was that it would be easier for the IRN going forward to be completely independent – and not seek funding from the state once again. Then the organisation could have more say on what terms to engage with authorities and external actors.

But that is probably not the only option available. Looking at the Muslim council in Austria, the IGGÖ, we saw that it was stable and well-functioning for many years, even though it was closely connected to the Austrian state. Conflicts seem to have begun in earnest after 2011, when political pressure led to a restructuring of the organisational structure in the organisation. Given the lack of in-depth studies about the IGGÖ, we cannot be sure about why the organisation proved so stable. But one interpretation is that it was about stability and predictability in the conditions the organisation was facing. The rights and duties of the organisation were enshrined in the law. Its institutionalisation was stable, both internally and externally. When deep conflicts hit the organisation in the 2010s, the organisation nevertheless survived – possibly because it was so deeply institutionalised in Austrian society. This may hint that Muslim representation works better when it happens under stable conditions – be it connected to or at a distance from the state. If Muslim representation is going to work better in the years ahead, European states may be well-advised to grant Muslim councils rights and obligations which are deeply institutionalised and regulated by law, and not subject to changing political whims.

Finally, the story of the IRN is a testament to the complex effects of public and political pressure. The public and political pressure on IRN did not lead it to seek balancing solutions in the 2010s, in contrast with how it comported itself earlier when the pressure was less intense. When authorities interact with representative Muslim organisation, it may be crucial to strike a balance between demands, control and laissez-faire. To step back and let organisations undertake some actions the authorities and the public may not like in the short-term, may in the long-term ensure that Muslim councils become more representative, and that new groups over time become moulded into the logic and norms of society at large.

Appendix 1: Interview Guide

Example of interview guide (for interview with N)
First part: Introduction
Introduce myself and the project
Research ethics – you can withdraw at any time during the interview
Everything you say will be anonymized. I might ask to cite some parts by name in the thesis, but that will be fully voluntary, and if you say no I will fully respect that.
Do you have any questions before we proceed?
Second part: Warming up and generally about IRN
Ok, just to start, say a little bit about yourself (occupation, age, family, etc)
Ask more about mosque background if it is not already covered.
The topic of this interview is IRN. When did you become involved in that organisation? How did it happen? Why did you become involved?
You were involved in IRN from (year) to (year). When you think about that period now, what is the first thing that springs to your mind?
When you think about your time in IRN, was there anything which surprised you? Were there things you did not expect would be like that, before joining the organisation?
(follow up on any leads)
Third part: Specific questions
I heard that you were involved with (a certain project in IRN). Can you tell me a bit more about that?
During that project, were there any disagreements on the board about how you should proceed?
This might be a bit sensitive, but I heard that there was a conflict with (person B) during (year X). Could you say a bit about that?
IRN has cooperated with many external organisations during the years. How do you think this cooperation has worked?
(follow up on the leads and ask follow-up questions)
Wrapping it up
Ok, we're almost finished here, thank you so much. This has been very useful. Is there anything you would like to say we haven't spoken about?
... ok, that's interesting. Can you expand a bit?
Thank you!
(tell about the process with the thesis going forward. You can always contact me)

© OLAV ELGVIN, 2025 | DOI:10.1163/9789004701144_009

This is an open access chapter distributed under the terms of the CC BY-NC-ND 4.0 license.

Appendix 2: Persons Interviewed in Depth for This Project

Yasir Ahmed, 17.04.2019
Asghar Ali, 25.04.2019
Mehtab Afsar, 22.09.2017, 08.10.2017
Mohamed Bouras, 20.01.2018
Åse Brandvold, 12.05.2017
Abdelmounim Elamin, 17.04.2019
Bård Folke Fredriksen, 17.09.2018
Basim Ghozlan, 12.01.2018
Berit Agøy Hagen, 10.09.2019
Smaira Iqbal, 17.04.2019
Arshad Jamil, 16.04.2019, 12.02.2023
Ingrid Rosendorf Joys, 01.04.2018
Senaid Kobilica, 21.10.2019
Lena Larsen, 22.01.2018
Oddbjørn Leirvik, 19.01.2018
Marius Linge, 15.03.2017
Trond Ali Linstad, 10.05.2018
Lars Gunnar Lingås, 03.05.2019
Zahid Mukhtar, 24.10.2018
Irfan Mushtaq, 30.11.2018, 03.05.2019
Imran Mushtaq, 22.04.2017; 12.05.2020
Bente Sandvig, 20.05.2019
Zaeem Shaukat, 14.11.2019
Anne Sender, 01.04.2018
Maryam Trine Skogen, 05.04.2017
Shoaib Sultan, 05.06.2017, 12.09.2019
Olav Fykse Tveit, 24.08.2018
Bureaucrat 1 in the ministry of culture and religion, 18.01.2018
Bureaucrat 2 in the ministry of culture and religion, 18.01.2018
These interviewees were given following codes in order to be quoted anonymously (not all of them have been quoted in the thesis though):
A, B, C, D, E, F, G, H, I, J, K, L, M, N, O, P, Q, R, S, T, U, V, W, X, Y, Z, X2, Y2, Z2

© OLAV ELGVIN, 2025 | DOI:10.1163/9789004701144_010

This is an open access chapter distributed under the terms of the CC BY-NC-ND 4.0 license.

Appendix 3: Key Written Sources

The website and Facebook page of the IRN can be found at www.irn.no and https://www.facebook.com/islamskraadnorge/?locale=nb_NO. Earlier pages and blog posts which have now been deleted can often be found with the help of the Wayback Machine, http://web.archive.org.

The Norwegian media archive, Atekst, can be found here: https://www.retriever group.com/no/product-mediearkivet-atekst. This is a searchable archive of almost all Norwegian media outlets going back to 1945, with a few exceptions like the business newspaper Dagens Næringsliv.

Private archives: Oddbjørn Leirvik's archive is in his personal possession. Bente Sandvig's archive is in her personal possession.

I reproduce below a key written source from the IRN – the various iterations of the statutes These sources are reproduced in the original Norwegian language. Even though the majority of the sources I have used for this book are not publicly available, the fundamental development of the organization can be seen in how these statutes have developed over the years. I also include the statutes of MDN, as their statutes documents how their profile differs from IRN's.

© OLAV ELGVIN, 2025 | DOI:10.1163/9789004701144_011

This is an open access chapter distributed under the terms of the CC BY-NC-ND 4.0 license.

APPENDIX 3: KEY WRITTEN SOURCES

IRN's first statutes from 1993

Statutter for Islamsk Råd Norge

§ 1   Grunnbestemmelser, navn

1.1   *Riksorganisasjonens fulle navn er:*

Norsk: *Islamsk Råd Norge*
Engelsk: *Islamic Council Norway*
Arabisk:

1.2   *Islamsk Råd Norge, i forkortelsen IRN, er en Islamsk landsdekkende paraplyorganisasjon bestående av Islamske menigheter og foreninger som er virksomme i Norge og har fått innpass i IRN.*

1.3   *IRN er en parti-politisk uavhengig organisasjon.*

1.4   *IRN har ingen som helst rett til å vedta beslutninger som strider med Al-Quran og Sunnah.*

1.5   *IRN er en ideel, religiøs og demokratisk organisasjon i den grad denne distinksjon kan overføres til et samfunn og er i samsvar med Norges lover.*

1.6   *IRN har sitt hovedsete i Oslo.*

1.7   *IRN's offisielle språk er Norsk.*

1.8   *IRN koordinerer medlemsforeningenes arbeid og representerer dem overfor myndighetene, organisasjoner, og institusjoner i Norge og utlandet i samsvar med statuttene.*

1.9   *IRN's statutter begrenser ikke medlemsforeningenes suvernitet og selvstendighet i arbeidet, og foreningene kan, innenfor rammene av statuttene, selvstendig arbeide og opprettholde kontakter med myndigheter, organisasjoner i Norge og i utlandet. En enkelt forening kan også føre sin egen som ikke strider med IRN's retningslinjer.*

§ 2   Definisjoner

2.1   *En __muslim__ defineres som en som offentlig bekjenner den Islamske Trosbekjennelsen Ash-Shahadat og som tror på endeligheten av Mohammed's (fred være med ham) Profetskap. Videre skal en muslim godta det Guddommelige Budskapet Al-Quranen mottat av Profeten Mohammed (fred være med ham) i dens helhet sammen med Profetens (fred være med ham) lære Sunnah.*

APPENDIX 3: KEY WRITTEN SOURCES

§ 3   Målsettinger

3.1   *Å forene alle muslimer boende i Norge til et Islamsk samhold.*

3.2   *Å fremme, beskytte, bevare og forsterke vår Islamske identitet.*

3.3   *Å skape ytre forhold som gjør det mulig for muslimer å leve i samsvar med Islamsk lære.*

3.4   *Å spre kunnskap om Islam i Norge ved informasjonsvirksomhet.*

3.5   *Å møte og besvare alle angrep mot Islam slik som forvrengelser/propaganda eller vanskeliggjøringer av den muslimske kultur og levesett.*

3.6   *Å streve for å styrke solidaritets og brorskapsbåndene med den muslimske verdens Ummah.*

3.7   *Å bevare Al-Quran's språk og dens nøkkelposisjon som det fremste middelet for å bevare det muslimske religiøse, kulturelle og politiske enhet ved å tilby alle muslimer i Norge muligheten til å kunne tilkjenne seg grunnleggende kunnskaper i arabisk.*

3.8   *Å gi alle muslimske barn i Norge en grundig utdannelse i Islamsk tro, lære, historie og kultur.*

§ 4   Virksomhet

4.1   *- Organisere og opprettholde ett sentralt kontor for informasjon og samordning av aktiviteter foreninger imellom.*

4.2   *- Representere Norges muslimske foreninger overfor norske myndigheter og institusjoner.*

4.3   *- Å være muslimenes offisielle talerør overfor den norske regjeringen.*

4.4   *- Representere IRN's medlemsforeninger i internasjonale sammenheng, dvs. konferanser, seminarer og sammenkomster som berører muslimenes interesser i Norge eller har betydning for Islam i den videre bemerkelse.*

4.5   *- Arrangere felles kulturelle aktiviteter som seminarer, konferanser, forelesninger ol.*

4.6   *- Hjelpe og gi råd til medlemsforeningene.*

4.7   *- Drive felles proskjekter i foreningenes regning eller på oppdrag av dem.*

4.8   *- Søke og samle okonomisk bistand både innen- og utenlands under forutsetning av at disse bidrag gis uten vilkår og uten innblanding i IRN's indre anliggender.*

4.9   *- Følge med samfunnsutviklingen i Norge og gi uttrykk for sine oppfatninger og meninger, gi forslag til losninger og gjennom det, eventuelt påvirke fremtidige beslutninger, spesielt i sporsmål som berører muslimenes Islamske interesser.*

4.10   *- Være et middel som skaper gjensidig informasjon mellom det norske folket og muslimene når det gjelder deres respektive kulturhistorie, religiøsitet og andre verdier.*

§ 5 Medlemskap

Enhver Islamsk forening eller senter har rett til å ha medlemskap i IRN om den er stiftet i samsvar med følgende punkter og oppfyller følgende krav,

5.1 *Foreningen må være stiftet i samsvar med den gjeldende norske ideelle foreningsprinsipp og drive Islamske aktiviteter på ett bestemt sted.*

5.2 *Foreningens statutter må stå i overenstemmelse med IRN's egne.*

5.3 *Foreningen skal oppgi medlemsantallet sammen med søkanden om medlemskap i IRN.*

5.4 *Foreningen skal drive regelmessig Koranskole for barn og voksne. Styret kan gi dispensasjon fra dette punktet.*

5.5 *Ved ønske om medlemskap i IRN skal foreningen/senteret levere følgende handlinger til IRN's styre,*

    - søknad om medlemskap.

    - årsmøteprotokoll der det fremgår at foreningen har gjort vedtak om å søke medlemskap i IRN.

    - oversikt over foreningens aktiviteter.

    - foreningens statutter vedtatt/godkjent på siste årsmøte.

5.6 *Styret i IRN skal behandle alle søknader om medlemskap, og avslå eller bevilge midlertidig medlemskap. Den endelige beslutningen tas ved IRN's årsmøte og fra da av trer alle plikter og rettigheter fullstendig i kraft.*

5.7 *Hver medlemsforening skal betale innmeldingsavgift på 1000,- kroner og videre betale minst 600,- kr årlig medlemsavgift til IRN.*

5.8 *Foreningen har adgang til å klage på IRN styret's og IRN's årsmøte vedtak innen 30 dager fra vedtaksdato.*

5.9 *Medlemskapet i IRN opphører hvis,*

    - foreningen nedlegger/stanser sin virksomhet.

    - foreningen driver med aktiviteter som strider mot de statutter som er blitt levert til IRN eller IRN's egne statutter.

5.10 *Foreninger som bryter sine egne eller IRN's statutter kan utelukkes intermittent eller midlertidig av IRN's ledelse.*

5.11 *Definitivt utestengelse av en forening blir vedtatt på IRN's årsmøte.*

APPENDIX 3: KEY WRITTEN SOURCES

5.12 *Om det oppstår tvister eller konflikter mellom ledelse og medlemmer i en forening som er tilsluttet IRN skal tvisten først prøvd løst internt.Om det viser seg å være umulig å løse det internt skal IRN's ledelse umiddelbart opprette en komite som skal prøve å løse tvisten gjennom megling.Foreningen skal respektere og akseptere det resultatet som meglingskomiteen kommer frem til.Hvis dette ikke skjer blir foreningens status som medlem i IRN opphevet umiddelbart til foreningen gjør rett for seg.*

5.13 *Om en forening vil slutte sin medlemskap i IRN skal en skriftlig søknad fremlegges IRN ved foreningens årsmøte.IRN's årsmøte fastslår avskjeden.*

§ 6 Årsmøte

6.1 *Årsmøte er IRN's høyeste besluttende organ.*

6.2 *IRN's ordinære årsmøte holdes årlig i oktober måned på tid og sted som IRN's styre bestemmer.*

6.3 *Styret kan innkalle til ekstraordinært årsmøte ved behov.*

6.4 *På ordinære årsmøter skal følgende behandles,*

   - Deltageropprop.

   - Valg av møteleder for årsmøtet.

   - Valg av protokollfører/referatskriver for årsmøtet.

   - Valg av en kontrollmann som bestemt skal justere protokollen/referatet.

   - Ledelsens virksomhetsberettelse for det foregående år.

   - Revisjonsberettelse.

   - Bevilgning av ansvarsfrihet / mandat for ledelsen.

   - Fastslå aktivitetsplan og budsjett for kommende år.

   - Forslag.

   - Valg av formann og styremedlemmer for to års mandat.

   - Valg av revisorer for to års mandat.

   - Øvrige saker.

6.5 *Inkalling til årsmøte ordnes av IRN's ledelse pr. brev som sendes foreningene pr. post senest to uker før ordinær årsmøte og en uke for ekstra årsmøte.*

6.6 *I innkallelsen skal det oppgis hvilken dagsorden som gjelder for årsmotet, eventuelle forslag og IRN's aktivitets- og revisjonsbeskrivelse.*

6.7   Vedtak på årsmøtet fattes med håndsopprekning hvis ikke noe annet kreves.

- Majoriteten av deltagernes stemmer blir årsmøtets beslutning.

- Ved likt stemmetall blir møtelederens stemme avgjørende.

- Antall stemmer for de ulike alternativer i avstemninger skal protokollføres.

§ 7   Representasjon

Medlemskapet til en forening innebærer at den skal velge en representant og en vararepresentant som fører ordet på vegne av foreningen i IRN. Representant og vararepresentant skal oppnevnes for to år. Representanten representerer sin forening på årsmøtet såvel som i alle andre spørsmål. Representanten har stemmerett ved avstemninger i IRN mens varamannen ikke har stemme rett. Ved forfall av representanten overtar vararepresentanten status som representant inkl. retter og plikter intil videre.

Om representanten ikke lenger har foreningens tillit skal dette umidelbart meddeles til IRN, og oppnevne en ny representant.

Representanten skal ikke føre sin egen sak i IRN men foreningen's.

§ 8   Styret

8.1   Styret er IRN's virkende organ

8.2   Styret velges på ordinær årsmøte av medlemsforeningenes representanter for to års mandatperiode.

8.3   IRN's styre består av 9 styremedlemmer (helst en fra hvert trossamfunn) og 3 varastyrerepresentanter.

8.4   Styret skal ha følgende sammensetning; Formann, Vise formann, General sekretær Kasserer, Vise kasserer, Proskjektleder, Utdanningsleder, og Leder for sosiale saker.

8.5   Formannen velges direkte på årsmøtet av medlemsforeningenes representanter, øvrige styremedlemmer velges også på årsmøtet men fordeler øvrige poster efter beste ønske.

8.6   Styret skal:

- Forvalte IRN's tilganger.

- Føre redelighet over IRN's regskap.

- Føre medlemsregister over IRN's medlemsforeninger.

APPENDIX 3: KEY WRITTEN SOURCES

195

- Behandle IRN's løpende kontakter med myndigheter og foreninger innen- og utenriks.

- Fullføre de oppdrag som medlemsforeningene har gitt til styret.

- Virkeliggjøre IRN's målsettinger og arbeide for IRN's beste.

8.7 *Styret skal ha styremøter minst en gang i kvartalet. Innkalling til styremøte, som skal inneholde opplysninger om kommende dagsorden, skal tilsendes styremedlemmer minst 14 dager før styremøtet.*

8.8 *Styret bør redegjøre sin virksomhet for medlemsforeningene hver andre kvartal.*

8.9 *Styret er beslutningsdyktig når innkallelsen er mottat i god orden og minst 50 % av styret er tilstede.*

8.10 *Som styrebeslutning gjelder den mening majoriteten av deltagerne har stemt for. Ved likt stemmetall har formannen den avgjørende stemmen.*

8.11 *Styrets vedtak protokollføres, justeres av en kontrollmann og meddeles til samtlige medlemsforeninger.*

8.12 *IRN's styre kan gjennom vedtak, når den finner nødvendig, sammenkalle til ekstraordinært årsmøte.*

8.13 *Styret har ikke stemmerett i spørsmål som berører deres ansvarsfrihet/mandat. Revisorene har uttalelses og forslagsrett.*

§ 9 Revisjon

9.1 *Til kontroll av styrets økonomiske forvaltning skal årsmøtet oppnevne en revisor og en vararevisor.*

9.2 *Revisjonsbeskrivelsen skal overlates til styret senest en måned før ordinært årsmøte.*

9.3 *Regnskapsår omfatter kalenderåret 1 januar t.o.m 31 desember.*

9.4 *Alle transaksjoner som utføres i IRN's navn skal bokføres i et offentlig register. Den og andre handlinger bør kontrolleres av en autorisert revisor hvert år.*

§ 10 Stempel

IRN har sitt eget stempel med organisasjonens navn. Et stempel er forvart hos general sekretæren og et hos formannen. Styret avgjør hvordan stempelet og eventuell logo skal se ut.

§ 11   Statutt forandringer

Endringer i disse statuttene skjer gjennom vedtak på to årsmøter etter hverandre med minst en måneds mellomrom, der en av årsmøtene er ekstraordinært årsmøte.Satuttendringer må godkjennes av minst 2/3 av årsmøtets deltagere respektivt.

§ 12   Oppløsning

IRN oppløses hvis medlemsforeningenes representanter på to årsmøter etter hverandre vedtar IRN's oppløsning. Beslutningen må fattes med 3/4 majoritet ved det første årsmøtet og en enkel majoritet ved det andre årsmøtet. Ved vedtak om IRN's oppløsning skal dens eiendeler fordeles slik som medlemsforeningene beslutter.

Følgende menigheter / foreninger danner herved Islamsk Råd Norge og vedtar og godkjenner statuttene ovenfor for Islamsk Råd Norge på første årsmøte den 22 oktober 1993.

Central Jamaat-e Ahl-e Sunnat Norway

Det Islamske Forbundet

Det Marokkanske Kultursamfunn

OSLO
KÜLTÜR SAMFUNN

Islamske Kultur Senter Union Norge

Tanzeemul Muslimeen
TANZEEMUL MUSLIMEEN
(Regd.)
Postboks 60 Bøler
0620 OSLO 6
Norway

APPENDIX 3: KEY WRITTEN SOURCES

IRN's second statutes from 2002

Statutter for Islamsk Råd Norge
[Sist endret og stemt over for andre gang 2002].

§ 1 Grunnbestemmelser

1.1 Organisasjonens fulle navn er:
Norsk: Islamsk Råd Norge
Engelsk: Islamic Council Norway

1.2 Islamsk Råd Norge, heretter skrevet som IRN, er en islamsk landsdekkende paraplyorganisasjon bestående av islamske trossamfunn og organisasjoner som er virksomme i Norge og er medlemmer i IRN.

1.3 IRN er en partipolitisk uavhengig organisasjon.

1.4 IRNs virksomhet og beslutninger skal være i samsvar med Koranen og Profeten Muhammads (fred og barmhjertighet være med Ham) sunnah.

1.5 IRN er en ideell, religiøs og demokratisk organisasjon hvis virksomhet er i samsvar med Norges lover.

1.6 IRN har sitt hovedsete i Oslo.

1.7 IRNs offisielle språk er norsk.

1.8 IRN koordinerer medlemsorganisasjonenes interesser og representerer dem overfor norske myndigheter, organisasjoner og institusjoner i Norge og i utlandet i samsvar med statuttene.

1.9 IRNs statutter begrenser ikke medlemsorganisasjonenes suverenitet og selvstendighet i sitt arbeid, og organisasjonene kan, innenfor rammene av statuttene, selvstendig arbeide og opprettholde kontakter med norske myndigheter, organisasjoner i Norge og i utlandet.

§ 2 Definisjoner

2.1 En muslim defineres som en som offentlig bekjenner den islamske trosbekjennelsen, shahada, som innebærer å tro på én Gud og på Muhammad (fred og barmhjertighet være med Ham) som den siste profet. En muslim skal godta hele Koranen som Guds åpenbaring og profeten Muhammads (fred og barmhjertighet være med Ham) sunnah.

§ 3 Målsettinger

3.1 Å fremme samhold blant alle muslimer som er bosatt i Norge.

3.2 Å fremme og bevare islamsk identitet blant alle muslimer bosatt i Norge.

3.3 Å arbeide for at muslimer kan leve i samsvar med islamsk lære i det norske samfunnet.

3.4 Å spre kunnskap og forståelse om islam i Norge gjennom informasjonsvirksomhet.

3.5 Vise solidaritet med det muslimske ummah verden over.

3.6 Å fremme at alle muslimske barn og ungdom i Norge skal få et tilbud om utdannelse i islamsk tro, lære, historie og kultur.

Statutter for Islamsk Råd Norge
[Sist endret og stemt over for andre gang 2002].

Landsdekkende
paraplyorganisasjon
for islamske trossamfunn
og organisasjoner i Norge

§ 4 Virksomhet
IRN skal:

4.1 Stå for driften av et sentralkontor for informasjon og samordning av IRNs aktiviteter.

4.2 Koordinere og representere islamske trossamfunn og organisasjoner overfor norske myndigheter og institusjoner.

4.3 Å være muslimenes offisielle talerør overfor norske myndigheter.

4.4 Representere IRNs medlemsorganisasjoner i internasjonale sammenhenger, dvs. konferanser, seminarer og sammenkomster som berører muslimenes interesser i Norge.

4.5 Arrangere felles kulturelle aktiviteter som seminarer, konferanser, forelesninger og lignende.

4.6 Gi veiledning til medlemsorganisasjonene ved behov.

4.7 Drive felles prosjekter på oppdrag av medlemsorganisasjonene.

4.8 Søke å samle økonomisk bistand til IRNs arbeid både innen- og utenlands under forutsetning av at disse bidrag gis uten vilkår og uten innblanding i IRNs indre anliggender.

4.9 Følge med samfunnsutviklingen i Norge og gi uttrykk for IRNs oppfatninger, gi forslag til løsninger og eventuelt påvirke fremtidige beslutninger. Dette gjelder spesielt i spørsmål som berører muslimenes interesser i Norge.

4.10 Være brobygger som skaper gjensidig forståelse og respekt mellom muslimene og det norske folk med hensyn til religion, kultur og moralske verdier.

§ 5 Medlemskap

Ethvert islamsk trossamfunn eller organisasjon har rett til å være medlem i IRN om det oppfyller følgende krav:

5.1 Trossamfunnet eller organisasjonen må være stiftet i samsvar med gjeldende norske lover og drive islamske aktiviteter på ett bestemt sted.

5.2 Trossamfunnet eller organisasjonen skal oppgi medlemstallet sammen med søknaden om medlemskap i IRN. Oppdatert medlemstall sendes IRN én gang årlig.

5.3 Trossamfunnet eller organisasjonen skal drive regelmessig koranundervisning for barn og voksne. Styret i IRN kan gi dispensasjon fra dette punktet.

5.4 Ved søknad om medlemskap i IRN skal trossamfunnet/organisasjonen levere følgende dokumenter til IRNs styre, - søknad om medlemskap, - kopi av styrevedtak der det fremgår at trossamfunnet/organisasjonen har gjort vedtak om å søke medlemskap i IRN. - oversikt over trossamfunnets/organisasjonens aktiviteter. - trossamfunnets/organisasjonens statutter.

Adresse: Calmeyer gt 8 - 0183 Oslo, Norge • Fax: 850 22 050 • epost: post@irn.no • url: http://www.irn.no
• Kontonummer: 0530 423 0454 • Organisasjonsnummer: 9828 42 840

APPENDIX 3: KEY WRITTEN SOURCES

Statutter for Islamsk Råd Norge
[Sist endret og stemt over for andre gang 2002].

Landsdekkende
paraplyorganisasjon
for islamske trossamfunn
og organisasjoner i Norge

5.5 Styret i IRN skal behandle alle søknader om medlemskap, og avslå eller bevilge midlertidig medlemskap. Den endelige beslutningen tas på IRNs årsmøte og fra da av trer alle plikter og rettigheter i kraft.

5.6 Hvert trossamfunn eller organisasjon skal betale innmeldingsavgift på 1000,- kroner og videre en årlig medlemsavgift til IRN basert på medlemstall, etter satser fastsatt på IRNs årsmøte. Det kan gis dispensasjon fra dette kravet.

5.7 Trossamfunnet/organisasjonen har adgang til å klage på IRNs vedtak vedrørende medlemskap som er fattet på styremøte og/eller årsmøte innen 30 dager fra vedtaksdato.

5.8 Medlemskap i IRN opphører hvis: - trossamfunnets/ organisasjonens virksomhet opphører – trossamfunnet/organisasjonen driver med aktiviteter som strider mot IRNs statutter.

5.9 IRNs styre kan midlertidig utelukke trossamfunn/organisasjoner som bryter IRNs statutter.

5.10 Definitiv utestengelse av et trossamfunn/organisasjon foretas på IRNs årsmøte.

5.11 Om foreningen vil melde seg ut av IRN skal en skriftlig utmelding fremlegges IRN. IRNs årsmøte bekrefter utmeldingen.

§ 6 Årsmøte

6.1 Årsmøtet er IRNs høyeste organ.

6.2 IRNs ordinære årsmøte holdes årlig på tid og sted som IRNs styre bestemmer.

6.3 Styret kan innkalle til ekstraordinært årsmøte ved behov.

6.4 På ordinære årsmøter skal følgende behandles, - Deltakeropprop, - Valg av møteleder. - Valg av sekretær. - Valg av to personer som skal underskrive protokollen. - Ledelsens virksomhetsberetning for det foregående år. - Regnskapsberetning. Bevilgning av ansvarsfrihet for styret. - Presentasjon av aktivitetsplan og budsjett for kommende år. - Andre saker. – Valg.

6.5 Innkalling til årsmøte må være postlagt senest to uker før ordinært årsmøte og minst en uke før ekstraordinært årsmøte.

6.6 I innkallelsen skal inngå: Dagsorden for årsmøtet, IRNs aktivitets- og regnskapberetning, samt forslag til aktivitetsplan og budsjett.

6.7 Vedtak på årsmøtet fattes med håndsoppregning hvis ikke noe annet kreves. - Majoriteten av deltakernes stemmer blir årsmøtets beslutning. - Ved likt stemmetall blir møtelederens stemme avgjørende. - Antall stemmer for de ulike alternativer i avstemninger skal protokollføres.

§ 7 Representasjon

7.1 Medlemskapet til et trossamfunn/organisasjon innebærer at det skal velge en representant og en vararepresentant som fører ordet på vegne av foreningen i IRN. Representant og vararepresentant skal oppnevnes for to år ad gangen. Representanten representerer sin organisasjon på årsmøtet så vel som i andre spørsmål. Representanten har stemmerett ved avstemninger i IRN mens

Statutter for Islamsk Råd Norge
[Sist endret og stemt over for andre gang 2002].

Landsdekkende
paraplyorganisasjon
for islamske trossamfunn
og organisasjoner i Norge

varamannen ikke har stemmerett. Ved forfall av representanten overtar vararepresentanten status som representant.

7.2 Om representanten ikke lenger har trossamfunnets/organisasjonens tillit, skal dette umiddelbart meddeles til IRN, og en ny representant oppnevnes.

7.3 Representanten skal ikke føre sin egen sak i IRN, men trossamfunnets/organisasjonens

§ 8 Styret

8.1 Styret er IRNs virkende organ. Det skal effektuere vedtak gjort av rådet (shura), som består av alle medlemsorganisasjonene.

8.2 Styret velges på ordinært årsmøte for to år av gangen.

8.3 IRNs styre består av 4 medlemmer.

8.4 IRNs styre består av leder, nestleder, sekretær, kasserer, samt ledere for komiteene.

8.5 Styre og komitéledere velges på ordinert årsmøte. Styret velges for to år av gangen.

8.6 Styret skal: - Forvalte IRNs økonomiske midler. - Føre IRNs regnskap. - Føre medlemsregister over IRN's medlemsorganisasjoner. - stå for IRNs løpende kontakter med myndigheter og foreninger innen- og utenlands.

8.7 Styret skal holde rådsmøte minst én gang i kvartalet. Innkalling til rådsmøte, som skal inneholde opplysninger om dagsorden, skal sendes rådsmedlemmene senest 7 dager før rådsmøtet.

8.8 Styret skal redegjøre for IRNs virksomhet overfor medlemsorganisasjonene gjennom å sende referat fra alle rådsmøter som finner sted.

8.9 Rådet er beslutningsdyktig når innkallelsen er mottatt innen fristen og minst 50% av rådet er tilstede.

8.10 Som rådsbeslutning gjelder den mening majoriteten av deltakerne har stemt for. Ved likt stemmetall har lederen dobbeltstemme.

8.11 Rådets vedtak skrives ned i referat.

8.12 IRNs styre kan, når det finner det nødvendig, sammenkalle til ekstraordinært årsmøte.

8.13 Styret har ikke stemmerett i spørsmål som berører deres ansvarsfrihet.

§ 9 Revisjon

9.1 Til kontroll av styrets økonomiske forvaltning skal årsmøtet oppnevne en revisor.

9.2 Revisjonsberetningen skal overlates til styret senest en måned før ordinært årsmøte.

9.3 Regnskapsår omfatter kalenderåret 1 januar t.o.m. 31 desember.

Adresse: Calmeyer gt 8 · 0183 Oslo, Norge · Fax: 650 22 050 · epost: post@irn.no · url: http://www.irn.no
· Kontonummer: 0530 423 0454 · Organisasjonsnummer: 9828 42 840

APPENDIX 3: KEY WRITTEN SOURCES 201

Statutter for Islamsk Råd Norge
[Sist endret og stemt over for andre gang 2002].

Landsdekkende
paraplyorganisasjon
for islamske trossamfunn
og organisasjoner i Norge

§ 10 Stempel

10.1 IRN har sitt eget stempel med trossamfunnets/organisasjonens navn. Et stempel er forvart hos lederen og et hos sekretæren. Rådet avgjør hvordan stempelet og eventuell logo skal se ut.

§ 11 Endring av statutter

11.1 Endringer av statutter skjer gjennom vedtak på årsmøte. Endringer av statutter krever minst 2/3 flertall.

§ 12 Oppløsning

12.1 IRN oppløses hvis medlemsorganisasjonenes representanter på to årsmøter etter hverandre vedtar IRNs oppløsning. Beslutningen må fattes med ¾ flertall ved et første årsmøtet og en simpelt flertall ved det andre årsmøtet. Ved vedtak om IRNs oppløsning skal dens eiendeler fordeles slik som medlemsorganisasjonene beslutter.

§ 13 Samarbeidsrådet for tros- og livssynssamfunn, STL

13.1 IRN representeres av to personer i STL, den til enhver tid sittende leder av IRN, samt en person som er valgt på IRNs årsmøte.

IRN's third/fourth statutes, from 2005/2006

Vedtekter

Islamsk Råd Norge
Landsdekkende paraplyorganisasjon for islamske trossamfunn og organisasjoner i Norge

Calmeyersgt. 8, 0183 Oslo
post@irn.no – www.irn.no

Organisasjonsnummer: 9828 42 840

APPENDIX 3: KEY WRITTEN SOURCES

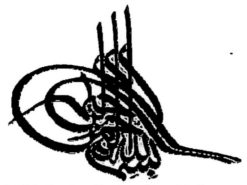

I Allah Den barmhjertiges, Den nåderikes navn
In The Name Of Allah, Most Gracious, Most Merciful

وَاعْتَصِمُوا بِحَبْلِ اللَّهِ جَمِيعًا وَلاَ تَفَرَّقُوا

"Hold dere alle fast i Guds rep, og unngå splittelser."

"Hold fast, all together, to the bond with Allah and be not divided."
Koranen 3:103

وَتَعَاوَنُوا عَلَى الْبِرِّ وَالتَّقْوَى وَلاَ تَعَاوَنُوا عَلَى الإِثْمِ وَالْعُدْوَانِ

"Hjelp hverandre henimot fromhet og gudsfrykt, ikke mot synd og fiendskap."

"Help one another to virtue and God-consciousness and do not help one other to sin and transgression."
Koranen 5:2

Vedtekter for Islamsk Råd Norge

§ 1 Navn, adresse og status

1. Organisasjonens navn skal være Islamsk Råd Norge (Engelsk: Islamic Council of Norway), heretter forkortet til IRN. IRNs offisielle språk skal være norsk.

2. IRN skal være landsdekkende paraplyorganisasjon for islamske trossamfunn og andre ideelle islamske organisasjoner som er virksomme i Norge. IRN skal ha sitt hovedkontor i Oslo som skal samordne alle aktiviteter.

3. IRN skal være en ideell, religiøs, demokratisk og partipolitisk uavhengig organisasjon hvis virksomhet er i samsvar med Norges lover.

4. IRNs virksomhet og beslutninger skal være i samsvar med Koranen og profeten Muhammeds (fred være med ham) *sunnah*.

5. IRN skal ikke begrense medlemsorganisasjonenes suverenitet og selvstendighet i sitt arbeid, og organisasjonene kan selvstendig arbeide og opprettholde kontakter med norske myndigheter og organisasjoner i Norge og i utlandet.

§ 2 Formål

1. Arbeide for at muslimer kan leve i samsvar med islamsk lære i det norske samfunnet og bidra til å bygge opp en norsk-muslimsk identitet.

2. Fremme samhold blant muslimer i Norge og ivareta medlemsorganisasjonenes rettigheter og interesser.

3. Være brobygger og dialogpartner som skaper gjensidig forståelse og respekt mellom muslimer og ikke-muslimer i Norge, med hensyn til religion, kultur og moralske verdier.

§ 3 Målsettinger og aktiviteter

IRN skal:

1. Holde seg orientert om samfunnsutviklingen og gi uttrykk for muslimenes oppfatninger overfor myndigheter og offentlighet, og fremme forslag til løsninger.

2. Koordinere medlemsorganisasjonenes interesser og representere dem overfor norske myndigheter, offentlighet, organisasjoner og institusjoner i Norge og i utlandet.

3. Drive fellesprosjekter på oppdrag av medlemsorganisasjonene og arrangere fellesaktiviteter som utredninger, høringer, seminarer, konferanser og lignende. I tillegg representere IRNs medlemsorganisasjoner i nasjonale og internasjonale konferanser, seminarer og lignende.

4. Søke samarbeid og dialog med andre organisasjoner for å jobbe mot mål som er i samsvar med IRNs formål.

5. Spre kunnskap og forståelse om islam i Norge.

6. Arbeide for inkludering av muslimer i det norske samfunnet og at muslimer blir verdsatt som en viktig ressurs for Norge.

7. Arbeide for at alle muslimske barn og ungdom i Norge skal få et tilbud om utdannelse i islamsk tro, lære, historie og kultur.

§ 4 Organisasjonsstruktur

IRNs organisasjonsstruktur skal bestå av:

- Rådet
- Styret
- Komiteer

APPENDIX 3: KEY WRITTEN SOURCES 205

§ 5 Rådet

1. Rådet består av en hovedrepresentant og en vararepresentant fra medlemsorganisasjonene. Hovedrepresentanten bør være styrelederen fra medlemsorganisasjonen.

2. Innkalling til rådsmøtet må sendes ut minst to uker i forveien.

3. Rådet skal ha minst 4 møter i året hvorav ett møte skal være årsmøte. Alle rådsmøter og årsmøter skal velge en møteleder, en referent og to personer til å underskrive protokollen samt godkjenne innkallingen og den endelige dagsorden. Rådsmøtet skal:

    o gjøre vedtak i alle saker som etter vedtekter ikke hører under årsmøtet
    o instruere styret og komiteer i deres arbeid
    o bestemme IRNs samarbeid og medlemskap med andre organisasjoner
    o oppnevne valgkomité på tre medlemmer

4. Ekstraordinært rådsmøtet skal innkalles dersom styret eller minst halvparten av medlemsorganisasjonene ber om det.

5. Alle avgjørelser i rådsmøter tas ved alminnelig flertall. Ved stemmelikhet skal stemmen til rådets leder være avgjørende.

6. Rådsmøte er beslutningsdyktig når innkallelsen er sendt ut innen fristen og minst halvparten av rådsmedlemmene er tilstedet.

7. Saker til rådsmøter må fremmes til styret. Forslag som ikke er utsendt i endelig innkalling, kan tas opp under "eventuelt", dersom minst halvparten av fremmøtte rådsrepresentanter godkjenner det.

§ 6 Årsmøtet

1. Rådets årsmøte skal holdes innen utgangen av mars. Innkalling til rådets årsmøte må sendes ut senest fire uker i forveien. I innkallelsen skal det inngå dagsorden for møtet og nødvendig bakgrunnsmateriale som årsberetning, årsregnskap, årsplan og budsjett.

2. Årsmøtet skal bl.a. behandle følgende saker:

    o årsberetning, årsregnskap og styrets ansvarsfrihet
    o årsplan og budsjett
    o valg av revisor
    o valg av styret for en periode på to år
    o fastsettelse av kontingent for en periode på to år
    o godkjenne endringer i vedtektene
    o opptak av nye medlemmer
    o andre saker som etter vedtekter hører under årsmøtet

3. Ekstraordinært årsmøtet skal innkalles dersom styret eller minst halvparten av medlemsorganisasjonene ber om det.

4. Alle avgjørelser i årsmøter tas ved alminnelig flertall, unntatt vedtektsendringer og oppløsning (§12). Ved stemmelikhet skal stemmen til rådets leder være avgjørende.

5. Årsmøte er beslutningsdyktig når innkallelsen er sendt ut innen fristen og minst halvparten av rådsmedlemmene er tilstedet.

6. Medlemmer av styret har ikke stemmerett i spørsmål som berører deres ansvarsfrihet. Styremedlemmer som ikke er medlemmer av rådet har tale- og forslagsrett.

7. Saker til årsmøtet må fremmes til styret.

§ 7 Styret

1. Styret for IRN velges av årsmøtet for to år av gangen og skal bestå av rådets leder, nestleder, sekretær, økonomiansvarlig og komitéledere. For å være valgbar til styret må man være medlem av en medlemsorganisasjon.

2. Styremøte skal holdes så ofte det er nødvendig av hensyn til saksmengden - minimum hver annen måned.

3. Alle avgjørelser i styret tas ved alminnelig flertall. Ved stemmelikhet skal stemmen til styreleder være avgjørende.

4. Styret skal:
   o effektuere vedtak gjort av rådet og ta seg av løpende saker mellom rådsmøtene
   o forberede og innkalle rådsmøter
   o forvalte økonomiske midler i IRN og føre regnskap
   o føre medlemsregister over IRNs medlemsorganisasjoner
   o bestemme ansettelse av medarbeidere

5. Styret skal avgi årsregnskap og årsberetning for foregående år i god tid slik at dette kan behandles av årsmøtet. Årsregnskap og årsberetning skal være underskrevet av alle medlemmer av styret. Dersom noen har innvendinger mot årsregnskap og årsberetning, skal vedkommende underskrive med påtegnet forbehold og gi nærmere redegjørelse i årsberetningen.

6. Når styret finner det nødvendig, kan det innkalle til konsultasjonsmøter med rådsmedlemmer, imamer eller andre personer.

§ 8 Komiteer

1. Opprettelse av komiteer bestemmes av årsmøtet.

2. Alle komiteer skal ha en leder som velges av årsmøtet.

3. Lederen for komiteen velger selv komitémedlemmer og orienterer styret om sammensetning av komiteen. Komitémedlemmer trenger ikke være medlemmer av en medlemsorganisasjon.

4. Alle prosjekter og arbeidsgrupper i komiteene skal godkjennes av styret.

§ 9 Medlemskap

Islamske trossamfunn og andre ideelle islamske organisasjoner kan bli medlemmer i IRN om de oppfyller følgende:

1. Støtter IRNs formål og er enig i at en muslim er en som offentlig bekjenner den islamske trosbekjennelsen, *shahada*, som innebærer å tro på én Gud og på Muhammed (fred og barmhjertighet være med ham) som den aller siste profet, dvs. profetenes segl. En muslim skal godta hele Koranen som Guds åpenbaring og profeten Muhammeds *sunnah*.

2. Er stiftet i samsvar med gjeldende norske lover og driver sine aktiviteter på ett bestemt sted.

3. Har minst 500 medlemmer. Rådet kan gi dispensasjon i særtilfeller.

4. Arrangerer fredagsbønn og tilrettelegger for fem daglige bønner.

5. Skal betale årlig medlemskontingent fastsatt på årsmøtet, som er en betingelse for stemmerett.

6. For opptak av medlemmer skal søknaden inneholde følgende:
   o vedtekter
   o styrevedtak der det fremgår at organisasjonen har vedtatt å søke medlemskap i IRN

7. Rådet kan i særtilfeller innvilge medlemskap til ideelle islamske organisasjoner selv om de ikke oppfyller § 9.3 og § 9.4 ovenfor. Disse organisasjonene skal ha tale og forslagsrett men ikke stemmerett på råds- og årsmøtet. Årsmøtet kan gi dispensasjon fra kontingentkravet.

8. Alle stemmeberettigede organisasjoner har en stemme hver.

9. Alle søknader om medlemskap blir behandlet av styret. Styret fremlegger søknaden, sammen med sin innstilling, på årsmøtet, som tar beslutning om medlemskap.

APPENDIX 3: KEY WRITTEN SOURCES

§ 10 Utmelding/opphør av medlemskap

1. Utmelding skal skje skriftlig og det skal foreligge styrevedtak fra organisasjonen om utmelding. Utmelding gir ingen rett til refusjon av innbetalt kontingent.

2. Medlemskapet i IRN opphører hvis organisasjonens virksomhet opphører.

3. Rådet tar en organisasjons medlemskap opp til diskusjon hvis organisasjonen ikke lenger oppfyller kravene i § 9. Utmelding og opphør av medlemskap skal bekreftes av rådet med 2/3 flertall av de fremmøtte rådsrepresentanter.

4. Årsmøtet kan til enhver tid suspendere eller ekskludere en medlemsorganisasjon med 2/3 flertall av de fremmøtte rådsrepresentanter, hvis organisasjonen har skadet IRNs interesser eller motarbeidet IRNs formål.

§ 11 Økonomi/regnskap

1. IRNs virksomhet finansieres ved medlemskontingent, tilskudd og gaver, under forutsetning at de gis uten innblanding i IRNs virksomhet. Alle midler skal brukes i henhold til IRNs formål.

2. Revisjonsberetningen skal overlates til styret senest en måned før årsmøtet som skal godkjenne regnskapet.

3. Regnskapsår omfatter 1. januar - 31. desember.

§ 12 Vedtektsendringer og oppløsning

1. Endring av vedtekter skal skje gjennom vedtak på årsmøtet med ⅔ flertall av de fremmøtte rådsrepresentanter etter at endringsforslagene har vært forelagt medlemsorganisasjonene sammen med innkalling til årsmøtet.

2. IRN oppløses hvis medlemmene på to etterfølgende ordinære årsmøter vedtar organisasjonens oppløsning. Denne beslutningen må fattes med ⅔ flertall av de fremmøtte rådsrepresentanter på hvert av årsmøtene. Ved vedtak om IRNs oppløsning skal dens eiendeler anvendes i henhold til IRNs formål.

***

Vedtatt 30.04.2006. Erstatter vedtekter sist endret 17.12.2005.

NOTATER:

IRN's most recent statutes, from 2021

Vedtekter for Islamsk Råd Norge (IRN)
Vedtatt på ekstraordinært årsmøte 2021

§ 1 Navn, adresse og status

1.1 Organisasjonens navn skal være Islamsk Råd Norge, heretter forkortet til IRN. På engelsk skal dette oversettes til The Islamic Council of Norway, heretter forkortet til ICN. IRNs offisielle språk skal være norsk.

1.2 IRN skal være landsdekkende paraplyorganisasjon for islamske trossamfunn og andre ideelle islamske organisasjoner som er virksomme i Norge. IRN skal ha sitt hovedkontor i Oslo som skal samordne alle aktiviteter.

1.3 IRN skal være en ideell, religiøs, demokratisk og partipolitisk uavhengig organisasjon hvis virksomhet er i samsvar med Norges lover.

1.4 IRNs virksomhet og beslutninger skal være i samsvar med Koranen og profeten Muhammeds (fred være med ham) sunnah.

1.5 IRN skal ikke begrense medlemsorganisasjonenes suverenitet og selvstendighet i sitt arbeid, og organisasjonene kan selvstendig arbeide og opprettholde kontakter med norske myndigheter og organisasjoner i Norge og i utlandet.

1.6 Medlemsorganisasjonene bør holde IRNs styret oppdatert om deres aktivitet ovenfor statlige myndigheter.

§ 2 Formål

2.1 Arbeide for at muslimer kan leve i samsvar med islamsk lære i det norske samfunnet og bidra til å bygge opp en norsk-muslimsk identitet.

2.2 Fremme samhold blant muslimer i Norge og ivareta medlemsorganisasjonenes rettigheter og interesser.

2.3 Være brobygger og dialogpartner som skaper gjensidig forståelse og respekt mellom muslimer og ikke-muslimer i Norge, med hensyn til religion, kultur og moralske verdier.

§ 3 Målsettinger og aktiviteter

IRN skal:

3.1 Holde seg orientert om samfunnsutviklingen og gi uttrykk for muslimenes oppfatninger overfor myndigheter og offentlighet, samt fremme forslag til løsninger på aktuelle problemstillinger

3.2 Koordinere medlemsorganisasjonenes interesser og representere dem overfor norske myndigheter, offentlighet, organisasjoner og institusjoner i Norge og i utlandet.

APPENDIX 3: KEY WRITTEN SOURCES

3.3 Tilby fellestjenester og bistand i form av kompetanse, kurs og lignende til medlemsorganisasjonene i samsvar med IRN's formål.

3.4 Drive fellesprosjekter på oppdrag av medlemsorganisasjonene og arrangere fellesaktiviteter som utredninger, høringer, seminarer, konferanser og lignende. I tillegg representere IRNs medlemsorganisasjoner i nasjonale og internasjonale konferanser, seminarer og lignende.

3.5 Ivareta muslimenes interesser, behov og rettigheter i det norske samfunnet

3.6 Søke samarbeid og dialog med andre organisasjoner for å jobbe mot mål som er i samsvar med IRNs formål.

3.7 Spre kunnskap og forståelse om islam i Norge.

3.8 Arbeide for inkludering av muslimer i det norske samfunnet og at muslimer blir verdsatt som en viktig ressurs for Norge.

3.9 Arbeide for at alle muslimske barn og ungdom i Norge skal få et tilbud om utdannelse i islamsk tro, lære, historie og kultur.

§ 4 Organisasjonsstruktur

4.1 IRNs organisasjonsstruktur skal bestå av:
- Rådet
- Styret
- IMAM KOMITEEN
- Sekretariatet
- Komiteer

4.2 Rådet er det øverste organ i IRN og velger et styret for 2 år. Rådet har ansvar for å verve ressurser til styret.

4.3 Styret er ledelsesorganet i IRN, som forvalter IRN i henhold til IRNs formål. Styret har ansvar for å verve ressurser til sekretariatet.

4.4 Sekretariat er utførende organ og må følge planene og retningslinjene de er underlagt fra styret, og melde status i forhold til det.

4.5 Imam komiteens oppgave er å behandle de teologiske problemstillinger og være et rådgivende organ.

§ 5 Rådet

5.1 Rådet består av inntil to representanter fra hver av medlemsorganisasjonene, en representant fra de ideelle islamske organisasjonene som ikke er en paraplyorganisasjon som representerer trossamfunn, som møter på vegne av, og med autorisasjon fra sin organisasjon. Medlemsorganisasjonene plikter å holde IRNs styre og sekretariat oppdatert om deres rådsrepresentanter og styremedlemmer før råds- og årsmøte.

5.2 Rådet skal møtes minst en gang i året, i tillegg til årsmøtet. Det skal velges en møteleder, referent, og to protokollvitner. Rådet skal godkjenne innkallelse og dagsorden. Daglig leder eller noen fra styret eller sekretariatet kan bli valgt som referent, protokollfører og tellekorps.

§ 6 Styret

6.1 Styremedlemmer velges av årsmøtet for 2 år av gangen og skal bestå av styreleder, nestleder, imamkomiteleder, økonomiansvarlig og inntil 5 andre styremedlemmer som besluttes av rådet. Styreleder, økonomiansvarlig og imamkomiteens leder og et styremedlem velges oddetall år. Mens nestleder og de 4 øvrige styremedlemmene velges partall år. Ved bytte av styremedlem skal avtroppende styremedlem delta i to første styremøter og overføre kunnskap og informasjon relatert til vervet. Det bør søkes å ha minst et styremedlem fra distrikt Norge.

6.2 Rådsrepresentanter, styremedlemmer og medlemmer av valgkomiteen har nominasjonsrett til styreverv. Enhver kandidat til styreverv må være medlem i en medlemsorganisasjon, medlemsorganisasjonen må bekrefte kandidatens medlemskap i medlemsorganisasjonen før vedkommende kan stille til valg. Ideelle islamske organisasjoner som ikke er en paraplyorganisasjon som representerer trossamfunn kan ikke stille sine medlemmer til styrevalg, og har heller ikke nominasjonsrett til styreverv. Kandidatene til styreverv bør søke å være praktiserende muslimer, og det bør søkes å ha kvinner representert i styret. Valgkomiteen skal forsikre seg om at det ikke er noen skriftlige innvendinger mot de nominerte fra deres medlemsorganisasjons ledelse.

6.3 Et styremedlem kan velges inntil 4 sammenhengende perioder etter hverandre. Vedkommende må ha en periode fri, etter 4 perioders tjeneste, før vedkommende på nytt kan velges som styremedlem.

6.4 Det året ny styreleder velges, kan styret fremme forslag til endring i årsplan og budsjett, dette må gjøres innen en måned etter tiltredelse av vervet. Endringer kan foretas slik:

6.4.1 I førstkommende rådsmøte/årsmøte kan rådet vedta endringene, eller
6.4.2 Avstemning om endringene i årsplan kan foretas elektronisk av rådsmedlemmene, etter forutgående elektronisk avstemning om slik votering kan foretas elektronisk av rådsmedlemmene.

6.5 Hver medlemsorganisasjon kan maksimalt få 1 av sine medlemmer valgt til styret. Unntak til denne regel kan gjøres hvis det ikke foreligger tilstrekkelig innmeldte kandidater til å muliggjøre det.

APPENDIX 3: KEY WRITTEN SOURCES

6.6 Valg av et styreverv der det er flere kandidater til vervet skal gjennomføres skriftlig. Valg av leder gjennomføres først, deretter nestleder, imamkomite leder, økonomiansvarlig og deretter inntil 5 styreverv i separate runder i nevnte rekkefølge.

6.7 Styremøte skal avholdes så ofte det er nødvendig av hensyn til saksmengden, ordinære styremøter avholdes hver annen måned. Styremøter kalles inn av styreleder eller den vedkommende bemyndiger fra styre eller sekretariatet. Styremøter er beslutningsdyktige med de tilstedeværende antall styremedlemmer, når de er innkalt med minst 1 ukes frist. Ekstraordinære styremøter som kalles inn med kortere frist og er beslutningsdyktige når minst halvparten av styret er representert.

6.8 Alle avgjørelser i styret tas ved alminnelig flertall. Ved stemmelikhet skal stemmen til styreleder være avgjørende.

6.9 Styrets arbeidsoppgaver:

6.9.1 Forvalte IRN i henhold til IRNs formål, årsplan og retningslinjer fra rådet.
6.9.2 Utarbeide arbeidsplan, strategi og interne retningslinjer for sekretariatet.
6.9.3 Følge opp sekretariatets arbeid
6.9.4 Styret skal løpende underrette Rådet om sitt arbeid.
6.9.5 Effektuere rådsvedtak
6.9.6 Forberede og innkalle til rådsmøter.
6.9.7 Utarbeide rekrutteringsplan og rekruttere ressurser til sekretariatet og komiteer.
6.9.8 Forvalte IRNs økonomiske midler og føre regnskap.
6.9.9 Føre register over IRNs medlemsorganisasjoner.
6.9.10 Foreta ansettelser/oppsigelser i sekretariatet.
6.9.11 Velge revisor

6.10 Styret skal avgi årsregnskap og årsberetning for foregående år i god tid slik at dette kan behandles av årsmøtet. Årsregnskap og årsberetning skal være underskrevet av alle medlemmer av styret. Dersom noen har innvendinger mot årsregnskap og årsberetning, skal vedkommende underskrive med påtegnet forbehold og gi nærmere redegjørelse i årsberetningen.

6.11 Når styret finner det nødvendig, kan det innkalle til konsultasjonsmøter med rådsmedlemmer, imamer, komiteer eller øvrige personer.

6.12 Styret kan bestemme at faste styremedlemmer som er fraværende i over tre sammenhengende ordinære styremøter uten gyldig fravær mister sine styreverv. Ved fravær av styreleder rykker nestleder opp, ved nestleders fravær velger styret i flertall hvem av øvrige styremedlemmene som rykker opp, sistnevnte gjelder også de øvrige styremedlemmene.

6.13 Oppsigelse fra hele styret skal behandles på råds- eller årsmøte for å være gyldig. Alle oppsigelser fra enkelte styremedlemmer og sekretariatet skal leveres skriftlig til styret med begrunnelse.

6.14 Styret kan etter eget skjønn delegere arbeidsoppgaver til sekretariatetsleder

§ 7 Sekretariatet

7.1 Sekretariatet består av de stillinger og frivillig verv styret oppretter og plikter til enhver tid å følge de planene styret har lagt.

7.2 Sekretariatas leder betegnes daglig leder.

7.3 Styreleder innehar personalansvaret for de ansatte i sekretariatet.

7.4 Alle stillinger og verv skal i det minste utlyses internt blant medlemsorganisasjonene. Kandidater til disse stillingene eller vervene vurderes av styret.

7.5 Styret og sekretariatetsleder skal ha faste status møter en gang i måned, og skal ha effektiv kommunikasjon mellom seg i form av elektronisk korrespondanse.

7.6 Sekretariatet er underlagt styret, dagligleder styreleder er til enhver tid sekretariatets overordne.

7.7 dagligleder kan ikke være et av rådets styremedlemmer.

7.8 Medlemmer av sekretariatet trenger ikke å være medlemmer av en medlemsorganisasjon.

7.9 Alle prosjekter og arbeidsoppgaver i sekretariatet skal godkjennes av daglig leder, ved vedkommendes fravær, av styret.

7.10 sekretariatetsleder kan opprette komiteer i sekretariatet etter behov, og de kan ledes av den sekretariatet utpeker til å lede. Komiteens leder kan velge selv deltakere i sine komiteer.

7.10 Ved ekstraordinære tilfeller kan styret pålegge sekretariatetsleder oppgaver.

7.11 Det bør søkes å ha kvinner representert i sekretariatet, samt medlemmer fra distrikt Norge.

§ 8 Komiteer

8.1 Råds- eller årsmøte kan opprette komiteer, dog kun to komiteer med styrerepresentasjon kan opprettes.

8.2 Komiteleder velger selv komitemedlemmer og orienterer styret om sammensetning av komiteen. Komitemedlemmer trenger ikke å være medlemmer av en medlemsorganisasjon.

8.3 Samtlige komiteer skal til enhver tid jobbe i henhold til IRNs formål, og styret forbeholder retten til å instruere komiteene.

8.4 Med unntak av komiteer med styrerepresentasjon og de vedtatte komiteer på råds- og årsmøte, kan øvrige komiteer oppløses av styret eller organisasjonsenheten som har opprettet komiteen.

Side 5 av 10

APPENDIX 3: KEY WRITTEN SOURCES

ORGANISASJONSBESTEMMELSER

§ 9 Rådsmøte

9.1 Rådsmøtet innkalles av styret. Ekstraordinært rådsmøte kan innkalles av styret ved behov eller dersom minst 1/3 av stemmeberettigede medlemsorganisasjoner ber om det. Innkalling til rådsmøtet med nødvendig sakspapirer må sendes ut minst to uker i forveien. Med nødvendige sakspapirer menes nominasjoner til verv, forslag til vedtektsendringer og andre saksdokumenter som er nødvendig for å kunne ta beslutning.

9.2 Rådsmøtet er beslutningsdyktig når innkallelsen er sendt ut innen fristen og minst halvparten av stemmeberettigede organisasjoner er representert, enten ved oppmøte eller med gyldig fullmakt. Kun skriftlig fullmakt fra medlemsorganisasjonens styreleder eller rådsrepresentant er gyldig, fullmakten kan være elektronisk.

9.3 Saker til rådsmøtet fremmes av styret, med eventuelle innspill fra rådsrepresentantene, sekretariatet eller komiteene. Saker som fremmes etter innkallelsesfristen kan bare tas opp under "eventuelt" med godkjenning fra 2/3 av representerte stemmeberettigede organisasjoner (dvs at hver organisasjon teller likt).

9.4 Alle avgjørelser i rådsmøter tas ved alminnelig stemmeflertall der ikke annet er spesifisert. Ved stemmelikhet skal stemmen til møteleder være avgjørende. Det er adgang til skriftlig votering i alle saker, etter krav fra majoriteten av representerte stemmeberettigede organisasjoner.

9.5 Rådsmøtet skal:

9.5.1 Gjøre vedtak i alle saker som etter vedtekter ikke hører under årsmøtet, eller annet følger av vedtektene
9.5.2 Instruere styret, sekretariatet og komiteer i deres arbeid ved behov.
9.5.3 Føre oversyn med styrets og sekretariatets arbeid
9.5.4 Bestemme IRNs samarbeid med og medlemskap i andre organisasjoner
9.5.5 Oppnevne valgkomité på minimum 3 medlemmer

9.6 Årsmøtet

9.6.1 Årsmøte skal holdes innen utgangen av april. Innkalling til årsmøtet må sendes ut senest fire uker i forveien. I innkallelsen skal det inngå dagsorden for møtet. Nødvendige sakspapirer som årsberetning, årsregnskap, årsplan, budsjett, samt valgkomiteens nominasjoner til styreverv og forslag til vedtektsendringer (når det er aktuelt), skal sendes medlemmene senest 2 uker før årsmøtets avvikling. Kun saker angitt i innkallelsen skal behandles, i øvrige saker som ikke følger med sakspapirene tillates kun orientering.

9.6.2 Årsmøtet skal behandle følgende saker:

9.6.2.1 Koranresitering (Tilawat).
9.6.2.2 Godkjenning av om innkallelse er lovlig.
9.6.2.3 Valg av møteleder og referent
9.6.2.4 Valg av to protokollførere

9.6.2.5 Valg av to tellekorps
9.6.2.6 Godkjenning av dagsorden.
9.6.2.7 Godkjenning av årsregnskap og årsberetning
9.6.2.8 Godkjenning av styrets ansvarsfrihet
9.6.2.9 Godkjenning av årsplan og budsjetter
9.6.2.10 Godkjenning av ressursplan
9.6.2.11 Vedtektsendringer
9.6.2.12 Fastsettelse av medlemskontingent.
9.6.2.13 Opptak av nye medlemmer
9.6.2.14 Valg av styre
9.6.2.15 Valg av valgkomite
9.6.2.16 Øvrige saker som medfølger sakspapirene
9.6.2.17 Øvrige saker – kun orientering
9.6.2.18 Bønn (Dua).

9.6.3 Alle avgjørelser i årsmøter tas ved alminnelig stemmeflertall, der ikke annet er spesifisert. Ved stemmelikhet skal stemmen til møteleder være avgjørende. Kun skriftlig fullmakt fra medlemsorganisasjonens styreleder og rådsrepresentant er gyldig, fullmakten kan være elektronisk.

9.6.4 Årsmøte er beslutningsdyktig når innkallelsen og sakspapirer er sendt ut innen fristen og minst halvparten av stemmeberettigede organisasjoner er representert, enten ved oppmøte eller med gyldig fullmakt.

9.6.5 Medlemmer av styret har ikke stemmerett i spørsmål som berører deres ansvarsfrihet. Styremedlemmer som ikke er medlemmer av rådet har tale- og forslagsrett.

9.6.6 Saker til årsmøtet må fremmes til styret.

9.6.7 Ideelle islamske organisasjoner som ikke er trossamfunn eller paraplyorganisasjoner som representerer trossamfunn, har talerett men ikke forslags- og stemmerett på råds- og årsmøtet. Årsmøte avgjør kontingentskravet til disse.

§ 10 Mistillitsforslag

10.1 Rådet kan vedta mistillitsforslag mot hele styret eller mot enkelte styremedlemmer i råds- og årsmøte. Mistillitsforslaget krever alminnelig flertall av representerte stemmer. Mistillitsforslag mot hele styret må foreligge eksplisitt i sakslisten, med begrunnelse. Dersom mistillitsforslaget blir vedtatt, blir sittende styret oppløst. Rådsmøte må velge nytt styre på samme årsmøte.

§ 11 Taushetsplikt

11.1 Det påhviler taushetsplikt for alle i IRN, rådet, styret, sekretariat og komiteene som ut fra sin stilling, tillitsverv eller på annen måte tilegner seg kunnskap om IRN, enkeltindivider, medlemmer og samarbeidspartnere.

11.2 Personer i styre, sekretariat og komiteer i IRN må signere taushetserklæring.

APPENDIX 3: KEY WRITTEN SOURCES

11.3 Ved særlige tilfeller kan styret også kreve at rådsmedlemmer eller øvrige signerer taushetserklæring.

11.4 For rådets medlemmer kan ikke taushetserklæringen begrense deling av opplysninger og informasjon med sin medlemsorganisasjon.

11.5 Taushetserklæringen utarbeides av styret.

§ 12 Kommunikasjon og elektronisk avstemming

12.1 Kommunikasjon og avstemning skal primært foregå elektronisk, der ikke annet er fastsatt.

12.2 Under møter skal avstemning skje ved håndsopprekning, der ikke annet er fastsatt.

12.3 Ved særlige tilfeller kan skriftlig avstemming foretas.

§ 13 Medlemskap

13.1 Islamske trossamfunn og andre ideelle islamske organisasjoner kan bli medlemmer i IRN om de oppfyller følgende vilkår:

13.1.1 Støtter IRNs formål og er enig i at en muslim er en som offentlig bekjenner den islamske trosbekjennelsen, *shahada*, som innebærer å tro på én Gud og på Muhammed (fred og barmhjertighet være med ham) som den aller siste profet, dvs. profetenes segl. En muslim skal godta hele Koranen som Guds åpenbaring og profeten Muhammeds (fred og barmhjertighet være med ham) sunnah.

13.1.2 Er stiftet i samsvar med gjeldende norske lover og driver sine aktiviteter på ett bestemt sted.

13.1.3 Arrangerer fredagsbønn og tilrettelegger for fem daglige bønner. Dette kravet gjelder ikke ideelle islamske organisasjoner, og rådet kan i særtilfeller gi dispensasjon fra dette kravet.

13.2 For opptak av medlemmer skal søknaden inneholde følgende:

13.2.1 Gjeldende vedtekter.
13.2.2 Gyldig organisasjonsnummer
13.2.3 Styrevedtak der det fremgår at organisasjonen har vedtatt å søke medlemskap i IRN.

13.3 Alle søknader om medlemskap blir behandlet av styret. Styret fremlegger sin innstilling på råds eller årsmøte med underlag, som tar beslutning om medlemskap.

13.4 Stemmeberettigede organisasjoner kan ha inntil 5 stemmer, avhengig av deres medlemsmasse. Endring av grenseverdiene for de ulike medlemsklassene foretas som vanlig vedtektsendring. Grunnlaget for stemmetildeling skal være offentlige data for organisasjonenes medlemstall ved inngangen til årsmøtets kalenderår. Endring av grenseverdier for etablerte medlemsklasser krever alminnelig flertall av representerte stemmer.

13.5 Som minimum førende gjelder følgende:

Medlemmer	Antall stemmer
<500	1
<501 – 1000>	2
<1001 – 2000>	3
<2001 – 4000>	4
>4001	5
Ideelle islamske organisasjoner som ikke er paraplyorganisasjoner som representerer trossamfunn.	0

13.6 Årsmøtet bestemmer medlemsklassenes tilhørende årskontingent, som skal være proporsjonalt med stemmetallet.

13.7 Stemmerett ved års- og rådsmøte forutsetter at medlemskontingent for det aktuelle kalenderår, samt eventuell annen utestående kontingent, er innbetalt senest 1 uke før avvikling av årsmøtet.

§ 14 Utmelding/opphør av medlemskap

14.1 Utmelding skal skje skriftlig og det skal foreligge styrevedtak fra organisasjonen om utmelding. utmelding gir ingen rett til refusjon, av innbetalt kontingent. Ingen fradragsrett på gaveinnberetning i medlemsorganisasjonen i utmeldingsåret.

14.2 Medlemskapet i IRN opphører hvis organisasjonens virksomhet opphører.

14.3 Rådet tar en organisasjons medlemskap opp til vurdering hvis organisasjonen ikke lenger oppfyller kravene til medlemskap i § 13.1, har skadet IRNs interesser, eller motarbeider dets formål. Rådet kan suspendere en slik organisasjon med 2/3 flertall av representerte stemmeberettigede organisasjoner. Eksklusjon krever tilsvarende flertallsbeslutning på årsmøtet. Begjæring om suspensjon eller eksklusjon må fremmes som egen sak i innkallelsen til råds- eller årsmøte, med en begrunnelse.

§ 15 Økonomi/regnskap

15.1 IRNs virksomhet finansieres ved medlemskontingent, tilskudd, inntekt og gaver, under forutsetning at de gis uten innblanding i IRNs virksomhet. Alle midler skal brukes i henhold til IRNs formål.

15.2 Revisjonsberetningen skal overlates til styret senest en måned før årsmøtet som skal godkjenne regnskapet.

15.3 Regnskapsår omfatter kalenderår, fra og med, 1. januar - 31. desember.

APPENDIX 3: KEY WRITTEN SOURCES

§ 16 Vedtektsendring og oppløsning

16.1 Endring av vedtekter skal skje gjennom vedtak på årsmøtet med 2/3 flertall av representerte stemmeberettigede medlemsorganisasjoner. Vedtektene trer i kraft straks de blir godkjent på årsmøtet / ekstraordinært årsmøtet.

16.2 IRN oppløses hvis medlemmene på to etterfølgende ordinære årsmøter vedtar organisasjonens oppløsning. Denne beslutningen må fattes med 3/4 flertall av representerte stemmeberettigede medlemsorganisasjoner på hvert av årsmøtene. Ved vedtak om IRNs oppløsning skal dens eiendeler anvendes etter årsmøtets beslutning, i henhold til IRNs formål.

MDN's most recent statutes, from 2022

VEDTEKTER FOR MUSLIMSK DIALOGNETTVERK (MDN)

§ 1. Navn og adresse
1. Muslimsk Dialognettverk (MDN)
2. MDN skal ha sitt hovedkontor i Oslo.

§ 2. Formål & verdier
- MDN skal være en paraply- og dialogorganisasjon.
- MDN skal være en nasjonal arena for religionsmøter, kunnskapsbasert dialog og samarbeid med andre tros- og livssynsorganisasjoner, offentlige myndigheter og det øvrige samfunnet.
- MDN skal fremme et felleskap hvor muslimer og ikke-muslimer møter hverandre med åpenhet, likeverd og respekt, og hvor uenigheter diskuteres med god dialog.
- MDN skal være forankret i den muslimske troen og fremme fredfull sameksistens og et pluralistisk samfunn.

§3 MDN består av følgende organer
1. Årsmøtet
2. Rådet
3. Styret
4. Administrasjonen

§ 4. Medlemskap
1. Medlemskap i MDN er åpen for offentlig godkjente islamske trossamfunn og paraplyorganisasjoner, med minst 1000 medlemmer og som støtter og fremmer MDNs formål og verdier.
2. Trossamfunn kan ikke være medlem av andre muslimske paraplyorganisasjoner.
3. Trossamfunn må ha eksistert i minst tre år og styres etter demokratiske prosesser.
4. Opptak av nye medlemmer besluttes av Årsmøtet, med 2/3 flertall. Søknaden vurderes ut fra søkersamfunnets historie, samt formål og betydning i det norske samfunnet.
5. Nye medlemmer som er trossamfunn, skal ha observatørstatus i ett år før medlemskap eventuelt innvilges.
6. Medlemmer kan suspenderes eller ekskluderes etter 2/3 flertallsvedtak under årsmøte. Krav om suspensjon eller eksklusjon fremmes av Styret, med detaljert begrunnelse, og skal være egen sak på Årsmøtet.
7. Dersom det foreligger særlige grunner, kan Årsmøtet beslutte å gi dispensasjon til trossamfunn som ikke oppfyller kriteriene i punkt 1, 3 og 5.

side 1

§ 5. Observatørstatus

1. Observatørstatus i MDN gir ikke stemmerett, men talerett på rådsmøter og Årsmøtet.
2. Har mulighet til deltakelse i administrasjonsarbeid, som inkluderer verv i administrasjonen, komité- og prosjektarbeid.

§ 7. Rådet

1. MDNs Råd består av inntil to navngitte representanter fra hver av medlemsorganisasjonens ledelse hvor minst én må være leder, nestleder, generalsekretær eller daglig leder, og den andre må være styremedlem.
2. Begge representanter fra medlemsorganisasjoner har en stemme hver, og stemmegivning kan ikke skje ved fullmakt.
3. Alle avgjørelser bør tilstrebes å bli fattet etter konsensus, men på den andre påfølgende behandlingen kan saken avgjøres med 2/3 flertall.
4. Rådet skal ha minst to møter i året hvorav ett skal være årsmøte.

§ 6. Årsmøtet

5. Årsmøtet er MDNs øverste myndighet
6. Årsmøtet avholdes innen utgangen av april og innkalles av styret med minst tre ukers varsel. Forslag som behandles på Årsmøtet skal være sendt til styret innen en uke fra innkallingen ble sendt. Fullstendig saksliste må være tilgjengelig for medlemmene senest en uke før Årsmøtet.
1. Ekstraordinært årsmøte skal avholdes når Styret bestemmer det, eller minst 1/3 av de stemmeberettigede medlemmene krever det.
2. Innkalling og gjennomføring av ekstraordinært årsmøte kan foregå med kortere varsel dersom hele Årsmøtet aksepterer det. Hvis ikke, følges samme prosedyre som for ordinært Årsmøte.
1. Medlemsorganisasjonene må ha betalt all utestående medlemskontingent før Årsmøtet finner sted for å være stemmeberettiget.
2. Årsmøtet er vedtaksdyktig når 50% av antall stemmeberettigede medlemmer møter opp.
3. MDN skal i størst mulig grad basere seg på konsensusbeslutninger. Vedtak er gyldige med 2/3 flertall av oppmøtte medlemmer, så lenge ikke noe annet er angitt.
4. Årsmøtet behandler følgende saker:
    - Konstituering
        - Godkjenning av møteinnkalling
        - Valg av møteleder, referent og to protokollunderskrivere
        - Godkjenning av dagsorden
    - Behandle årsmelding for foregående kalenderår
    - Behandle regnskap og revisjon
    - Fastsette kontingent

- o Behandle handlingsplan og budsjett for inneværende kalenderår
- o Velge revisor
- o Opptak av nye medlemmer
- o Valg av valgkomiteen, samt antall styremedlemmer året før styrevalg
- o Valg av styreleder og styremedlemmer skjer hvert 2. år

§ 8. Styret

1. Styret er ansvarlig for organisasjonens administrasjon, strategisk utvikling, forvalte og videreutvikle MDNs verdier i samsvar med vedtekter og Årsmøtets vedtak.
2. Styret har ansvaret for utarbeidelse av handlingsplanen.
3. Styret skal bestå av leder, nestleder og andre styremedlemmer.
4. Styret skal være representert av medlemmer fra minst tre forskjellige medlemsorganisasjoner.
5. Styret skal bestå av minimum fem personer.
6. For å kunne bli valgt som styremedlem må man ha hatt et verv i sin moské i minst ett år.
7. Ved leders fravær trer nestleder automatisk inn som fungerende leder. I fravær av begge, plikter leder å utpeke en fungerende leder.
8. Styremøter innkalles av styreleder.
9. Styret oppretter administrasjonen og har organisasjons- og instruksjonsmyndighet.
10. Alle avgjørelser bør tilstrebes å bli fattet etter konsensus, men på den andre styrebehandlingen kan saken avgjøres med 2/3 flertall.
11. Styret, ved dets leder, har personalansvar for ansatte.
12. Styret godkjenner opprettelse av nye stillinger og fastsetter instruks for stillinger. Det skal kun være adgang til åremåls- og prosjektbaserte ansettelser. Styret ansetter og avsetter.

§ 9. Administrasjonen

Administrasjonen har ansvaret for daglig drift i organisasjonen. Administrasjonen rapporterer til styret ved styrets leder. Administrasjonen skal bestå av minimum:

- Sekretariat
- Økonomiansvarlig
- Informasjonsansvarlig
- Leder for dialogavdeling
- Leder for imam- og kunnskapskomité

§ 10. Økonomi og ansvar

1. MDNs virksomhet finansieres av medlemskontingent, tilskudd og gaver under forutsetning at de gis uten innblanding i organisasjonens virksomhet.
2. Revisjonsberetning skal sendes til styret senest en uke før Årsmøtet som skal godkjenne regnskapet.
3. Minst to personer, inkludert økonomiansvarlig, skal ha tilgang til organisasjonens konti.
4. Regnskapsår omfatter 1. januar – 31. desember.
5. Prokura- og signaturrett gis styreleder og nestleder, hver for seg.
6. Alle utbetalinger over kr. 20.000,- må godkjennes av styrets leder.

APPENDIX 3: KEY WRITTEN SOURCES

§ 11. Vedtektsendring

Endringer i vedtekter kan bare foretas på ordinært eller ekstraordinært Årsmøte etter å ha vært på sakslisten, og det kreves 2/3 flertall av de avgitte stemmene.

§ 12. Oppløsning

1. Oppløsning av organisasjonen krever 2/3 flertallsvedtak av de avgitte stemmene på to etterfølgende ordinære eller ekstraordinære årsmøter.
2. Ved oppløsning skal eventuelle restmidler avhendes av Styret i tråd med organisasjonens formål og verdier.

Godkjent ver 1.0: Stiftelsesmøte 22.05.2017
Godkjent ver 2.0: Årsmøte 20.03.2022

Bibliography

AFP. 2022. 'Islam en France : les instances représentatives en pleine restructuration'. *Middle East Eye édition française*, 9 January 2022. http://www.middleeasteye.net/fr/actu-et-enquetes/forum-islam-france-cfcm-moussaoui-algerie-maroc-turquie-macron.

Aguilar, Luis Hernandez. 2018. *Governing Muslims and Islam in Contemporary Germany*. Leiden : Brill.

Ahlberg, N. L. 1992. *New Challenges – Old Strategies: Themes of Variation and Conflict among Pakistani Muslims in Norway*. Helsinki: Finnish Antropological Society.

Ahmed, Shahab. 2015. *What Is Islam? The Importance of Being Islamic*. Princeton University Press.

Ahmed, Shahab. 2017. *Before Orthodoxy: The Satanic Verses in Early Islam*. Harvard University Press.

Ahmed, Shahab, and Nenad Filipovic. 2004. 'The Sultan's Syllabus: A Curriculum for the Ottoman Imperial Medreses Prescribed in a Fermān of Qānūnī I Süleymān, Dated 973 (1565)'. *Studia Islamica*, no. 98/99, 183–218.

Ahrne, Göran, and Nils Brunsson. 2005. 'Organizations and Meta-Organizations'. *Scandinavian Journal of Management* 21 (4): 429–49.

Ahrne, Göran, and Nils Brunsson. 2008. *Meta-Organizations*. Edward Elgar Publishing.

Akerhaug, Lars. 2016. 'Strup støtten til Islamsk Råd'. *Dagbladet*, 20 June 2016. https://www.dagbladet.no/kultur/strup-stotten-til-islamsk-rad/60243553.

Aldrich, Howard. 2008. *Organizations and Environments*. Stanford University Press.

Alibasic, Ahmet. 2016. 'Apostasy'. In *Encyclopedia of Islam and the Muslim World*, edited by Richard C. Martin, Second edition. Farmington Hills: Gale.

Al-Qaradawi, Yusuf. 2003. *Fiqh of Muslim Minorities: Contentious Issues and Recommended Solutions*. Cairo: Al-Falah Foundation.

Amir-Moazami, Schirin. 2011. 'Dialogue as a Governmental Technique: Managing Gendered Islam in Germany'. *Feminist Review* 98 (1): 9–27.

Anckar, Carsten. 2008. 'On the Applicability of the Most Similar Systems Design and the Most Different Systems Design in Comparative Research'. *International Journal of Social Research Methodology* 11 (5): 389–401.

Anonymous. 2008. 'IRN 2008-2018'. In author's private archive.

Anthony, Sean W. 2019. 'The Satanic Verses in Early Shi'ite Literature: A Minority Report on Shahab Ahmed's Before Orthodoxy'. *Shii Studies Review* 3 (1–2): 215–52.

AP. 2019. 'Moon Sightings, Politics Play a Part in Muslim Holiday'. *Ap News*, 4 June 2019, https://apnews.com/85106d29271a409882de5dfef3d1793c.

Arens, Christoph. 2016. 'Koordinationsrat der Muslime erfüllt bislang kaum seine Funktion', 2 February 2016. https://www.domradio.de/themen/islam-und-kirche/2016-02-02/koordinationsrat-der-muslime-erfuellt-bislang-kaum-seine-funktion.

BIBLIOGRAPHY

Arnesen, Daniel. 2019. 'Nonprofit Advocacy Reconfigured? Resource Mobilization, Political Opportunity and Organizational Change'. PhD thesis, University of Oslo.

Arnesen, Hans Olav. 2011. 'Det faller underlig frukt fra Islamsk Råd Norge-bygningen'. *Religioner. No*, 5 February 2011. https://religioner.no/aktuelt/det-faller-underlig -frukt-fra-islamsk-rad-norge-bygningen/.

Arslan, Leyla, and Mohamed-Ali Adraoui. 2013. *L'Islam En France Pour Les Nuls*. Paris: Actu. First.

Ashraf, Mohammad. 1992. 'Kontakt mellom Den Norske Kirke og Muslimske Organisations i Norge', 18 April 1992. Leirvik's archive.

Atkinson, Mary. 2016. 'Dutch Islamic Groups Resist Becoming Informers in Surveillance Drive'. *Middle East Eye*, 8 August 2016. http://www.middleeasteye.net /features/dutch-islamic-groups-resist-becoming-informers-surveillance-drive.

Austena, Ann Magrit. 2011. *Arven Etter Sataniske Vers*. Oslo: Cappelen Damm.

Azzam, Jamal Eddine, and Héloïse Berkowitz. 2018. 'Patterns of Coopetition in Meta-Organizations'. *Routledge Companion to Coopetition Strategies*, 280–91.

Babayan, Kathryn. 1996. 'Sufis, Dervishes and Mullas: The Controversy over Spiritual and Temporal Dominion in Seventeenth-Century Iran'. In *Safavid Persia: History and Politics of an Islamic Society*, edited by Charles Melville, 117–39. London: I. B. Tauris.

Bakke-Lorentzen, Elin. 2000. 'Skolefag som politisk konstruksjon: En sosiologisk analyse av den politiske prosessesen bak grunnskolefaget "Kristendomskunnskap med religions- og livssynsorientering"'. Master's thesis, University of Bergen. http://bora .uib.no/bitstream/handle/1956/1277/Hovedoppgave-lorentzen.pdf?sequence=1.

Bakken, Laila Ø. 2010. 'Anti-snillismen som endret Norge'. NRK. 26 September 2010. https://www.nrk.no/urix/anti-snillismen-som-endret-norge-1.7305686.

Bakkevig, Trond, and Olav Fykse Tveit. 'Invitation letter from the Church of Norway to the mosques of Norway, January 1992', 20 January 1992. Leirvik's archive.

Bakkevig, Trond, and Olav Fykse Tveit 1992b. 'Untitled 2', 28 October 1992. Leirvik's archive.

Bangstad, Sindre. 2009. *Sekularismens Ansikter*. Universitetsforl.

Bangstad, Sindre. 2016. 'Recoding Nationalism: Islam, Muslims and Islamophobia in Norway Before and After July 22 2011'. *Islamophobia Studies Yearbook* 7:44–65.

Bar-Tal, Daniel. 2013. *Intractable Conflicts: Socio-Psychological Foundations and Dynamics*. Cambridge: Cambridge University Press.

Bauer, Thomas. 2011. *Die Kultur Der Ambiguität. Eine andere Geschichte des Islams*. Berlin: Verlag der Weltreligionen.

Bayrakli, Enes, Farid Hafez, and Leonard Faytre. 2018. 'Engineering a European Islam: An Analysis of Attempts to Domesticate European Muslims in Austria, France, and Germany'. *Insight Turkey* 20 (3): 131–56.

Beach, Derek, and Rasmus Brun Pedersen. 2013. *Process-Tracing Methods: Foundations and Guidelines*. Ann Arbor: University of Michigan Press.

Bech, Emily Cochran. 2010. 'From Blowback to Incorporation: Muslim Council Consolidation and Influence in Europe'. Unpublished manuscript. https://www .researchgate.net/publication/270898550_From_Blowback_to_Incorporation _Muslim_Council_Consolidation_in_Europe

Belanger, Paul, and Munroe Eagles. 2007. 'Partisan Cross-Pressure and Voter Turnout: The Influence of Micro and Macro Environments'. *Social Science Quarterly* 88 (3): 850–67.

Ben Rouma, Hanan. 2018. 'Les Fédérations font front commun autour du CFCM pour lancer l'association pour le financement du culte musulman'. *Saphir News*, 9 July 2018. https://www.saphirnews.com/Les-federations-font-front-commun-autour -du-CFCM-pour-lancer-l-Association-pour-le-financement-du-culte-musulman _a25395.html.

Bleskestad, Maren Thorsen. 2010. 'Livet i Tøyengata'. *Nettavisen*, 12 June 2010. https:// www.nettavisen.no/dittoslo/livet-i-tyengata/3422888196.html.

Bourget, Carine. 2019. *Islamic Schools in France: Minority Integration and Separatism in Western Society*. Cham: Palgrave Macmillan.

Braginskaia, Ekaterina. 2015. 'Muslim Councils in Britain and Russia: Challenges of Cooperation and Representation in Contrasting Institutional Contexts'. PhD thesis, University of Edinburgh. https://era.ed.ac.uk/handle/1842/16456

Brandvol, Ivar. 2007. 'Strid om avlivingsmetode for kylling'. *Nationen*, 16 March 2007.

Brandvold, Åse. 2009. 'Våre nye kulturradikalere'. *Klassekampen*, 12 September 2009.

Brandvold, Åse. 2010. 'Angrer på uklarhet'. *Klassekampen*, 22 September 2010.

Brandvold, Åse. 2012. 'I dialog med Arfan Bhatti'. *Klassekampen*, 22 February 2012. https://www.klassekampen.no/article/20120222/ARTICLE/302229999.

Brandvold, Åse. 2016a. 'Boikottet valget'. *Klassekampen*, 19 October 2016.

Brandvold, Åse. 2016b. 'Tøff strid i Islamsk Råd'. *Klassekampen*, 15 October 2016. http://www.klassekampen.no/article/20161015/PLUSS/161019766.

Brandvold, Åse. 2017a. 'Får dialogpenger'. *Klassekampen*, 20 December 2017.

Brandvold, Åse. 2017b. 'Konflikt kan ende i retten'. *Klassekampen*, 3 April 2017. https:// www.klassekampen.no/article/20170403/ARTICLE/170409993.

Brandvold, Åse. 2017c. 'Kritiserer Islamsk Råd'. *Klassekampen*, 20 April 2017.

Bråten, Beret, and Olav Elgvin. 2014. 'Forskningsbasert politikk. En gjennomgang av forskningen på tvangsekteskap, kjønnslemlestelse og alvorlige begrensninger av unges frihet, og av de politiske tiltakene på feltet'. Oslo: Fafo.

Brottveit, Ånund, Ann Kristin Gresaker, and Nina Hoel. 2015. 'Det handler om verdensfreden. Evaluering av rollen Samarbeidsrådet for tros- og livssynssamfunn. Trossamfunn som arena for forebygging av radikalisering og voldelig ekstremisme'. Oslo: KIFO.

Brubaker, Rogers. 2013. 'Categories of Analysis and Categories of Practice: A Note on the Study of Muslims in European Countries of Immigration'. *Ethnic and Racial Studies* 36 (1): 1–8.

BIBLIOGRAPHY

Bruce, Benjamin. 2018. *Governing Islam Abroad: Turkish and Moroccan Muslims in Western Europe*. Cham: Palgrave Macmillan.

Brudevold, Else. 1995. 'Muslimsk gen.sekretær drev solospill'. *Aftenposten*, 27 February 1995.

Brun, Ellen, and Jacques Hersh. 2008. 'The Danish Disease: A Political Culture of Islamophobia'. *Monthly Review* 60 (2): 11.

Bygnes, Susanne. 2013. 'Ambivalent multiculturalism'. *Sociology* 47 (1): 126–41.

Capar, Robin-Ivan. 2021. 'Islamic Council of Norway Certifies Several Slaughterhouses'. *Norway Today*, 26 July 2021. https://norwaytoday.info/news/islamic-council-of-norway-certifies-several-slaughterhouses/.

Casciani, Dominic. 2010. 'Islamic Scholar Tahir Ul-Qadri Issues Terrorism Fatwa'. BBC *News*, 2 March 2010. http://news.bbc.co.uk/2/hi/uk_news/8544531.stm

Chaudhry, Ayesha S. 2013. *Domestic Violence and the Islamic Tradition*. Oxford: Oxford University Press

Chaudhry, Ayesha Siddiqua. 2009. 'Wife-Beating in the Pre-Modern Islamic Tradition: An Inter-Disciplinary Study of Hadīth, Qur'anic Exegesis and Islamic Jurisprudence'. PhD thesis, New York University.

Christensen, Johan, and Stine Hesstvedt. 2019. 'Expertisation or Greater Representation? Evidence from Norwegian Advisory Commissions'. *European Politics and Society* 20 (1): 83–100.

Christensen, Johan, and Cathrine Holst. 2017. 'Advisory Commissions, Academic Expertise and Democratic Legitimacy: The Case of Norway'. *Science and Public Policy* 44 (6): 821–33.

Christiansen, Peter Munk, and Hilmar Rommetvedt. 1999. 'From Corporatism to Lobbyism? – Parliaments, Executives, and Organized Interests in Denmark and Norway'. *Scandinavian Political Studies* 22 (3): 195–220.

Ciciora, Alice. 2018. 'Varieties of Muslim Councils in Europe'. *Comparative European Politics* 16 (2): 330–49.

Dagsavisen. 2011. 'Beholder statsstøtte tross homosyn', 8 February 2011.

Dahlburg, John-Thor. 1995. 'Death Sentence for Boy, 14, Roils Pakistan'. *Los Angeles Times*, 19 February 1995.

Danermark, Berth, Mats Ekstrom, and Liselotte Jakobsen. 2005. *Explaining Society: An Introduction to Critical Realism in the Social Sciences*. London: Routledge.

Daugstad, Gunnlaug, and Lars Østby. 2009. 'Et mangfold av tro og livssyn'. *Samfunnsspeilet* 23 (3): 14–22.

Dazey, Margot. 2021a. 'Polite Responses to Stigmatization: Ethics of Exemplarity among French Muslim Elites'. *Ethnic and Racial Studies*, 1–21.

Dazey, Margot. 2021b. 'Rethinking Respectability Politics'. *The British Journal of Sociology* 72 (3): 580–93.

Decap, Alejandro. 2013. 'Krever fordømmelse'. *Utrop*, 31 January 2013. https://www.utrop.no/nyheter/nytt/24510/.

Den norske kirke. 2011. 'Islamsk/kristen fellesuttalelse mot religiøs ekstremisme'. 22 November 2011. http://www.gammel.kirken.no/?event=dolink&famID=223367.

Det Islamske Forbundet – Rabita. 2019. 'Det Islamske Forbundet – Rabita – Innlegg Om Eid'. 3 June 2019. https://www.facebook.com/detislamske.forbundet/photos/a.8537 64701341588/2388475857870457/?type=3&theater.

Deutschen Bischofskonferenz. 2022. 'Begegnung zwischen der Deutschen Bischofskonferenz und dem Koordinationsrat der Muslime'. Deutsche Bischofskonferenz. 3 February 2022. https://www.dbk.de/presse/aktuelles/meldung/begegnung-zwi schen-der-deutschen-bischofskonferenz-und-dem-koordinationsrat-der-muslime.

Devereaux, Bret. 2022. 'New Acquisitions: On the Wisdom of Noah Smith'. A Collection of Unmitigated Pedantry. 29 August 2022. https://acoup.blog/2022/08/29 /new-acquisitions-on-the-wisdom-of-noah-smith/.

Diouf, Mamadou. 2013. *Tolerance, Democracy, and Sufis in Senegal*. New York: Columbia University Press.

Djuve, Anne Britt. 2016. 'Multikulturalisme på norsk – er anerkjennelse til hinder for utjevning?' *Agora* 32 (02–03): 85–109.

Domes et minarets. 2019. 'Huit écoles musulmanes parmi les plus performantes du Royaume-Uni'. *Des Dômes & Des Minarets*, 28 October 2019. https://www.desdome setdesminarets.fr/2019/10/28/huit-ecoles-musulmanes-parmi-les-plus-perfor mantes-du-royaume-uni/.

Døving, Cora Alexa. 2016. 'Pluralismens voktere. Samarbeidsrådet for tros -og livssynssamfunn som politisk aktør gjennom 20 år'. *Kirke og kultur* 120 (04): 362–85.

Dupont, Gilbert. 2024. '"Ce projet a été torpillé par le ministre": pourquoi le torchon brûle entre l'Exécutif des Musulmans et le Conseil musulman de Belgique'. *DHnet*, 27 August 2024. https://www.dhnet.be/actu/belgique/2024/08/27/ce-projet -a-ete-torpille-par-le-ministre-pourquoi-le-torchon-brule-entre-lexecutif-des -musulmans-et-le-conseil-musulman-de-belgique-F6ZSZSZVZNGTBMYIZV BBEHXCYI/.

Egeberg, Kristoffer. 2006. 'Tror Muhammed-meklingen hjalp'. *Dagbladet*, 19 February 2006. https://www.dagbladet.no/a/66186490.

Eggen, Nora S. 2021. 'Profetsitater i koronavirus-pandemiens tid: Om hvordan muslimer i Norge forvalter profeten Muhammads arv'. *DIN-Tidsskrift for religion og kultur*, no. 2: 13–40.

Eidsvåg, Inge, ed. 1993. *Fellesskapsetikk i et Flerkulturelt Norge*. Oslo: Universitetsforlaget.

EKD. 2022. 'Armut gemeinsam begegnen: EKD und KRM ermuntern zu interreligiösen Kooperationen'. 29 October 2022. https://www.ekd.de/armut-gemeinsam -begegnen-ekd-und-krm-ermuntern-zu-75894.htm.

Ekström, Sören. 2006. 'Staten, trossamfunden och samhällets grundläggande värderingar – en bakgrund'. In *Samfunden och bidragen. «De grundläggande värderingar som samhället vilar på» – om förutsättningarna för statsbidrag till trossamfund*. Stockholm: Proprius förlag AB.

BIBLIOGRAPHY

Elgvin, Johannes. 2007. 'Koranskolens folk: En kvalitativ studie av en tyrkiskdominert islamsk menighet i Oslo'. Master's thesis, University of Oslo.

Elgvin, Olav. 2011. 'Secularists, Democratic Islamists and Utopian Dreamers: How Muslim Religious Leaders in Norway Fit Islam into the Norwegian Political System'. Master's thesis, University of Oslo.

Elgvin, Olav. 2020. 'Between a Rock and a Hard Place : The Islamic Council of Norway and the Challenge of Representing Islam in Europe'. PhD thesis, University of Bergen.

Elgvin, Olav. 2022. 'Regulations in Flux: Theology, Politics, and Halal Slaughter in Norway'. *Tidsskrift for Islamforskning* 16 (2): 136–55.

Elgvin, Olav. 2023a. 'Den Norske dialogmodellen: Representasjon og dialog som svar på kulturell ulikhet'. In *Ulikhetens Drivere Og Dilemmaer*, 311–23. Oslo: Universitetsforlaget.

Elgvin, Olav. 2023b. 'For the Greater Good: Common Goals and Institutional Sunni–Shi'a Cooperation in Norway'. *Journal of Muslims in Europe* 12 (1): 15–35.

El-Rouayheb, Khaled. 2009. *Before Homosexuality in the Arab-Islamic World, 1500-1800*. Chicago: University of Chicago Press.

Engelstad, Marianne. 2013. 'Sataniske vers og Muhammed-karikaturer: En analyse av de muslimske miljøenes og myndighetenes reaksjoner på og håndtering av Rushdie-saken og karikaturstriden i Norge Og Danmark'. Master's thesis, University of Oslo.

Engström, Josefin. 2007. '- Dør på feil vis'. *Aftenposten*, 9 June 2007.

Eriksen, Thomas Hylland. 1995. *Det nye fiendebildet*. Oslo: Cappelen.

Figenschou, Tine Ustad, and Audun Beyer. 2014. 'The Limits of the Debate: How the Oslo Terror Shook the Norwegian Immigration Debate'. *The International Journal of Press/Politics* 19 (4): 430–52.

Fındıklı, Burhan. 2022. 'Rethinking Ancient Centers of Higher Learning: Madrasa in a Comparative-Historical Perspective'. *British Journal of Educational Studies* 70 (2): 129–44.

Flatøe, Geir. 2003. '- Suldal bør tenke seg om'. *Stavanger Aftenblad*, 16 October 2003.

Fleck, Denise. 2007. 'Institutionalization and Organizational Long-Term Success'. *BAR-Brazilian Administration Review* 4:64–80.

Flyvbjerg, Bent. 2006. 'Five Misunderstandings about Case-Study Research'. *Qualitative Inquiry* 12 (2): 219–45.

Fosse, Anders. 2006. '– Respekter våre verdier'. *VG*, 11 February 2006. https://www.vg.no/i/od54m.

Fox, Nick J. 2008. 'Post-Positivism'. *The SAGE Encyclopedia of Qualitative Research Methods* 2:659–64.

Friskolornas riksförbund. 2017. 'Sveriges bästa och sämsta grundskolor 2017'. https://www.mynewsdesk.com/se/friskolornas_riksforbund/documents/sveriges-baesta-och-saemsta-grundskolor-2017-72416.

Geard, Kathrine. 2006. '– Islamsk råd representerer ikke oss'. *Journalisten*, 3 March 2006. https://journalisten.no/islamsk-rad-representerer-ikke-oss/206852.

Gehring, Thomas, and Johannes Marx. 2023. 'Group Actors. Why Social Science Should Care About Collective Agency'. *Historical Social Research/Historische Sozialforschung* 48 (3): 7–39.

Gerring, John. 2007. 'Is There a (Viable) Crucial-Case Method?' *Comparative Political Studies* 40 (3): 231–53.

Gerring, John. 2012. 'Mere Description'. *British Journal of Political Science* 42 (4): 721–46.

Gilje, Caroline Teinum. 2019. 'Vil ha muslimske barnevernsinstitusjoner'. *Vårt Land*, 4 November 2019. https://www.vl.no/nyhet/vil-ha-muslimske-barneverns-institus joner-1.1612514?paywall=true.

Godard, Bernard. 2015. *La Question Musulmane En France*. Paris: Fayard.

Godard, Bernard, and Sylvie Taussig. 2007. *Les Musulmans en France: Courants, institutions, communautés; Un état des lieux*. Paris: R. Laffont.

Goffman, Erving. 1959. *The Presentation of Self in Everyday Life*. New York: Bantam Doubleday Dell

Gottschalk, Sebastian. 2017. *Kolonialismus und Islam: Deutsche und Britische Herrschaft in Westafrika (1900-1914)*. Weinheim: Campus Verlag.

Gran, Even. 2007. '- Homofili er synd, men dødsstraff er feil'. *Fri tanke*, 9 November 2007. https://fritanke.no/homofili-er-synd-men-dodsstraff-er-feil/19.7491.

Gran, Even. 2012. 'Azmeh Rasmussen fornøyd med Islamsk Råd ett år etter: – Aksjonen har gått inn i en ny fase'. *Fri tanke*, 30 January 2012. https://fritanke.no/aksjonen -har-gatt-inn-i-en-ny-fase/19.8742.

Granbo, Kristin. 2010. 'Advarte mot norsk 11. september'. NRK, 12 February 2010. https://www.nrk.no/norge/advarte-mot-norsk-11.-september-1.6991394.

Grimstad, Grunde. 2006. 'Rolig, men høylydt'. *Aftenposten*, 12 June 2006. https://www .aftenposten.no/article/ap-8Qk9d.html.

Gripsrud, Jostein. 2018. *Norsk hamskifte. En kritikk av Terje Tvedt, et betinget forsvar for godheten og en etterlysning av midtbanen i innvandringsdebatten*. Bergen: Vigmostad & Bjørke.

Grung, Anne Hege, and Lena Larsen. 2000. *Dialog Med Og Uten Slør*. Oslo: Pax.

Guttormsen, Arne. 1994. 'Først må muslimske barns problemer løses'. *Vårt Land*, 30 June 1994.

Haakaas, Einar, Alf Endre Magnussen, and Olga Stokke. 2010. 'Sier nei til statlig støtte'. *Aftenposten*, 25 February 2010.

Haddad, Yvonne. 1992. 'Islamists and the" Problem of Israel": The 1967 Awakening'. *The Middle East Journal*, 266–85.

Haddad, Yvonne Yazbeck, and Tyler Golson. 2007. 'Overhauling Islam: Representation, Construction, and Cooption of "Moderate Islam" in Western Europe'. *Journal of Church and State*, 487–515.

BIBLIOGRAPHY

229

Hagelund, Anniken. 2003. *The Importance of Being Decent: Political Discourse on Immigration in Norway 1970-2002*. Oslo: Unipax.

Hamdan, Mohammad. 2006. 'Rapport fra reisen til Midt-Østen i forbindelse med karikatursaken (12-23 februar 2006)'. http://folk.uio.no/leirvik/tekster/IRNdelegas jonMA.pdf.

Hauge, Johanna, Fouad Acharki, and Jenny Dahl Bakken. 2022. 'Ny kalender gir like bønnetider: – Ønsker å samle norske muslimer'. *NRK*, 22 March 2022, sec. dk. https://www.nrk.no/stor-oslo/ramadan-2022_-kalender-gir-like-bonnetider-for -muslimer-i-norge-1.15902809.

Haugen, Hans Morten. 2015. 'Fra statskonform kirke til sosial omformer? Sju teser om Den Norske Kirkes rolle fra 1800-Tallet til i dag'. *Teologisk Tidsskrift* 4 (2): 164–82.

Hegstad, Harald. 1999. *Kirke i forandring: Fellesskap, tilhørighet og mangfold i Den Norske Kirke*. Oslo: Luther.

Henriksen, Anita Bakk. 2017. 'Twitter koker etter Islamsk Råds ansettelse'. *Nettavisen*, 28 March 2017. http://nettavisen.no/artikkel/3423327059.

Hilalkomiteen. 2000. 'Hijrikalender avtalen i Norge'. Author's private archive.

Hirsti, Kristine. 2012. 'Norske muslimer mot Muhammed-film'. NRK. 21 September 2012. https://www.nrk.no/norge/norske-muslimer-mot-muhammed-film-1.8331401.

Hoffner, Anne-Benedicte. 2019. 'Une nouvelle organisation se veut « au service des fidèles et citoyens musulmans »'. *La Croix*, 21 January 2019. https://www.la-croix .com/Religion/Islam/nouvelle-organisation-veut-service-fideles-citoyens-musul mans-2019-01-21-1200996971.

Horsfjord, Vebjørn. 2013. 'Dialog etter karikaturkrisen: Sammen er vi Forskjellige?' *Kirke Og Kultur* 117 (04): 405–22.

Horsfjord, Vebjørn. Letter to Oddbjørn Leirvik. 2005a. 'Kontaktgruppe og veiledning', 27 October 2005. Leirvik's archive.

Horsfjord, Vebjørn. Letter to Medlemmer av kontaktgruppa med Islamsk Råd. 2005b. 'Kontaktgruppa IRN-MKR', 7 November 2005. Leirvik's archive.

Houten, Maaike van. 2019. 'De voorzitter van moskeekoepel CMO houdt er alweer mee op'. *Trouw*, 22 February 2019, sec. religie&filosofie. https://www.trouw.nl/gs -bdo6fb5d.

Hovland, Siri Lundberg. 2012. 'Ytringsfrihetens grenser. Krenke eller respektere religiøse følelser? Debatten i norske aviser fra 1. Oktober 2005 til 31. Mars 2006, og fra 1. januar til 31. Mars 2010'. Master's thesis, University of Oslo.

Hultgreen, Gunnar. 2010. 'Hysj-politiet lenker til sider som framstiller profeten som en gris'. *Dagbladet*, 3 February 2010. https://www.dagbladet.no/a/64938791.

Huseby, Vilde Blix. 2016. 'Afsar: Ble vingeklippet av tidligere styre'. *Vårt Land*, 15 October 2016. https://www.vl.no/reportasjer/reportasje/afsar-ble-vingeklippet-av-tidligere -styre-1.791511.

BIBLIOGRAPHY

Huseby, Vilde Blix. 2017. 'Begeret er fullt: Kan kaste ut Islamsk Råd'. *Dagsavisen*, 5 September 2017. https://www.dagsavisen.no/nyheter/innenriks/begeret-er-fullt -mehtab-afsar-og-islamsk-rad-kan-kastes-ut-1.1020050.

Ihlebæk, Elisabeth Rodum Jostein, and reas Bakke Foss Halvor Tjønn Arild Færaas. 2012. 'Video truer kronprinsen, Støre og Stoltenberg'. *Aftenposten*, 17 January 2012. https://www.aftenposten.no/article/ap-Jo5z8.html.

IRN. 2000. 'Pressemelding fra Islamsk Råd Norge'. https://web.archive.org/web/200 11129123344/http://www.irn.no/.

IRN. 2006a. Bakgrunnsnotat for søknad om driftssøtte Til Islamsk Råd Norge'. Departemental archives.

IRN. 2006b. 'Søknad om driftsstøtte til IRN'. Departemental archives.

IRN. 2008a. 'IRN lanserer Trygg Muslim'. Www.Irn.No. 11 April 2008. https://web .archive.org/web/20120601193006/http://irn.no/.

IRN. 2008b. 'Islamsk Råd Norge inngår avtale om halalslakt med nortura'. Halalmat. No. 15 September 2008. https://web.archive.org/web/20080921005354/https:// halalmat.no/avtale.html.

IRN. 2012. 'Trygg Muslim – Islamsk Råd Norge'. 2 October 2012. https://web.archive.org /web/20121002061156/http://www.irn.no/trygg-muslim.

IRN. 2019a. 'Islamsk Råd Norge – Innlegg Om Barnevern'. 7 November 2019. https://www.facebook.com/islamskraadnorge/posts/2953263791352807?_xts_[0] =68.ARCdj_0-Xgg9m6PKNmZJ_n8rVuUjejPAmj8jwtOCZHI5IQ1A9qKF1ionD nqbrRfo7XHXVqapyeMEnyDzmDw3KCOm0nw7M54Qv59sWE4VBATJE mEJA5Lsfctpmvq8segFzh6ykTDToPlMPNM6JMD6JAbpsiRmNbza3S2DJI F6Oy8svVNktfULMr4Y3BeSk1On6ml5FVlhJzDMAmwEN_CuDtRDU8_uKHY eaqUpc8szfPJnpALYqAPY-PLO7RZ_nEBVbeXVwjJszcfS8PFv2SqDlvYzLHeqf FsEUugQTCzQOy_btcXQvXjPQLhE7tV-Ji9lOBE_OA8qw7fomUtfMqRIIfQ& _tn_=-R.

IRN. 2019b. 'Islamsk Råd Norge – Innlegg om Eid'. 4 June 2019. https://www.facebook .com/islamskraadnorge/photos/a.877097372302803/2645297518816104/?type=3 &theater.

IRN. 2019c. 'Trygg Muslim'. Islamsk Råd Norge. 2019. https://www.irn.no/trygg-muslim -forside/.

IRN. 2021. 'Vedtekter'. https://irn.no/wp-content/uploads/2022/10/VEDTATT-VEDTEK TER-IRN-2021.pdf.

IRN. 2022. 'Hvem vi er – Islamsk Råd Norge'. 29 July 2022. https://web.archive.org /web/20220729144821/https://irn.no/om-oss/hvem-vi-er/.

IRN. 2023. 'Innspill til ekstremismekommisjonen'. *Islamsk Råd Norge* (blog). 7 April 2023. https://irn.no/innspill-til-ekstremismekommisjonen/.

IRN. 2024. 'SLUTT PÅ NORSK HALALSLAKTET KYLLING'. *Islamsk Råd Norge* (blog). 12 July 2024. https://irn.no/slutt-pa-norsk-halalslaktet-kylling/.

BIBLIOGRAPHY

IRN and MKR. 2006. Fellesuttalelse Fra Kontaktgruppen Mellom Islamsk Råd Norge Og Mellomkirkelig Råd'. 23 January 2006. http://folk.uio.no/leirvik/tekster /UttalelseMKR-IRN230106.htm.

IRN and MKR. 2007. 'Joint Declaration on the Freedom of Religion and the Right to Conversion'. Church of Norway. 22 August 2007. http://www.gammel.kirken.no /english/news.cfm?artid=149142.

IRN and MKR. 2009. 'Joint Statement on Violence in the Family and in Close Relationships by Islamic Council of Norway and Church of Norway Council on Ecumenical and International Relations'. 9 November 2009. http://www.gammel .kirken.no/english/doc/engelsk/Joint_declaration_violence_relations_0911.pdf.

Islamic Culture Centre Norway. 2016. 'Imam Mehboob ur Rehman går av med pensjon'. ICC – Islamic Culture Centre. 29 December 2016. https://www.islamic.no/2016 /imam-mehboob-ur-rehman-gar-pensjon/.

IslamiQ. 2019. 'KRM Plant Aufbau von Landesstrukturen – IslamiQ'. *IslamiQ – Nachrichten- Und Debattenmagazin Zu Islam Und Muslimen*, 2 July 2019. http:// www.islamiq.de/2019/07/02/koordinationsrat-der-muslime-plant-aufbau-von -landesstrukturen/.

Ispahani, Farahnaz. 2017. *Purifying the Land of the Pure: A History of Pakistan's Religious Minorities*. Oxford: Oxford University Press.

Isungset, Odd. 2010. *Hvem skjøt William Nygaard?* Oslo: Tiden.

Isungset, Odd. 2018. 'Skuddene mot William Nygaard: Flere siktet for attentatet'. NRK. 9 October 2018. https://www.nrk.no/dokumentar/skuddene-mot-william-nygaard _-flere-siktet-for-attentatet-1.14237346.

Ivarsflaten, Elisabeth, and Paul M. Sniderman. 2022. *The Struggle for Inclusion: Muslim Minorities and the Democratic Ethos*. Chicao: University of Chicago Press.

Jackson, William Kesler. 2013. 'A Subcontinent's Sunni Schism: The Deobandi-Barelvi Rivalry and the Creation of Modern South Asia'. PhD thesis, Syracuse University.

Jacobsen, Christine. 2002. *Tilhørighetens mange former: Unge muslimer i Norge*. Oslo: Unipax.

Jacobsen, Christine. 2010. *Islamic Traditions and Muslim Youth in Norway*. Leiden: Brill.

Joppke, Christian. 2013. *Legal Integration of Islam*. Cambridge, MA: Harvard University Press.

Jouanneau, Solenne. 2013. *Les Imams en France: Une autorité religieuse sous contrôle*. Paris: Agone.

Jupskås, Anders Ravik. 2015. 'The Persistence of Populism. The Norwegian Progress Party 1973–2009'. PhD thesis, University of Oslo.

Jurkovich, Ray. 1974. 'A Core Typology of Organizational Environments'. *Administrative Science Quarterly*, 380–94.

Khan, Adil Hussain. 2013. 'Creating the Image of European Islam: The European Council for Fatwa and Research and Ireland'. In *Muslim Political Participation in Europe*, 215–38.

Khoury, Jack. 2019. 'Caught between the Moon, Iran and Saudi Arabia: Muslims Divided over Ramadan's End'. *Haaretz*, 6 July 2019. https://www.haaretz.com/world -news/.premium-caught-between-iran-saudi-arabia-and-the-moon-muslims -divided-over-ramadan-s-end-1.7330808.

Kirknes, Hanne, and Rolf Widerøe. 2007. 'Muslimer vil ha Kylling-BOIKOTT'. *VG*, 22 July 2007.

Klausen, Jytte. 2005. *The Islamic Challenge: Politics and Religion in Western Europe*. Oxford: Oxford University Press.

Klausen, Jytte. 2009. *The Cartoons That Shook the World*. New Haven: Yale University Press.

KNA. 2019. 'Koordinationsrat der Muslime mit neuen Mitgliedern'. *domradio.de*, 2 July 2019. https://www.domradio.de/themen/interreligi%C3%B6ser-dialog/2019-07-02 /im-sinne-einer-gemeinsamen-muslimischen-repraesentanz-koordinationsrat-der -muslime-mit-neuen.

KNA. 2023. 'Islamverband VIKZ: Wollen Unseren Weg Alleine Gehen'. *Evangelische Zeitung*, 10 November 2023. https://www.evangelische-zeitung.de/islamverband -wir-schulden-deutschland-politische-neutralitaet.

Kobilica, Senaid. 2006. 'Rapport fra reisen til Pakistan i forbindelse med karikatursaken (16–19 Februar 2006)'. http://folk.uio.no/leirvik/tekster/IRNdelegasjonPak.pdf.

Kobilica, Senaid, and Masoom Zubair. 2024. 'Dehumanisering muliggjør utslettelse av Palestina'. *Aftenposten*, 2 January 2024. https://www.aftenposten.no/meninger /kronikk/i/y6PvoE/dehumanisering-muliggjoer-utslettelse-av-palestina.

Korbøl, Aud, and Arnfinn Midtbøen. 2018. *Den kritiske fase. Innvandring fra Norge Til Pakistan 1970-1973*. Oslo: Universitetsforlaget.

Kraatz, Matthew S., and Emily S. Block. 2008. 'Organizational Implications of Institutional Pluralism'. *The Sage Handbook of Organizational Institutionalism* 840:243–75.

Kristoffersen, Asbjørn. 1995. 'Feige muslimar?' *Bergens Tidende*, 25 February 1995.

Kruse, Elise. 2019. 'STL holder dørene åpne for Islamsk råd'. *Vårt Land*, 19 October 2019. https://www.vl.no/nyhet/stl-holder-dorene-apne-for-islamsk-rad-1.1603706.

KUF. 1995. *NOU 1995:9. Identitet og Dialog*. https://www.regjeringen.no/no/dokumenter /nou-1995-9/id140223/

Kultur- og kirkedepartementet. 2007. 'Statstilskudd 2007 – tilskuddsbrev'. Departemental archives.

Kulturdepartementet. 2017. 'Prop. 9 S (2017–2018). Samtykke til ikke å utbetale andre rate av driftstilskuddet til Islamsk Råd Norge for 2017'. https://www.regjeringen .no/no/dokumenter/prop.-9-s-20172018/id2577390/.

BIBLIOGRAPHY

Kumano-Ensby, Anne Linn. 2007. 'Avviser ikke homo-dødsstraff'. *NRK*, 8 November 2007. https://www.nrk.no/osloogviken/avviser-ikke-homo-dodsstraff-1.3988084.

Kurier. 2018. 'Löste Intrigen in IGGÖ Moscheen-Schliessung auf?' *Kurier*, 10 June 2018. https://kurier.at/politik/inland/loeste-intrige-in-iggioe-moscheen-schlies sung-aus/400048808.

Kvamme, Kjell. 2017. 'Nytt Muslim-Nettverk'. *Vårt Land*, 31 October 2017.

Lapidus, Ira M. 2014. *A History of Islamic Societies*. Ebook edition. Cambridge University Press.

Larsen, Lena. 2009. 'Lena Larsen om religion'. *morgenbladet.no*, 23 October 2009, sec. Aktuelt. https://morgenbladet.no/2015/06/stub-1601.

Larsen, Lena. 2018. *How Muftis Think: Islamic Legal Thought and Muslim Women in Western Europe*. Leiden: Brill.

Larson, Jeff A. 2009. *Why Change? Organizational Adaptation and Stability in a Social Movement Field*. Tuson: The University of Arizona.

Laurence, Jonathan. 2005. 'From the Élysée Salon to the Table of the Republic: State-Islam Relations and the Integration of Muslims in France'. *French Politics, Culture & Society* 23 (1): 37–64.

Larsen, Lena. 2006. 'Managing Transnational Islam: Muslims and the State in Western Europe'. In *Immigration and the Transformation of Europe* 251-269.

Larsen, Lena. 2009. 'The Corporatist Antecedent of Contemporary State-Islam Relations'. *European Political Science* 8 (3): 301–15.

Larsen, Lena. 2012. *The Emancipation of Europe's Muslims: The State's Role in Minority Integration*. Princeton: Princeton University Press.

Larsen, Lena. 2015. 'Muslim Mobilization Between Self-Organization, State-Recognized Consultative Bodies and Political Participation'. In *After Integration*, 59–78. Springer.

Laurence, Jonathan, and Justin Vaisse. 2007. *Integrating Islam: Political and Religious Challenges in Contemporary France*. Brookings Institution Press.

Laurent, Adrien, Pierre Garaudel, Géraldine Schmidt, and Philippe Eynaud. 2020. 'Civil Society Meta-Organizations and Legitimating Processes: The Case of the Addiction Field in France'. *VOLUNTAS: International Journal of Voluntary and Nonprofit Organizations* 31 (1): 19–38.

Lazarsfeld, Paul Felix, Bernard Berelson, and Hazel Gaudet. 1948. *The People's Choice: How the Voter Makes up His Mind in a Presidential Campaign*. New York: Columbia University Press.

Le Priol, Mélinée. 2019. 'La plateforme « L.E.S. musulmans » lance une Union des imams'. *La Croix*, 4 November 2019. https://www.la-croix.com/Religion/Islam/plateforme -L-E-S-musulmans-lance-Union-imams-2019-11-04-1201058414.

Leirvik, Oddbjørn. 1995a. 'Arbeidet Med Skolespørsmål i Kontaktgruppen Mellom-kirkelig Råd/Islamsk Råd'. Leirvik's archive.

Leirvik, Oddbjørn. 1995b. 'Untitled', 21 February 1995. Leirvik's archive.

Leirvik, Oddbjørn. 1995c. 'Letter to Kontaktgruppa Mellomkirkelig Råd / Islamsk Råd'. 7 April 1995. Leirvik's archive.

Leirvik, Oddbjørn. Letter to Statsministerens kontor. 1998. 'Ang. "Verdikommisjonen"', 4 January 1998. Leirvik's archive.

Leirvik, Oddbjørn. 2003. 'Rapport til Mellomkirkelig Råd frå kontaktgruppa med Islamsk Råd'. Leirvik's archive.

Leirvik, Oddbjørn. 2006a. 'Kva Var Karikatursaka Eit Bilete På'. *Kirke Og Kultur* 11 (2): 147–60.

Leirvik, Oddbjørn. Letter to Ingrid Næss. 2006b. 'Dialog Mellom Kristne Og Muslimer i Norge', 2 April 2006. Leirvik's archive.

Leirvik, Oddbjørn, and Erling Birkedal. 1994. 'Et større rom for etikk og religion i skolen'. Leirvik's archive.

Lindekleiv, Heidi Marie. 2015. 'Dialogen stanset etter dialogtur'. *Vårt Land*, 27 March 2015. https://www.vl.no/nyheter/2015/03/27/dialogen-stanset-etter-dialogtur/.

Loobuyck, Patrick, Jonathan Debeer, and Petra Meier. 2013. 'Church–State Regimes and Their Impact on the Institutionalization of Islamic Organizations in Western Europe: A Comparative Analysis'. *Journal of Muslim Minority Affairs* 33 (1): 61–76.

Malik, Kenan. 2010. *From Fatwa to Jihad: The Rushdie Affair and Its Aftermath*. New York: Melville House Publications.

March, Andrew F. 2011. 'Theocrats Living under Secular Law: An External Engagement with Islamic Legal Theory'. *Journal of Political Philosophy* 19 (1): 28–51.

Maréchal, Brigitte. 2008. *The Muslim Brothers in Europe: Roots and Discourse*. Leiden: Brill.

Maréchal, Brigitte, Stefano Allievi, Felice Dassetto, and Jørgen Nielsen. 2003. *Muslims in the Enlarged Europe: Religion and Society*. Leiden: Brill.

Masood, Ehsan. 2006. 'Muslim Council Phases in Lunar Calendar'. *Nature*, 1 September 2006.

Matpunkt. 2020. 'Kylling naturell – Curry Cut 16+ biter u/skinn, singelfryst, ca.1kg'. MatpunktTM Halalmat levert på døra. 2020. https://matpunkt.no/produkt/kjott-og -kylling/kylling-1/curry-cut-16-biter-over-1kg-2.

Mattes, Astrid, and Sieglinde Rosenberger. 2015. 'Islam and Muslims in Austria'. In *After Integration*, 129–52. Wiesbaden: Springer.

Mawaqeet Norway, dir. 2022. *Hvorfor vi ikke skal følge den nye IRN tabellen – Imam Rizwan Dawood*. https://www.youtube.com/watch?v=F6fX6SDweks.

MDN. 2019. 'Muslimsk Dialognettverk – Innlegg'. 28 January 2019. https://www.face book.com/MuslimskDialog/photos/a.276853022982563/279782949356237/?type =1&theater.

MDN. 2022. Vedtekter for Muslimsk Dialognettverk.

BIBLIOGRAPHY

MDN. 2024. 'Strategi 2025-2028'. Muslimsk Dialognettverk. Author's personal archive.

Medlemmer og ledere i Islamsk råd i Norge, Norges kristne råd og Den norske kirke. 2006. 'Muslimsk-Kristen Fellesuttalelse'. 3 February 2006. http://folk.uio.no/leirvik /tekster/Fellesuttalelse-karikaturstriden2006.pdf.

Merton, Robert K. 1957. 'The Role-Set: Problems in Sociological Theory'. *British Journal of Sociology*, 106–20.

Metcalf, Barbara Daly. 2002. 'Traditionalist'Islamic Activism: Deoband, Tablighis, and Talibs'. *ISIM Paper*, 1.

Midtbøen, Arnfinn H. 2017. 'Innvandringshistorie som faghistorie: Kontroverser i norsk migrasjonsforskning'. *Nytt Norsk Tidsskrift* 34 (2): 130–49.

MKR. 1991. 'Forslag om å opprette en "ordnet kontakt" med norske muslimer'. Leirvik's archive.

MKR. 2008. 'Protokoll Fra Møte i kontakgruppa for Mellomkirkelig Råd og Islamsk Råd Norge, 6. Mars 2008'. Leirvik's archive.

MKR. 2010. 'Protokoll Fra Møte i Kontaktgruppa Mellom IRN Og MKR 04. Mars 2010'. Leirvik's archive.

MKR, IRN, and DMT. 2013. 'Rapport Fra Jødisk-Kristen-Muslimsk Delegasjonsreise Israel Og Palestina 4.-10. Februar 2013'. Privat arkiv.

Moosa, Ebrahim. 1998. 'Shaykh Aḥmad Shākir and the Adoption of a Scientifically-Based Lunar Calendar'. *Islamic Law and Society* 5 (1): 57–89.

Moravcsik, Andrew. 2014. 'Transparency: The Revolution in Qualitative Research'. *PS: Political Science & Politics* 47 (1): 48–53.

Morgenbladet. 2010. 'Rocka talsmann'. *morgenbladet.no*, 17 December 2010. https:// morgenbladet.no/samfunn/2010/rocka_talsmann.

Morrow, Amanda. 2022. 'France Dumps Muslim Advisory Council That Is "Under Foreign Influence"'. *RFI*, 1 February 2022, sec. france. https://www.rfi.fr/en/france /20220201-france-dumps-muslim-advisory-council-under-foreign-influence-cfcm -islam-darmanin.

Mujtaba, Hasan, Stephen O. Murray, Will Roscoe, Eric Allyn, Louis Crompton, Mildred Dickemann, and Badruddin Khan. 1997. *Islamic Homosexualities: Culture, History, and Literature*. New York: NYU Press.

Mukhtar, Zahid. 1992a. 'Untitled2', 4 December 1992. Leirvik's archive.

Mukhtar, Zahid. Letter to Mellomkirkelig råd. 1992b. 'Letter to MKR', 18 August 1992. Leirvik's archive.

Mukhtar, Zahid. Letter to Mellomkirkelig råd. 1994. 'Invitasjon til møte mellom Islamsk Råd og Mellomkirkelig Råd', 10 January 1994. Leirvik's archive.

Mushtaq, Irfan. 2012. 'Halalkjøtt og aalalslakting i Norge – Muslimposten'. Www .Irn.No. 21 October 2012. https://web.archive.org/web/20121231204719/http://www .irn.no/siste-nytt-om-halalmat/entry/halalkjott-og-halalslakting-i-norge.

Mukhtar, Zahid. 2013a. 'Halalmat seminar 2013 – Islamsk Råd Norge'. Www.Irn.No. 4 April 2013. https://web.archive.org/web/20160322043310/http://www.irn.no/entry /halalmat-seminar-2013.

Mukhtar, Zahid. 2013b. 'Villedende bruk av halalmerking'. Www.Irn.No. 14 March 2013. https://web.archive.org/web/20160612080309/http://www.irn.no/entry/villedende -bruk-av-halalmerking.

Mutz, Diana C. 2002. 'The Consequences of Cross-Cutting Networks for Political Participation'. *American Journal of Political Science*, 838–55.

Navestad, Lars. 1995. 'Dødsdom i strid med koranen'. *Vårt Land*, 22 February 1995.

Nawal. 2020a. 'NAWAL – En Fornøyd Kunde Har Sendt Oss Bildet Av Sin Fryseboks... | Facebook'. 9 June 2020. https://www.facebook.com/permalink.php?story_fbid =pfbidoYdxCwbcszugmZresdChxGjVQm9uZaKm2T7JkUtsuhGoTLFs5qnaUq K2kYfiVFPs2l&id=1046681272201922.

Nawal. 2020b. 'Nawal Posting 24.01.2020'. 24 January 2020. https://www.facebook .com/permalink.php?story_fbid=1331564160380297&id=1046681272201922.

Nesser, Petter. 2019. 'Military Interventions, Jihadi Networks, and Terrorist Entrepreneurs: How the Islamic State Terror Wave Rose So High in Europe'. *CTC Sentinel* 12 (3). https://ctc.usma.edu/wp-content/uploads/2019/03/CTC-SENTINEL-032019 .pdf.

Nordhaug, Halvor, ed. 1991. *Når tro møter tro*. Oslo: Verbum.

Norges Imam Råd. 2019. 'Norges Imam Råd | Facebook'. 2019. https://www.facebook .com/NorgesImamRad/?ref=py_c.

Nortura. 2017. 'Nortura sier opp avtalen med Islamsk Råd Norge'. Nortura. 2 October 2017. http://www.nortura.no/pressesenter/nortura-sier-opp-avtalen-med -islamsk-rad-norge/.

Norwegian National Research Ethics Committee. 2016. *Guidelines for Research Ethics in the Social Sciences, Humanities, Law and Theology*.

NTB. 1992. 'Muslimske ledere tar avstand fra Rushdie-besøk'. *NTB*, 14 August 1992.

NTB. 2011. 'Avsluttet homoprotest mot Islamsk Råd'. *NTB*, 5 February 2011.

NTB. 2017a. '30000 står klare til å danne ny norsk islamsk organisasjon'. *NTB*, 31 March 2017.

NTB. 2017b. 'Sterke reaksjoner mot nikabkledd rådgiver i Islamsk Råd'. *NTB*, 28 March 2017.

Oliver, Christine. 1991. 'Strategic Responses to Institutional Processes'. *Academy of Management Review* 16 (1): 145–79.

Opsal, J. 2013. 'Representasjon og representativitet i kristen-muslimsk dialog i Norge'. *Norsk Tidsskrift for Misjonsvitenskap* 4:197–212.

Østberg, Sissel. 1998. 'Pakistani Children in Oslo: Islamic Nurture in a Secular Context'. University of Warwick.

Østberg, Sissel. 2003. *Muslim i Norge: Religion og hverdagsliv blant unge norskpakistanere*. Oslo: Universitetsforlaget.

BIBLIOGRAPHY

Pache, Anne-Claire, and Filipe Santos. 2010. 'When Worlds Collide: The Internal Dynamics of Organizational Responses to Conflicting Institutional Demands'. *Academy of Management Review* 35 (3): 455–76.

Parsons, Talcott. 2005. *The Social System*. London: Routledge.

Pellegrino, Chiara. 2017. 'Morocco: The Apostate No Longer Faces Death'. Oasis. 10 April 2017. https://www.oasiscenter.eu/en/morocco-apostate-no-longer-faces-death.

Perduco. 2011. 'Kartlegging av kunnskaper og holdninger på området rasisme og antisemittisme'. Oslo: Perduco. https://web.archive.org/web/20110617180015/http://www.utdanningsetaten.oslo.kommune.no/getfile.php/utdanningsetaten%20(UDE)/Internett%20(UDE)/PED/Dok/Rapport_UDA_7.6.2011.pdf.

Peter, Frank, and Rafael Ortega. 2014. *Islamic Movements of Europe*. London: IB Tauris.

Peters, Rudolph, and Gert JJ De Vries. 1976. 'Apostasy in Islam'. *Die Welt Des Islams*, 1–25.

Pfaff, Steven, and Anthony J Gill. 2006. 'Will a Million Muslims March? Muslim Interest Organizations and Political Integration in Europe'. *Comparative Political Studies* 39 (7): 803–28.

Philippon, Alix. 2014. 'L'apport Différentiel Du Soufisme Au Registre Islamiste Pakistanais'. *Revue Internationale de Politique Comparee* 21 (1): 33–64.

Piser, Karina. 2019. 'The Battle for a "French Islam"'. *Institute of Current World Affairs*, 12 July 2019. https://www.icwa.org/the-battle-for-a-french-islam/.

Proff. 2020. 'Norwegian M Import AS – Oslo – Roller og kunngjøringer'. https://www.proff.no/roller/norwegian-m-import-as/oslo/kj%C3%B8tt-og-vilt-engros/IF8SJ7D10OV/.

Purbrick-Thompson, Katherine Emily. 2019. 'Mahomet ou la république versus Mahomet et la république: Islam and Republicanism in France since 1989'. Birmingham: University of Birmingham.

Qadhi, Yasir. 2014. 'On Salafi Islam'. https://muslimmatters.org/wp-content/uploads/On-Salafi-Islam_Dr.-Yasir-Qadhi.pdf.

Qureishi, Tanveer ul-Islam. 1992. 'Åpningstale fra Islamsk Råd til Mellomkikrelig Råd'. Leirvik's archive.

Qureshi, Fahad. 2012. '- Sannheten vil alltid se lyset, selv om natten er mørk'. 5 March 2012. https://www.islamnet.no/aktuelt/samfunnsdebatten/item/68-sannheten-vil-alltid-se-lyset-selv-om-natten-er-mork.

Ramadan, Tariq. 2005. 'An International call for Moratorium on corporal punishment, stoning and the death penalty in the Islamic World'. Tariqramadan.com. 5 April 2005. https://tariqramadan.com:443/an-international-call-for-moratorium-on-corporal-punishment-stoning-and-the-death-penalty-in-the-islamic-world/.

Ramadan, Tariq. 2009. 'A Call for a Moratorium on Corporal Punishment—The Debate in Review'. In *New Directions in Islamic Thought: Exploring Reform and Muslim Tradition*, 163–74.

Rasch, Siril K. Herseth, Eiliv Frich Flydal, and Jonas Sverrisson. 2010. 'Bhatti vil være islams ansikt utad i Norge'. *Dagbladet*, 19 March 2010. https://www.dagbladet.no/a/65004302.

Rasmussen, Sara Azmeh. 2011. 'Brød, dadler og humanisme'. *Aftenposten*, 3 October 2011. https://www.aftenposten.no/article/ap-3MLXM.html.

Rebucini, Gianfranco. 2013. 'Hegemonic Masculinities and "Sexualities" Among Men in Morocco'. *Cahiers d'études Africaines*, no. 1, 387–415.

Reetz, Dietrich. 2010. "Alternate'Globalities? On the Cultures and Formats of Transnational Muslim Networks from South Asia'. In *Translocality*, 291–334. Brill.

Riaz, Wasim. 2007a. '- Imamene overdriver'. *Aftenposten*, 24 July 2007.

Riaz, Wasim. 2007b. 'Imamer: Å spise kylling = å synde'. *Aftenposten*, 21 July 2007.

Riaz, Wasim. 2008. 'Nå blir kyllingen halal'. *Aftenposten*, 17 September 2008.

Rodum, Elisabeth. 2006. 'Støre roste muslimene'. *Aftenposten*, 8 December 2006. https://www.aftenposten.no/article/ap-rE3PA.html.

Rommetvedt, Hilmar. 2005. 'Norway: Resources Count, but Votes Decide? From Neo-Corporatist Representation to Neo-Pluralist Parliamentarism'. *Western European Politics* 28 (4): 740–63.

Rommetvedt, Hilmar, Gunnar Thesen, Peter Munk Christiansen, and Asbjørn Sonne Nørgaard. 2013. 'Coping with Corporatism in Decline and the Revival of Parliament: Interest Group Lobbyism in Denmark and Norway, 1980–2005'. *Comparative Political Studies* 46 (4): 457–85.

Rosenow-Williams, Kerstin. 2012. *Organizing Muslims and Integrating Islam in Germany: New Developments in the 21st Century*. Leiden: Brill.

Rosenow-Williams, Kerstin. 2014. 'Organising Muslims and Integrating Islam: Applying Organisational Sociology to the Study of Islamic Organisations'. *Journal of Ethnic and Migration Studies* 40 (5): 759–77.

Saeed, Abdullah. 2017. *Freedom of Religion, Apostasy and Islam*. London: Routledge.

Saum, Veronika. 2010. '– Dagbladet ble brukt av Bhatti'. *TV 2*, 11 February 2010. https://www.tv2.no/a/3133732/.

Schiffauer, Werner. 2000. *Die Gottesmänner: Türkische Islamisten in Deutschland; Eine Studie Zur Herstellung Religiöser Evidenz*. Frankfurt/Main: Suhrkamp.

Schiffauer, Werner. 2010. *Nach Dem Islamismus. Eine Ethnografie Der Islamischen Gemeinschaft Milli Görüş*. Frankfurt/Main: Suhrkamp.

Schmidt, Nina, and Espen Egil Hansen. 1995. '30 Moskeer for Islam i Oslo'. *VG*, 24 July 1995

Schmidt, Ulla. 2015. 'Styring av religion. Tros- og livssynspolitiske tendenser etter det livssynsåpne samfunn'. *Teologisk Tidsskrift* 4 (03): 218–36.

Scott, W. Richard. 2013. *Institutions and Organizations: Ideas, Interests, and Identities*. Los Angeles: Sage publications.

BIBLIOGRAPHY

Seawright, Jason, and John Gerring. 2008. 'Case Selection Techniques in Case Study Research: A Menu of Qualitative and Quantitative Options'. *Political Research Quarterly* 61 (2): 294–308.

Seim, Turid Karlsen. Letter to Inger Nesvåg. 1986. 'Untitled', 23 May 1986. Leirvik's archive.

Selbekk, Vebjørn Kroll. 2006. *Truet av islamister*. Kjeller: Genesis.

Selznick, Philip. 1996. 'Institutionalism" Old" and" New"'. *Administrative Science Quarterly*, 270–77.

Selznick, Philip, and Leonard Broom. 1977. *Sociology: A Text with Adapted Readings. Sixth Edition*. 6th ed. New York: Harper & Row.

Shah, Zahra. 2016. 'Countering Radicalisation by Engaging Mosques and Imams: The UK's Case'. Master's thesis, Leiden University. https://openaccess.leidenuniv.nl/bit stream/handle/1887/38036/Zahra%20Shah%20-%20Thesis.pdf?sequence=1.

Shavit, Uriya. 2015. *Sharia and Muslim Minorities: The Wasati and Salafi Approaches to Fiqh al-Aqalliyyat al-Muslima*. Oxford: Oxford University Press.

Shavit, Uriya. 2016. 'Ramadan in Iceland: A Tale of Two Mosques'. *Islam and Christian–Muslim Relations* 27 (4): 397–417.

Sifaoui, Mohamed. 2020. 'Comment les islamistes ont sabordé "la charte des valeurs" de l'islam voulue par Macron'. *Le Journal du Dimanche*, 26 December 2020. https://www.lejdd.fr/Politique/comment-la-charte-des-valeurs-de-lislam-a-explose-en-vol-4014749.

Sil, Rudra, and Peter J. Katzenstein. 2010a. 'Analytic Eclecticism in the Study of World Politics: Reconfiguring Problems and Mechanisms across Research Traditions'. *Perspectives on Politics* 8 (2): 411–31.

Sil, Rudra, and Peter J. Katzenstein. 2010b. *Beyond Paradigms: Analytic Eclecticism in the Study of World Politics*. London: Macmillan International Higher Education.

Silvestri, Sara. 2007. 'Muslim Institutions and Political Mobilisation'. In *European Islam. Challenges for Public Policy and Society*, 169–82. CEPS Centre for European Policy Studies.

Silvestri, Sara. 2010. 'Public Policies towards Muslims and the Institutionalization of 'Moderate Islam' in Europe: Some Critical Reflections'. In *Muslims in 21st Century Europe*, 55–68. Routledge.

Simonnes, Kamilla. 2013. 'I stjålne klær? En analyse av endringer i Høyres, Arbeiderpartiets og Fremskrittspartiets innvandrings- og integreringspolitikk'. *Norsk Statsvitenskapelig Tidsskrift* 29 (02): 144–58.

Sleipnes, Per A. 2010. 'Skjeggerød blir storprodusent av halal-produkter'. *Kjøttbransjen*, March 2010.

Soifer, Hillel. 2020. 'Shadow Cases in Comparative Research'. *Qualitative and Multi-Method Research* 18(2), 9-18.

Soløy, Margrethe. 1995. 'Oslo-muslimer støtter dødsdom'. *Aftenposten*, 15 February 1995.

Sorgenfrei, Simon. 2018. *Islam i Sverige: De första 1300 åren*. Myndigheten för stöd till trossamfund.

Stanghelle, Harald. 1991. 'Nordhus trekker seg fra Rushdiesaken'. *Aftenposten*, 23 July 1991.

Steien, Solveig. 2008. '"Almost at War". The Mohammed Cartoon Crisis in Norwegian Media.' *Conflict & Communication* 7 (1), 1-14.

Steinsland, Arild. 1995. 'Møte i Kontaktgruppen Mellomkirkelig Råd / Islamsk Råd Norge'. Leirvik's archive.

'St.Melding Nr. 39 (2006-2007). Frivillighet for Alle.' 2007. https://www.regjeringen.no /contentassets/68b20a00c377479c98d8bac4c4e38cf6/no/pdfs/stm200620070039000dddpdfs.pdf.

Stokke, Olga. 1995. 'Islamsk Råd våger ikke ta avstand fra dødsdom'. *Aftenposten*, 22 February 1995.

Stokke, Olga, and Halvor Hegtun. 2006. 'Beklager trykking av tegningene'. *Aftenposten*, 10 February 2006. https://www.aftenposten.no/article/ap-2BGRq.html.

Sylte, Turid. 2011. '"Islamsk Råd tar for lett på jødehat'. *Vårt Land*, 10 June 2011.

Tajik, Hadia. 2013. 'Vår demokratiske beredskap'. *VG*, 25 June 2013. https://www .vg.no/i/7e2b4.

Tareen, SherAli. 2020. *Defending Muḥammad in Modernity*. Notre Dame: University of Notre Dame Pess.

Tassamma, Adan Hassan. 2024. 'Halalstrid kan endre det norske kjøttmarkedet'. *Aftenposten*, 24 July 2024. https://www.aftenposten.no/norge/i/qPPeo1/islamsk -raad-norge-trekker-halal-godkjenning-tusenvis-av-muslimer-kan-staa-uten -kylling.

Tavory, Iddo, and Stefan Timmermans. 2014. *Abductive Analysis: Theorizing Qualitative Research*. Chicago: University of Chicago Press.

Tayyeb, Ahmad al-. 2012. 'Declaration by Al-Azhar and the Intellectuals on the Legal Ordinances of Fundamental Freedoms'. Fondazione Internazionale Oasis. 28 February 2012. http://www.oasiscenter.eu/en/declaration-al-azhar-and-intel lectuals-legal-ordinances-fundamental-freedoms.

Therriault, Andrew, Joshua Aaron Tucker, and Ted Brader. 2011. 'Cross-Pressures and Political Participation'. Paper 23. http://opensiuc.lib.siu.edu/pnconfs_2011/23.

Thornton, Patricia H., William Ocasio, and Michael Lounsbury. 2015. 'The Institutional Logics Perspective'. In *Emerging Trends in the Social and Behavioral Sciences: An Interdisciplinary, Searchable, and Linkable Resource*, 1–22.

Thurston, Alexander. 2018. 'An Emerging Post-Salafi Current in West Africa and Beyond'. *Maydan* (blog). 15 October 2018. https://themaydan.com/2018/10/emerging -post-salafi-current-west-africa-beyond/.

Timmermans, Stefan, and Iddo Tavory. 2012. 'Theory Construction in Qualitative Research: From Grounded Theory to Abductive Analysis'. *Sociological Theory* 30 (3): 167–86.

BIBLIOGRAPHY

Triandafyllidou, Anna. 2010. 'Muslims in 21st Century Europe: Conceptual and Empirical Issues'. In *Muslims in 21st Century Europe*, 11–36. Routledge.

Tveit, Olav Fykse. Letter to Mellomkirkelig råd. 1993. 'Rapport frå møte med muslimske organisasjoner i Noreg 15. desember 1992 i Paulus menighetshus, Oslo', March 1993. Leirvik's archive.

Utrop. 2007. '-Kutt statsstøtten til Islamsk Råd Norge'. *Utrop*, 4 December 2007. https://www.utrop.no/nyheter/innenriks/14105/.

Vahed, Goolam, and Thembisa Waetjen. 2014. 'Moon Sightings and the Quest for Muslim Solidarities in Twentieth Century Natal.' *New Contree*, no. 71.

VG. 1995. 'Kan reddes av anke'. *VG*, 15 February 1995.

VG. 2013. 'Krever at Islamsk Råd tar oppgjør med Profetens Ummah'. 30 January 2013. https://www.vg.no/i/Lwmmx.

Vogl, Benjamin Hernes. 2024. 'Nortura: – Uaktuelt for oss å gå på kompromiss med norsk lov'. *Nationen*, 17 September 2024. https://www.nationen.no/5-148-607079.

Vogt, Kari. 2008. *Islam på norsk: Moskeer og islamske organisasjoner i Norge*. Oslo: Cappelen Damm.

Vogt, Kari. 2019. 'id al-fitr'. In *Store norske leksikon*. http://snl.no/id_al-fitr.

Vogt, Kari, and Zahoor Ahmad Chaudry. 2022. 'Ahmadiyya'. In *Store norske leksikon*. http://snl.no/ahmadiyya.

Vogt, Kari, Lena Larsen, and Christian Moe. 2011. *New Directions in Islamic Thought: Exploring Reform and Muslim Tradition*. London: IB Tauris.

Warner, Carolyn M., and Manfred W. Wenner. 2006. 'Religion and the Political Organization of Muslims in Europe'. *Perspectives on Politics* 4 (3): 457–79.

Zucker, Lynne G. 1977. 'The Role of Institutionalization in Cultural Persistence'. *American Sociological Review*, 726–43.

Index

Key concepts

Abduction 7
Analytic eclecticism 7
Causal mechanisms 5–6
Collective action 20–22, 30, 52, 75, 110, 170
Corporatist / corporatism 17, 71–73, 157–158, 163, 166, 178, 183, 184
Cross-pressures 5, 13–14, 51, 54–56, 91, 101, 112, 120, 136, 139, 171–173, 175, 177, 180, 184
Discourse 13, 28, 35, 51, 58–64, 69, 116, 145
Diversity and multipolarity 22–28, 30, 43–45, 53, 73, 139, 144–147, 170–171
Institutionalisation 14–15, 91–93, 116–117, 155–159, 172, 177–185
Islamophobia 1, 3, 35, 59, 111–112, 121–122, 132, 170, 174, 179
Meta-organisation. *See also* umbrella organisation 51–54, 56, 72, 120
Multiculturalism 28, 35, 64
Multiple institutional logics 54–55, 101–102
Organisational strategies 19, 55–56, 58, 84–85, 91, 113, 120, 123–128, 161, 163, 171–172, 175, 177, 184
Process tracing 5–6
Umbrella organisation 51–54, 76, 81, 95, 116–117, 136, 154, 158–165
Secularism 2, 69

Key organisations

ALIS (Alliance for liberty of faith in school) 67–73, 168–169
Central Jamaat-e Ahl-e Sunnat (CJAS), mosque 25, 30, 33, 38–46, 60–61, 78, 108–110, 146, 154
Council for Religious and Life Stance Communities in Norway (STL) 71–73, 84, 121, 125–126, 135, 154, 156, 158–159, 160
Council on Ecumenical and International Relations in the Church of Norway (MKR) 36–42, 44–45, 49, 54, 58, 60–62, 69, 72–73, 79–81, 94–98, 100, 104–105, 113, 115, 120–123, 125–126, 135–137, 154, 158, 160, 166, 168–169

Islamic Cultural Centre (ICC), mosque 24–26, 31, 50, 61, 75, 80, 96, 100, 106, 138, 144, 146, 148, 150, 155–156
Jewish Community of Oslo, The 11, 13, 67, 67–70, 121–122, 136–138
IslamNet 106, 109
Minhaj ul-Quran, mosque 43, 108–110, 117
Norwegian Humanist Association, The 9, 65–70
Norwegian Imam Council (Norges imam råd) 107–110
Rabita, mosque 26, 42, 45–50, 61, 69, 81, 83, 106, 108, 118–119, 138, 144, 147, 150, 154, 156, 164
Tablighi Jamaat, Islamic movement 25–26, 42, 59, 164
World Islamic Mission, mosque 25, 43–44, 61, 98, 149, 160

Key actors

Ali, Asghar 53–54, 102–104, 111, 128–129
Afsar, Mehtab 117, 118, 119, 120, 121, 122, 132, 138, 139, 147, 149, 150, 151, 152, 153, 154, 160, 161, 188
Bouras, Mohamed 46, 47, 52, 67, 70, 72, 136
Elamin, Abdelmounim 47, 63, 188
Larsen, Lena 70, 85–87, 105
Ghozlan, Basim 147
Grung, Anne Hege 105
Hamdan, Mohamed 94–96
Hasic, Leyla 133–134, 151–154
Jamil, Arshad 99, 147, 156
Joys, Ingrid 156
Kobilica, Senaid 94, 96, 125–127, 135, 143, 147, 164
Leirvik, Oddbjørn 8–9, 37–38, 40, 47–49, 61–62, 67, 79–80, 82–83, 105, 189
Linstad, Trond Ali 30–33, 60–61, 69–70
Mukhtar, Zahid 38, 40–41, 44–46, 57–60, 62, 84–85, 149–150
Mushtaq, Imran 88, 114, 188
Mushtaq, Irfan 88, 116, 117, 118, 124, 125, 127, 128, 129, 130, 131, 132, 137, 144, 147, 148, 149, 188
Secka, Kebba 46, 82–85, 87, 149–150

INDEX

243

Shaukat, Zaeem 150
Sultan, Shoaib 100–102, 105–106, 109, 117–118, 129, 132, 138, 152
Tveit, Olav Fykse 37, 40–41, 49, 60, 79, 125

Key events / critical junctures
Rushdie affair (1989) 28–34, 44, 56–58, 166, 181
Blasphemy in Pakistan controversy (1995) 77–81, 134, 166
Religion in Norwegian public school controversy (1995–1999)
FGM controversy ("Kadra affair", 2000) 82–84
Cartoon crisis (2005–2006) 93–99, 104, 111, 125, 135, 167, 171–172
Interfaith trip to Israel-Palestine (2012) 136–137
Niqab controversy (2016) 151–154
Gaza war (2023–2025) 164–165

Norwegian politics and society: Key topics and persons
Breivik, Anders Behring 141–142
Christian Democratic Party 66, 95–96
Dialogue, inter-religious 11, 32, 36–37, 104–105, 136–137, 140, 156, 161, 169–170
Human rights service / Hege Storhaug 142, 158
Immigration to Norway 34–35
Kvarme, Ole Christian 95, 143
Labour party 64, 66, 97–98, 142
Multiculturalism in Norway 35–36
Nygaard, William 56–58
Selbekk, Vebjørn 93–96
School system in Norway 60–73, 113, 120, 159, 166
State-church relations in Norway 27, 36, 65–66, 73
Støre, Jonas Gahr 95, 98

Key academic interlocutors
Ahmad, Shahab 7, 22, 28
Braginskaia, Ekaterina 1–2, 7, 18, 20, 182
Bruce, Benjamin 1–2, 7, 19–20, 157, 166, 173–174, 178–180
Ciciora, Alice 1–2, 7, 18–19, 173
Dazey, Margot 7, 112, 171

Døving, Cora Alexa 72–73, 168–169
Godard, Bernard 1–2, 7–8, 20, 170, 173–175
Jacobsen, Christine 7, 24, 88, 134–135
Laurence, Jonathan 1–2, 6–7, 16–18, 20, 174, 178, 183
Rosenow-Williams, Kerstin 1–2, 7–8, 19–20, 55, 178–180
Schiffauer, Werner 7–8, 26
Shavit, Uriya 2, 8, 21–22, 145, 170
Vogt, Kari 7, 24–27, 30, 44, 70, 73–76, 81, 106

Islamic debates, Islamic movements and Islamic figures
Ahmadiyya 27, 35, 39–40, 44
Apostasy 25, 40, 104–105
Barelwi 24–26, 29, 168, 170, 181
Blasphemy 28–33, 77–81, 85, 134–135, 166
Deobandi 24–26, 30, 31, 130
European Fatwa Council 103, 119
Gender-based violence 105–106
Halal slaughter and certification 106–110, 114–115, 127–132, 134, 136, 138, 144, 146–147, 151, 154–156, 160–163, 167–168, 170
Hadith 39–40
Hijab 24, 64, 86, 113, 118, 134, 169
Homosexuality 102–104, 112, 118–120, 142
Islamism 26, 31, 48–49
Jihadism 111–112, 141, 182
Law schools 104
Lunar calendar (hilal calendar) 73–77, 163–164, 168
Mawdudi, Abu al-A'la al- 48–49
Niqab 133–134, 151–153, 172
Post-Islamism 26, 31, 144
Post-Salafism 143
Prayer times 163–164
Qaradawi, Yusuf al- 69, 97, 103, 107
Quran 28, 39–40, 58, 60, 79–80, 89–90, 127
Shia 22, 44, 104, 156, 181–182
Sufis / Sufism 22–23, 108, 117, 130, 144–145, 178, 181–182
Ramadan fasting 21–22
Ramadan, Tariq 88–89
Salafi 143–145
Sunnah 89–90
Tolu-e-Islam 39–40, 44
Wahhabi 144–145

Printed in the United States
by Baker & Taylor Publisher Services